Globalization in Practice

Globalization in Practice

Edited by
Nigel Thrift, Adam Tickell,
Steve Woolgar, and William H. Rupp

OXFORD
UNIVERSITY PRESS

OXFORD

UNIVERSITY PRESS

Great Clarendon Street, Oxford, OX2 6DP,
United Kingdom

Oxford University Press is a department of the University of Oxford.
It furthers the University's objective of excellence in research, scholarship,
and education by publishing worldwide. Oxford is a registered trade mark of
Oxford University Press in the UK and in certain other countries

© Oxford University Press 2014

The moral rights of the authors have been asserted

First Edition published in 2014

Impression: 1

Published in the United States of America by Oxford University Press
198 Madison Avenue, New York, NY 10016, United States of America

British Library Cataloguing in Publication Data

Data available

Library of Congress Control Number: 2014938939

ISBN 978-0-19-921262-0 (hbk.)
ISBN 978-0-19-921263-7 (pbk.)

Printed and bound by
CPI Group (UK) Ltd, Croydon, CR0 4YY

▦ CONTENTS

▨ LIST OF FIGURES AND TABLES

Figures

Tables

LIST OF ABBREVIATIONS

9/11	al-Qaeda terrorist attacks on New York and Washington, 11 September 2001
AATF	Approved Authorized Treatment Facility
Acorn	A Classification of Residential Neighbourhoods
AML	anti-money laundering
ATM	automated teller machine
BBA	British Bankers' Association
BERR	Department for Business, Enterprise and Regulatory Reform
CBOT	Chicago Board of Trade
CCTV	closed-circuit television
CDO	collateralized debt obligation
CME	Chicago Mercantile Exchange
DCF	Designated Collection Facility
DRM	digital rights management
EBRD	European Bank for Reconstruction and Development
EPC	Electronic Product Code
EU	European Union
FSA	Financial Services Authority
G8	world's eight largest national economies: Canada, France, Germany, Italy, Japan, Russia, UK, USA
GAO	US General Accounting Office
GDP	gross domestic product
GKO	short-term Russian government bond
GMO	genetically modified organism
ICT	information and communication technology
IFC	International Finance Corporation
IIE	International Institute for Education
IMF	International Monetary Fund
INIBAP	International Network for the Improvement of Banana and Plantain
IO	international organization
IPGRI	International Institute of Plant Genetic Resources
IRN	International Rivers Network
ISBN	International Standards Book Numbering

ISO	International Organization for Standardization
KMT	Kuo-Min-Tung
LIBOR	London Interbank Offered Rate
MDG	Millennium Development Goal
NASS	National Asylum Support Service
NBA	Narmada Bachao Andolan (Save Narmada Movement)
NGO	non-governmental organization
OECD	Organization for Economic Co-operation and Development
ONS	Object Naming Service
PAFRAS	Positive Action for Refugees and Asylum Seekers
PCS	Producer Compliance Scheme
PGA	Asia People's Global Action (Asia)
PRIZM	Potential Rating Index for ZIP Markets
RFID	radio frequency identification
STS	science and technology studies
UD	urine diversion
UKMTA	UK Money Transmitters Association
UN	United Nations
UPC	universal product code
USAID	US Agency for International Development
WTO	World Trade Organization

NOTES ON THE EDITORS

Nigel Thrift is the Vice-Chancellor and President of the University of Warwick. He continues to maintain an active research career alongside his role as Vice-Chancellor and has been the recipient of a number of distinguished academic awards including the Royal Geographical Society Victoria Medal for contributions to geographic research in 2003, Distinguished Scholarship Honors from the Association of American Geographers in 2007, and the Royal Scottish Geographical Society Gold Medal in 2008. He was made a Fellow of the British Academy in 2003 and received Honorary LLDs from the University of Bristol in 2010 and Monash University in 2013. His current research spans a broad range of interests including international finance; cities and political life; non-representational theory; affective politics; and the history of time.

Adam Tickell is Provost at the University of Birmingham. He is an economic geographer whose work explores finance, English local governance, and the politics of ideas. He has served as both Dean of the Faculty of History and Social Sciences and as a Vice-President at Royal Holloway, University of London and was Research Director in the Faculty of Social Sciences and Law at the University of Bristol. He has also held chairs at the universities of Birmingham, Bristol, Southampton, and Royal Holloway, University of London, and lectureships at Leeds and Manchester. He is a member of the Council of the Academy of Social Sciences and maintains an active research and publishing portolio.

Steve Woolgar is Professor of Marketing and Director of Science and Technology Studies at Saïd Business School, University of Oxford. He has published widely in science and technology studies, and in social theory, and was awarded the J. D. Bernal Prize in 2008. His current research includes the effects of the neurosciences on the social sciences and humanities; and the nature of provocation and intervention in the social sciences. Recent books include *Mundane Governance: Ontology and Accountability* (with Dan Neyland; Oxford University Press, 2013), *Representation in Scientific Practice Revisited* (with Catelijne Coopmans, Janet Vertesi, and Michael Lynch; MIT Press, 2014), and *Visualization in the Age of Computerization* (with Annamaria Carusi, Aud Sissel Hoel, and Timothy Webmoor; Routledge, 2014).

William H. Rupp completed his doctorate at the University of Warwick, examining the creation of national identity in the late eighteenth-century world, and has also studied at the University of Toronto and Wilfrid Laurier University. Currently he works in the Student Admissions and Recruitment Office at the University of Warwick. He is the assistant editor of *The European World 1500–1800; An Introduction to Early Modern History* (2nd edition forthcoming).

NOTES ON THE CONTRIBUTORS

Peter Adey is Professor of Human Geography at the Department of Geography, Royal Holloway University of London. Peter is progamme director of an interdisciplinary MSc on Geopolitics and Security. He has published on the contours and cultures of mobility and aviation security, most notably in *Mobility* (2009), *Aerial Life* (2010), and the edited collections *From Above: War, Violence and Verticality* (2013) and the *Handbook of Mobilities* (2013). His new book *Air* is currently in press for 2014.

Andrew Barry is a Professor at University College London. He is author of *Political Machines: Governing a Technological Society* (2001) and co-editor of *Foucault and Political Reason* (1996), *The Technological Economy* (2005), and *Interdisciplinarity: Reconfigurations of the Social and Natural Sciences* (2011).

Geoffrey C. Bowker is Professor in the Department of Informatics, University of California at Irvine. There he directs the Evoke Laboratory (<http://evoke.ics.uci.edu/>), whose signature programme is an annual interdisciplinary workshop. His research is now concentrated on emerging modes of knowledge expression. His most recent book is *Memory Practices in the Sciences*.

Roger Burrows is Professor of Sociology and Head of the Department of Sociology at the University of York. He has research interests in the areas of urban studies, social informatics, health and illness, and methodological innovations in the social sciences. He has published over 100 articles, chapters, reports, and books on these and other topics.

Nick Clarke is Lecturer in Human Geography at the University of Southampton. He researches community in a global age and publishes on associated topics including travel and tourism, transnationalism, ethical consumption, moral geographies, political participation, policy mobility, and localism. Recent publications include *Globalizing Responsibility: The Political Rationalities of Ethical Consumption* (with Clive Barnett, Paul Cloke, and Alice Malpass; Oxford, Wiley-Blackwell).

Franck Cochoy is Professor of Sociology at the University of Toulouse and member of the CERTOP-CNRS, France, and a visiting professor at the University of Gothenburg, Sweden. His research is focused on the sociology of organizations and markets, and more precisely on the different mediations that frame the relation between supply and demand (marketing, packaging, self-service, standardization, corporate social responsibility, trade press, etc.).

Stephen J. Collier is Associate Professor in the Graduate Program in International Affairs at the New School in New York City. He is author of *Post-Soviet Social: Neoliberalism, Social Modernity, Biopolitics* (Princeton University Press, 2011), and co-editor *of Biosecurity Interventions* (Columbia University Press, 2008) and *Global Assemblages* (Blackwell, 2005). He is completing a book on the government of catastrophes in the United States during the twentieth century.

Catelijne Coopmans is a Fellow and Director of Studies at Tembusu College and a Research Fellow at the Asia Research Institute at the National University of Singapore. Catelijne's chapter on 'Mobility and the Medical Image' is related to her research on the contextual and technologically mediated arrangements in and through which visual evidence is valued. Her other publications on this theme have appeared in *Information, Communication & Society, Science Technology & Society*, and *Social Studies of Science*.

Martin Dodge is Senior Lecturer in Human Geography at the University of Manchester, where his research focuses on conceptualizing the socio-spatial power of digital technologies and urban infrastructures, virtual geographies, and the theorization of visual representations, cartographic knowledge, and novel methods of geographic visualization. He curated the well known Web-based *Atlas of Cyberspaces* and has co-authored with Rob Kitchin three books covering aspects of spatiality of computer technology: *Mapping Cyberspace* (Routledge, 2000), *Atlas of Cyberspace* (Addison-Wesley, 2001), *and Code/Space* (MIT Press, 2011). He has also co-edited two books, *Geographic Visualization* (Wiley, 2008) and *Rethinking Maps* (Routledge, 2009), focused on the social and cultural meanings of new kinds of mapping practice.

Rebecca M. Ellis is currently the director of an independent research consultancy, Digital Era Research, specializing in the area of ICTs and society. She was previously a researcher specializing in new media in the Department of Sociology, University of Essex. Rebecca has book chapters on the social and cultural aspects of eBay in *Everyday eBay: Culture, Collecting and Desire* (Routledge) and the *Handbook of Research on Socio-Technical Design and Social Networking Systems* (IGI Global).

Jürgen Gerhards is Professor of Sociology at the Free University, Berlin. His publications analysing the development of first names from a sociological perspective include *The Name Game; Cultural Modernization and First Names* (Transaction Publishers, 2005) and 'From Hasan to Herbert: Name-Giving Patterns of Immigrant Parents between Acculturation and Ethnic Maintenance' (*American Journal of Sociology*, 2009, with Silke Hans).

Nicholas Gill is Senior Lecturer in Human Geography at Exeter University. His research is concerned with the control of migration. He coordinates the Asylum Network research group and is presently leading a research project that critically examines the asylum appeal process in the UK. He has edited a book entitled *Carceral Spaces* with Drs Dominique Moran and Deirdre Conlon for Ashgate and has published articles in *Progress in Human Geography, Transactions of the Institute of British Geographers*, and *Political Geography*.

Stephen Graham is Professor of Cities and Society at the Global Urban Research Unit in Newcastle University's School of Architecture, Planning, and Landscape. His books include *Telecommunications* and *The City, Splintering Urbanism* (both with Simon Marvin), *The Cybercities Reader, Cities, War and Terrorism, Disrupted Cities: When Infrastructures Fail*, and, most recently, *Cities Under Siege: The New Military Urbanism*. His next book will be *Vertical: The Politics of Up and Down* and will be published by Verso (2015).

Christopher Hall is a social care researcher with a particular expertise in child welfare research at Durham University. He worked as a social worker and team manager in local authorities in London before taking up research posts at the National Foundation for Educational Research, Dartington Social Research Unit, and the Centre for Applied Childhood Studies at Huddersfield University. He is a founder member of the international research group, DANASWAC (Discourse and Narrative Approaches to Social Work and Counselling).

Christian Heath is Professor at King's College London and leads the Work, Interaction and Technology research centre. He specializes in fine-grained, video-based studies of social interaction, in particular in institutional environments drawing on ethnomethodology and conversation analysis. He is currently undertaking studies of operating theatres, command and control centres, auctions, and museums and galleries.

Alex Hughes is Reader in the School of Geography, Politics and Sociology at Newcastle University. She is co-editor (with Suzanne Reimer) of *Geographies of Commodity Chains* (Routledge, 2004) and (with Jane Pollard and Cheryl McEwan) of *Postcolonial Economies* (Zed, 2011). She has also published a range of journal articles on the subjects of global production networks, retailers, and ethical trade.

Tim Ingold is Professor of Social Anthropology at the University of Aberdeen. He has carried out ethnographic fieldwork in Lapland, and has written on environment, technology, and social organization in the circumpolar North, on evolutionary theory in anthropology, biology and history, on the role of animals in human society, on language and tool use, and on environmental perception and skilled practice. He is currently exploring issues on the interface between anthropology, archaeology, art, and architecture. He is the author of *The Perception of the Environment* (2000), *Lines* (2007), *Being Alive* (2011), and *Making* (2013), all published by Routledge.

Adrian Johns is Allan Grant Maclear Professor of History at the University of Chicago, where he also chairs the Committee on Conceptual and Historical Studies of Science. He was educated at Cambridge University, and taught at the University of Kent at Canterbury, Caltech, and the University of California, San Diego, before moving to Chicago. He is the author of *The Nature of the Book: Print and Knowledge in the Making* (1998), *Piracy: The Intellectual Property Wars from Gutenberg to Gates* (2009), and *Death of a Pirate: British Radio and the Making of the Information Age* (2010).

Nino Kemoklidze is a doctoral candidate at the Centre for Russian and East European Studies (CREES), University of Birmingham. Her PhD topic concerns issues of nationalism and ethnic violence in Georgia. She is one of the guest editors and co-authors of the special issue on 'Many Faces of the Caucasus', *Europe–Asia Studies* (64/9, 2012). Her other publications include 'The Kosovo Precedent and the "Moral Hazard" of Secession', *Journal of International Law and International Relations* (5/2, 2009).

Lucy Kimbell works as a designer, researcher, and educator. She is associate fellow at Said Business School, University of Oxford, where she has taught design practices to MBA students since 2005. Her artwork work has been shown internationally including at the TEDGlobal conference (2011) and in Making Things Public (2005).

Rob Kitchin is a Professor and ERC Advanced Investigator at the National Institute for Regional and Spatial Analysis at the National University of Ireland, Maynooth. He is author or editor of 21 books, co-editor-in-chief of the *International Encyclopedia of Human Geography*, and editor of *Progress in Human Geography* and *Dialogues in Human Geography*.

Wendy Larner is Professor of Human Geography and Sociology, and Research Director for the Faculty of Social Sciences and Law at the University of Bristol. Her research focuses on globalization, governance, and gender. Recent co-edited books include *Calculating the Social: Standards and the Reconfiguration of Governing* (Palgrave Macmillan, 2010), and *The Point is to Change It: Geographies of Hope and Survival in an Age of Crisis* (Wiley Blackwell, 2010).

Eric Laurier is Senior Lecturer in Geography and Interaction, School of GeoSciences, University of Edinburgh. Eric is currently involved in a number of research projects on mobility and technology. He has written previously on why people say where they are at the beginning of mobile phone calls.

Michael Levi has been Professor of Criminology at Cardiff University since 1991. He has been conducting international research on the control of white-collar and organized crime, corruption, and money laundering/financing of terrorism since 1972. In 2007–10 he was an ESRC Professorial Fellow, ESRC RES-051-27-0208, and examined the globalization of economic crime and its control. His most recent book is a revised monograph of his doctoral thesis, *The Phantom Capitalists*.

Celia Lury is Director of the Centre for Interdisciplinary Methodologies at the University of Warwick. Recent relevant publications include *Brands: The Logos of the Global Economy* (Routledge, 2004); *Global Culture Industry: The Mediation of Things* (with Scott Lash; Polity, 2007), and *Inventive Methods* (co-edited with Nina Wakeford; Routledge, 2012).

Donald MacKenzie works in the sociology of science and technology and in the sociology of markets, especially of financial markets. He holds a personal chair in sociology at the University of Edinburgh, where he has taught since 1975. His most recent books are *An Engine, Not a Camera: How Financial Models Shape Markets* (MIT Press, 2006), *Do Economists Make Markets? On the Performativity of Economics* (Princeton University Press, 2007), co-edited with Fabian Muniesa and Lucia Siu, and *Material Markets: How Economic Agents are Constructed* (Oxford University Press, 2009).

Peter Merriman is a Reader in Human Geography at Aberystwyth University. His research focuses on the histories and geographies of driving, and theories of space and spatiality. He is the author of *Driving Spaces: A Cultural-Historical Geography of England's M1 Motorway* (2007) and *Mobility, Space and Culture* (2012), and an editor of *Geographies of Mobilities* (2011) and *The Routledge Handbook of Mobilities* (2014).

Peter Miller is Professor of Management Accounting at the London School of Economics and Political Science, and an Associate of the Centre for Analysis of Risk and Regulation. He is an editor of *Accounting, Organizations and Society*, and has published in a wide range of accounting, management, and sociology journals.

University of Warwick. He is the author of *The New Masters of Capital: American Bond Rating Agencies and the Politics of Creditworthiness* (Cornell University Press, 2005), *The Problem with Banks*, co-authored with Lena Rethel (Zed, 2012), and *Global Governance* (Polity, 2012). He is a visiting professor at Kyung Hee University in Korea and during 2013/14 is a visiting fellow at the Sheffield Political Economy Research Institute at the University of Sheffield. His research focuses on the politics of global finance and approaches to global governance.

Gerard Toal is Professor of Government and International Affairs in the School of Public and International Affairs at Virginia Tech, National Capital Region.

John Torpey is Professor of Sociology and History and Director of the Ralph Bunche Institute for International Studies at the Graduate Center, City University of New York. Recent books include *The Invention of the Passport: Surveillance, Citizenship, and the State* (Cambridge University Press, 2000), *Old Europe, New Europe, Core Europe: Transatlantic Relations after the Iraq War* (edited with Daniel Levy and Max Pensky; Verso, 2005), *Making Whole What Has Been Smashed: On Reparations Politics* (Harvard University Press, 2006), and *Legal Integration of Islam: A Transatlantic Comparison* (with Christian Joppke; Harvard University Press, 2013).

Helen Verran taught History and Philosophy of Science at the University of Melbourne, Australia for 25 years. She now teaches at the ITU in Copenhagen. She is the author of the prize-winning *Science and an African Logic* (University of Chicago Press, 2001), an empirical philosophical study of numbers in Yorubaland, West Africa.

Sumei Wang holds a PhD in Sociology from Lancaster University. She is currently Assistant Professor at the Department of Journalism, National Chengchi University in Taiwan. Her research interests fall in the areas of cultural globalization, practices, and identities, and the use of ICTs in everyday life.

Michael J. Watts is Class of '63 Professor of Geography, and Director of Development Studies at the University of California, Berkeley, where he has taught for 30 years. He served as the Director of the Institute of International Studies at Berkeley from 1994 to 2004. His research has addressed a number of development issues, especially food security, resource development, and land reform in Africa, South Asia, and Vietnam.

Janine R. Wedel is University Professor in the School of Public Policy at George Mason University. Her publications include two award-winning and widely reviewed books: *Shadow Elite: How the World's New Power Brokers Undermine Democracy, Government, and the Free Market* (2009), and *Collision and Collusion: The Strange Case of Western Aid to Eastern Europe* (2001) (<http://janinewedel.info/books.html>). Her new book, *Unaccountable*, will be published by Pegasus Books in 2014. Winner of the prestigious Grawemeyer Award for Ideas Improving World Order, she is also a four-time Fulbright fellow and recipient of awards from the National Science Foundation and MacArthur Foundation, among others. She is President of the Association for the Anthropology of Policy, which is affiliated with the American Anthropological Association. A public intellectual, her contributions are featured here: <http://www.psmag.com/politics/meet-flexians-government-business-media-money-power-wall-street-65029/>.

Jackie West is Honorary Research Fellow in Sociology and former Senior Lecturer at the University of Bristol, where she was also Graduate Dean of Social Sciences and Law. Her research interests include prostitution, gambling, and the new economy, and she has written widely on gender and employment. She is a member of the UK Network of Sex Work Projects and is currently part of an EU-funded Action, Comparing European Prostitution Policies: Understanding Scales and Cultures of Governance.

Sue White is Professor of Social Work (Children and Families) at the University of Birmingham. Her research principally focuses on the analysis of everyday decision-making in professional practice. For the past five years she has been involved in the reform of social work in England.

Alexandra Woolgar is an Australian Research Council (ARC) Discovery Early Career Research Award fellow in the Department of Cognitive Science and ARC Centre of Excellence in Cognition and its Disorders at Macquarie University in Australia. Her research seeks to understand human behaviour from a cognitive neuroscience perspective.

Caitlin Zaloom is a cultural anthropologist and an associate professor of Social and Cultural Analysis and Business at New York University. Her book *Out of the Pits: Traders and Technology from Chicago to London* (University of Chicago, 2006) examines emerging forms of knowledge and practice related to financial risk. She is currently working on a book about the finances of middle-class families in the United States.

Ragna Zeiss is Assistant Professor in Science and Technology Studies at Maastricht University, the Netherlands. She obtained her PhD from the Department of Sociology at the University of York. Her research interests include standardization, regulation, and governance; knowledge brokerage and boundary work; risk governance; and sustainability—all in the areas of water, sanitation, nature, the environment, bio-objects, and nanotechnologies in the global north and south.

Introduction: Respecifying Globalization

An Editorial Essay for
Globalization in Practice

Nigel Thrift, Adam Tickell, and Steve Woolgar

Think of the ship or the stirrup or barbed wire. These are the mundane but remarkable stuff from which empires have been built. Without them, it would not have been possible to achieve the degree of extension in space and time needed to allow an empire to be constructed and maintained. Yet, until recently, what, in retrospect, are clearly crucial determinants of the process of building empire have only rarely been assayed, and often simply as an aside. And it is not just empire. The world has been through many waves of globalization, each of which has been spawned by their own material drivers and markers, but these have often been cast aside as mere flags of a deeper underlying process or thought of as 'little' things in comparison with much 'larger' happenings. As this book sets out to show, that position is wrong. Mundane objects and practices are deeply implicated in questions of governance and accountability.[1] These so-called little things[2] are the real material of globalization, the things that count, the things that guide or impose outcomes.

A few years ago, that would have been a deviant position. But, increasingly, such is not the case. There are many reasons for this state of affairs but we will mention just three. To begin with, what has been called 'analytic scepticism', a notion taken originally from science and technology studies (STS),[3] has become the order of the day in large parts of the social sciences, a position

---

[1] Steve Woolgar and Daniel Neyland, *Mundane Governance: Ontology and Accountability* (Oxford: Oxford University Press, 2013).

[2] Nigel Thrift, *Knowing Capitalism* (London: Sage, 2005).

[3] STS is a large multidisciplinary endeavour which draws on disciplines as varied as sociology, psychology, economics, philosophy, anthropology, and history. It is informed by and contributes to cross-cutting intellectual currents including feminism and gender studies, cultural studies, social constructivism, reflexivity, and actor network theory.

in which weighty topics and synoptic phenomena of transcendental scale are respecified as ordinary everyday mundane practices and activities:

[T]he best work in STS . . . addresses heady topics (knowledge, objectivity, natural order, experiment, measurement, and the like) in a way that disarms and deflates intellectual pretence. 'Knowledge' is de-Kanted and becomes pluralized and situated; Objectivity dissolves into historical usage; Natural Order is traced back to mundane practices; Mathematics becomes number-use.[4]

To understand the kind of deflation of either mystery or system which is deemed necessary in this stance we can take the analogous example of 'markets'. Like 'globalization', here is a notion which has permeated discourse in many and multitudinous areas of social and political life. But what is a market without market devices? In a set of volumes, Michel Callon and co-workers have addressed the crucial role of technical instruments and devices in the construction of markets.[5] From pricing models to merchandising tools, from trading protocols to aggregate indicators, the topic of market devices includes a wide array of objects that have been often overlooked in sociological analysis. Thus, Callon explores how market devices configure economic calculative capacities. He observes the part they play in the marketability of goods and services. He analyses the performative aspects of knowledge and expertise needed in adjusting and calibrating them.

Relatedly, the idea of scale as producing an easy correlate with global in the manner of 'global equals large, local equals small' has come under sustained examination, as it has become clear that to claim that things happen on a global level is to invoke a range of assumptions and implications about the phenomenon under study which stand in contrast with those which are 'merely' local. In talking of large and small, there is no easy correlation to be made between size and geographical extent. A 'large' entity might be relatively nebulous. Think of many international political organizations able to function only because of multiple and often fragile alliances. Equally, an entity can be 'small' and have remarkable and wide-ranging effects: think of the contraceptive pill or the credit card. Both these objects have been extruded from enormous and seemingly shadowy infrastructures: their 'footprint' is enormous.

Especially within the social sciences, it has been common to encounter fundamental splits in terms of scale: discussions are often organized in terms of the micro, macro, and meso, for example, as well as local and global. Often rancorous disputes are organized around a host of similar-sounding dualisms: micro/macro, large/small, global/local, particular/general, near/far, and so on. The framing and outcome of these disputes are crucial for academic

[4] Micheal Lynch, 4S Presidential Election Ballot, 6 May 2006.
[5] See, for example, Michel Callon, Yuval Millo, and Fabian Muniesa, eds, *Market Devices* (Oxford: Blackwell, 2007).

social science but also for all manner of interventions—in policy, management and business, and so on. Typically, adherents to 'micro' analysis are criticized for their resistance to broad generalization. Those in the 'macro' camp are criticized for their vagueness, for lack of rigour and for the ease with which they jump from particular examples to general conclusions. The questions then arise: Why should we consider certain actors, processes, categories, events as bigger or smaller than others? How are different scales of analysis and thought achieved? How is the 'macro' scale produced and maintained? What processes of miniaturization enable the creation and maintenance of 'micro' entities? These questions suggest the need for a close examination of the empirical, analytical, and conceptual practices entailed in the creation of different scales. We would expect to find such practices at work in academic inquiry. But we also need to ask how these practices differ, if at all, in the work of architects, designers, urban planners, public health officials, engineers, nanotechnologists, politicians, and so on. The work of constructing scale is a constantly unfinished project.[6]

Finally, and in turn, debates like those over analytic scepticism and scale have generated a vast amount of new theoretical and empirical work on globalization. In the rest of this introductory chapter, we point to five different but related kinds of literatures which have produced an intricate helix of thinking in which all have come to roughly the same conclusion: to think of the objects and practices of globalization as somehow secondary to a process of globalization is a category mistake. They are primary.

Objects

One of the most important intellectual currents of the last ten years has been the rediscovery of the object as having a presence in its own right, rather than as being simply a subsidiary of humanity. 'Things are back.'[7] All manner of disciplines have simultaneously rediscovered the object and put that rediscovery to work and yet, unlike the study of languages or places, there is no discipline devoted to the study of objects.

---

[6] Woolgar and colleagues have proposed the notion of 'scalography'—the sceptical ethnographic study of scalar objects and practices—as the methodological stance appropriate to highlighting the contingent features of what is so often taken for granted about scale. Steve Woolgar, 'From Scale to Scalography: A Provocation Piece' (presented at an international workshop on Scaleography, 8 July 2009), <http://www.sbs.ox.ac.uk/centres/insis/Documents/Scalography_provocation_22.pdf>. See also 'Scalography', Said School of Business, <http://www.sbs.ox.ac.uk/centres/insis/research/Pages/scalography.aspx>.

[7] Frank Trentmann, 'Crossing Divides: Consumption and Globalization in History', *Journal of Consumer Culture* 9, 2 (July 2009): 1.

To begin with, the growth of material culture studies in anthropology and archaeology[8] has pointed to the crucial role of objects in not only maintaining cultures but in many cases in founding them: without what Daniel Miller calls 'stuff' there is no civilization.[9] Things make us as much as we make things. Thus, we use objects not only to express ourselves and inhabit our environment but equally to define what it is to be alive and to cope with death. There are clear, but surely unconscious, echoes here with Marx's views on the relationship between productive forces and social relations, expressed in the most reductionist fashion in chapter two of *The Poverty of Philosophy*: 'The hand-mill gives you society with the feudal lord; the steam-mill, society with the industrial capitalist.'[10]

In STS, the object has had a chequered career. Early work in this tradition pursued a humanistic agenda in which it was argued that the objects of the natural world were not given, but socially constructed. Natural-world phenomena were shown to be the (socially constructed) upshot of the work of scientists operating in particular social and institutional contexts, rather than the cause of scientific knowledge. Subsequently, and especially with the advent of actor network theory, it was suggested that experimental objects had to have some degree of freedom to 'talk back', so to speak, to make their presence known in ways which were not expected.[11] But the tendency to give objects such degrees of freedom has only been reinforced by the growth of interest in STS in modern information and communications technologies, which have both shown up the issues that needed to be addressed—for example, by underlining the degree to which objects might have various kinds of sentience—and also pointed to new means of design of technologies which can allow objects to be both more active and less attended to. In particular, of late there has been a move to try to link objects and affect in more knowing and calculated ways, which has been an equal concern of STS and of industries like information and communications.

In history, objects have themselves become historical moments of enquiry—and all kinds of objects at that. Whereas, at one time, the objects that counted might have been those that were scattered around the eighteenth-century rooms of elites, now they can be any kind of mundane entity, as signalled by, for example, the move from an interest in the practices of elite practitioners of time like mathematicians and astrologers and of correspondingly expensive and often highly decorative clocks to an interest in the kinds of timekeeping

---

[8] Dan Hicks and Mary C. Beaudry, eds, *The Oxford Handbook of Material Culture Studies* (Oxford: Oxford University Press, 2012).

[9] David Miller, *Stuff* (Cambridge: Polity Press, 2010).

[10] Karl Marx, *The Poverty of Philosophy*, <http://www.marxists.org/archive/marx/works/1847/poverty-philosophy/ch02.htm#s2>.

[11] Bruno Latour, *We Have Never Been Modern*, trans. Catherine Porter (Cambridge, MA: Harvard University Press, 1993).

that ordinary people practised and of means of timekeeping that they could afford.[12] Equally, the range of sensory registers in which objects dwell has become as important, as evidenced by much recent work on the British Empire which stresses the role that objects played in its emotional maintenance.[13] Then there is the simple fact of the size of the flows of many objects around the world and their cultural effect, as the much-studied example of the porcelain trade out of China would demonstrate.[14] In his magisterial radio series, which used objects in the collection of the British Museum to illustrate both moments and trends in world history, Neil MacGregor showed how the Han Dynasty maintained its power 2,000 years ago through dispensing luxury goods, such as a highly intricate lacquer cup, to military commanders on the empire's edge.[15] This is a tradition that has been maintained into the present in China through ritualized gift-giving. In the history of art, again, the object has taken a prime place, no longer subject to the vagaries of interpretation but seen as something which stands by itself as part of a pictorial grammar.[16]

In geography and sociology, objects have become key through studies of the practice of consumer society. Increasingly, objects are seen as having 'degrees of freedom' from human intervention, neither leading separate lives nor being mere ciphers (see, for example, the large and growing study of the problem of waste, showing objects as having an afterlife outside human care, which is a potent driver of all kinds of change).[17] Similarly, the growth of objects which provide comfort for people has been shown to be a double-edged sword, as in the study of air conditioning or the growth of devices which use very large amounts of water.[18]

Finally, in philosophy, there has been the rise of so-called 'speculative realism', a movement intended to combat the anti-realist strain in philosophy

[12] Paul Glennie and Nigel Thrift, *Shaping the Day: A History of Timekeeping in England and Wales, 1300–1800* (Oxford: Oxford University Press, 2009).

[13] Margot C. Finn, 'Colonial Gifts: Family Politics and the Exchange of Goods in British India, c.1780–1820', *Modern Asian Studies* 40, 1 (February 2006): 203–32.

[14] Maxine Berg, 'Cargoes: The Trade in Luxuries from Asia to Europe', in *Empire, the Sea and Global History: Britain's Maritime World, c.1760–1840*, ed. David Cannadine (Basingstoke: Palgrave Macmillan, 2007).

[15] The whole radio series is available to listen to, and download, at <http://www.bbc.co.uk/ahistoryoftheworld>.

[16] Paul Smith, 'Pictoral Grammar: Chomsky, John Willats, and the Rules of Representation', *Art History* 34, 3 (June 2011): 563–93.

[17] Nicky Gregson and Mike Crang, 'Materiality and Waste: Inorganic Vitality in a Networked World', *Environment and Planning. A* 42, 5 (2010): 1026–32; N. Gregson, M. Crang, F. Ahamed, N. Akhtar, R. Ferdous, 'Following Things of Rubbish Value: End-of-life Ships, 'Chock-Chocky' Furniture and the Bangladeshi Middle Class Consumer', *Geoform* 41, 6 (November 2010): 846–54.

[18] Russell Hitchings and Shu Jun Lee, 'Air Conditioning and the Material Culture of Routine Human Encasement', *Journal of Material Culture* 13, 3 (November 2003): 251–65; Elizabeth Shove, *Comfort, Cleanliness and Convenience: The Social Organization of Normality* (Oxford: Berg, 2003).

which, though it gave considerable attention to such notions as text, culture, consciousness, and power as to what constitutes the world,

gave us less a critique of humanity's place in the world than a sweeping critique of the self-enclosed Cartesian subject. Humanity remains at the centre of these works, and reality appears in philosophy only as the correlate of human thought...In the face of the looming ecological catastrophe, and the increasing infiltration of technology into the world (including our own bodies), it is not clear that the antirealist position is equipped to face up to these developments.[19]

Not surprisingly, the speculative (in the sense of trying to get at something beyond the concerns of the critical or linguistic turns) realist turn has fuelled work on objects. In its earliest guise, this meant the vagaries of a symbiosis with movements like actor network theory. More recently, it has involved drawing upon the work of Claude Meillassoux and authors like Graham Harman who argue that objects have a life of their own and that the landscape of things must be imagined in a way that does not necessarily imply human access to the phenomenal realm in the shape of thought, memory, fantasy, dreams, and the like.[20] As Whitehead would have it, sentience is merely a difference in degree, not in kind, and reality can be apprehended as existing independently of human thought and, indeed, of humanity more generally.[21]

A whole slew of studies of the object has now manifested itself as these different threads have tangled together in these interdisciplinary times—far too many to enumerate. But two examples will suffice to illustrate the range of impulses and outputs. One particularly important manifestation of the object world is that whole set of material infrastructures that are often thought of as 'underlying' processes: intelligent energy systems, cables and pipes, software, telephone and wireless and electricity networks, airline networks, the multiple logistics of container traffic, and so on. In previous studies of globalization, these entities tended to be thought of as enabling technologies. However, it has become increasingly clear that this is not a viable position. These infrastructures are not passive and this is true in at least three ways. First, they are themselves manifestations of particular ambitions and representations of the world, although they might be seen as a model of impersonal rule. So—for example—a grand new freeway or a high-speed train line is clearly more than simply a link in a network. It is a cultural statement too. It can be understood as embodying social and political interests.[22] Second, these networks have their

---

[19] Levi Bryant, Nick Srnicek, and Graham Harman, eds, *The Speculative Turn: Continental Materialism and Realism* (Prahan, Australia: re.press, 2011).

[20] Claude Meillassoux, *Femmes, Greniers et Capitaux* (Paris: Maspero, 1975); Graham Harman, *Circus Philosophicus* (Winchester: 0 Books, 2010).

[21] Alfred Whitehead, *Science and the Modern World* (New York: The Free Press, 1925).

[22] See Langdon Winner, 'Do Artifacts Have Politics?', in *The Social Shaping of Technology*, ed. Donald MacKenzie and Judy Wajcam (2nd edn, Cambridge, MA: MIT Press, 1999): 28–40.

own degree of efficacy. This point becomes very apparent when they break down, something which is more common than is often perceived. When these breakdowns occur, the system is revealed for what it is: a vital component of the conduct of everyday life and, indeed, of globalization. Third, these systems are based to quite a large degree on the logic of improvization and tinkering. They continue to exist because of mundane acts of repair and maintenance which, though unsung, are vital to their operation.[23]

Then take, as the other example, pharmaceutical distribution networks. These can be hugely well organized and sometimes profitable for the mainly Western companies who invest in their research and development. But these networks can have immense problems in stabilizing the mundane objects that they offer to the market. Generic drugs run out of patent or face challenges in some developing countries from clones; more than this, many of the drugs on offer turn out to be counterfeits and, as a result of their dubious efficacy, threaten lives. This later point can be of more than marginal importance, as a report by the World Health Organization makes clear:

- Many countries in Africa and parts of Asia and Latin America have areas where more than thirty per cent of the medicines on sale can be counterfeit, while other developing countries have less than ten per cent; overall, a reasonable estimate is between ten and thirty per cent.
- In many of the countries of the former Soviet Union the proportion of counterfeit medicines is above twenty per cent of market value.[24]

Practices

A parallel intellectual rediscovery has been the importance of practices understood as concernful means of being in the world. Taken originally from philosophers like Heidegger and then strained through the work of writers like Bourdieu, the practice is understood as the elemental building block of human activity, the means by which people take hold of the world and make it work, the set of '-ings' which make up the quanta of meaningful activity. As this literature evolved, so it became increasingly clear that objects could not be seen as subsidiary moments in practice. Human being is, as Harman would put it, 'tool-being'.[25] There are very few practices which are not intermediated by objects and there are many practices where objects dictate the terms of trade.

---

[23] Stephen Graham and Nigel Thrift, 'Out of Order: Understanding Repair and Maintenance', *Theory, Culture & Society* 24, 3 (May 2007): 1–26.

[24] World Health Organization, 'Counterfeit Drugs Kill' (Geneva: World Health Organization, n.d.): 3.

[25] Graham Harman, *Tool-Being: Heidegger and the Metaphysics of Objects* (Chicago: Open Court, 2002).

The 'practice turn' has now infiltrated many parts of the social sciences, but especially those which involve objects.[26] Think only of fields like the study of consumption or of various different media, where this approach is fast becoming dominant. So far as this current of work is concerned, what globalization consists of is a set of new practices which are able to overcome propinquity whilst retaining credibility as means of interaction.

Take the example of modern finance which, no one could dispute, has been a driver of the current round of globalization. Nearly every practice that currently exists in the financial armoury has now been intermediated by a thick field of objects. Thus, certain practices would not—literally could not—exist without the object field. Modern practices of trading in derivatives (explored in Caitlin Zaloom's entry in this volume) and high frequency (algorithmic) trading in stocks and shares depend upon very fast computers and telecommunications. By the end of the nineteenth century, transatlantic cables allowed deals between London and New York to be executed within five minutes, enabling the development of internationally liquid capital markets.[27] Today, fibre optic cable networks are being constructed to give minute—but hugely significant—advantages in time that are actively reconstituting finance itself. For example, a fibre optic connection between Chicago and New York is reckoned to shave three microseconds off the 825-mile trading journey between the exchanges, whilst a transatlantic fibre optic link between Novia Scotia in Canada and Somerset in the UK is being built primarily to serve the needs of algorithmic traders and will send information between London and New York in 60 milliseconds (or 0.001 minutes). Taking advantage of such a time advantage, of course, requires both complex algorithms which can spot and trade a price advantage automatically and highly sophisticated supercomputers. As Donald MacKenzie points out:

Little of this has to do directly with human action. None of us can react to an event in a millisecond: the fastest we can achieve is around 140 milliseconds, and that's only for the simplest stimulus, a sudden sound...As recently as 20 years ago, the heart of most financial markets was a trading floor on which human beings did deals with each other face to face. The 'open outcry' trading pits at the Chicago Mercantile Exchange, for example, were often a mêlée of hundreds of sweating, shouting, gesticulating bodies. Now, the heart of many markets (at least in standard products such as shares) is an air-conditioned warehouse full of computers supervised by only a handful of maintenance staff.[28]

---

[26] Theodore R. Schatzki, Karin Knorr Cetina, Eike Von Savigny, eds, *The Practice Turn in Contemporary Theory* (London: Routledge, 2001).

[27] Anton A. Huurdeman, *A Worldwide History of Telecommunications* (New York: J. Wiley, 2003).

[28] Donald MacKenize, 'How to Make Money in Microseconds', *London Review of Books*, 19 May 2011, 16–18.

But we should not restrict our notion of the practices of globalization to the economic high frontier. Other practices are as important in cementing particular kinds of operation. For example, higher education is now a global industry which depends on a serried range of practices which span distance but give the impression of being local. Take the example of the graduation (or commencement) ceremony. At some point during the year, somewhere in the world, there will be a graduation ceremony taking place. At one time, it looked like these events might become a thing of the past—a dusty ceremony which many undergraduates wanted to avoid. But now the apparatus of gowns, music, certificates, photographs, and films seems to be remorselessly expanding. The massification and globalization of higher education have prompted a reinvention of this particular tradition, which is presenting dilemmas of content, presentation, and logistics which cannot just be ignored. As universities have grown in size and reach, so the challenge of mounting more and larger graduation ceremonies has become greater and greater. First, and most obviously, there is the issue of numbers: mounting a graduation ceremony is an intricate logistical exercise which becomes more difficult with size. Second, there is the problem of time: ceremonies have become longer, and innovations need to be introduced to prevent them being tedious for the participants. Third, there is the problem of cost: some universities now feel forced to charge for ceremonies and nearly all restrict the number of guests, often quite severely. Finally, the globalization of higher education means that it can no longer be assumed that all graduation ceremonies take place in one place. Making ceremonies in places which were not designed for the purpose can be a real challenge, and simply having robes to hand does not work.

Universities have adopted a number of solutions to these problems. One solution has been to expand the number of ceremonies but this can become its own problem as ceremonies occupy more and more time. Another solution is to find auditoria which can accommodate larger events. Again, this is not an easy task and can involve trade-offs between beautiful and grand older spaces which can only take limited numbers and newer spaces (sometimes not even the university's own) which can take larger numbers. Furthermore, if ceremonies become too big, the vital importance of what the political theorist Josiah Ober has called inter-visibility—the ability to see response, which creates meaning and common knowledge—starts to be threatened, even with (or indeed, because of) all the modern paraphernalia of amplification and big screens to hand. What is clear, then, is that the massification and globalization of higher education are leading to adjustment of all kinds of practices.

How can we put the insights from the rediscovery of objects and practices to work in understanding contemporary globalization differently? Certainly this trend is not without problems. We are conscious that the very move to re-establish the centrality of objects and practices carries with it the temptation to use summary descriptions of these phenomena which can all too easily sound like a recourse to simplistic determinism. In our own description, we have just recounted, for example, how 'objects determine the terms of trade', that 'transatlantic cables allowed deals to be executed' and so on. While these kinds of formulation justifiably bring ordinary objects to centre stage, we have yet to find a vocabulary which offsets the implication that the properties of such objects by themselves sufficiently account for major global change.

Bearing in mind the need to avoid overly summary depictions of the effects of objects and practices, in the following three sections we consider the objects and practices of globalization as elements of a new global history, and as the preserve of two different but dependent social segments, namely global elites and those populations that are creating globalization from below.[29]

Global History

One thing that has become clear to many historians is that globalization has been a constant through the history of humanity. There are very few spaces and times where human cultures have not been integrated one with another, in particular through networks of trade, distributed production, and flows of knowledge. Given that fact, it has become increasingly common to practise history without recourse to national and other kinds of boundaries that were prevalent in the past. History is about connection between places as much as it is about the places themselves. Given that viewpoint, objects can take on a new life as travellers on a world stage. From archaeological work showing the ways in which northern Europe was hyper-connected through networks of trade as early as the Bronze and Iron Ages,[30] through the spice route to the Roman Empire, through the vagaries of the Chinese or Venetian empires, through the rise of an Atlantic economy, and on to the multiple kinds of objects constantly being moved through vast logistical networks in the contemporary world, what we can see is a variegated history of object movement which pulls human beings along with it.[31]

But there is more. What global history shows us is that objects themselves mark cultures. Think of a contemporary object like the mouse. Intended by its 1964 inventor, Douglas Engelbart, to be a simple way of navigating the graphical user interface without a keyboard, it has now become a means of access to

---

[29] Jean-François Bayart, *Global Subjects: A Political Critique of Globalisation* (Cambridge: Polity Press, 2007).

[30] Barry Cunliffe, *Facing the Ocean: The Atlantic and Its Peoples, 8000BC–1500AD* (Oxford: Oxford University Press 2001).

[31] Trentmann, 'Crossing Divides', and 'Materiality in the Future of History: Things, Practices, and Politics', *Journal of British Studies* 48, 2 (April 2009): 283–307.

the world which cannot be gainsaid. At least until the time when the use of touch-screen technologies—the iPhone, the iPad, and so on—came to dominate our information worlds, the mouse remained an obligatory point of passage. And through its many clicks passed information, interpretation, moods, and new inventions of the world. Thus the mouse opens the user to the world of flows but, at the same time, these flows are often surprisingly specific as another example shows.

Thus, Daniel Miller, in his study of Facebook, shows that practices like Facebook, for all the rhetoric of hyper-connection, are actually much more limited but perhaps more powerful entities. Thus, he illustrates that this simple means of reorganization of web contacts which has become a basic household utility has actually produced a means of reintegrating and repairing social networks:

> My conclusion is that the secret of Facebook's success, along with that of similar social networks, lies not in change but in conservatism. Above all, Facebook really is quite literally a social network. Its importance lies in its perceived and actual ability to reconstruct relationships, especially within families and with absent friends, that have gradually been fading away due to the attrition of other aspects of modern life, such as mobility…So the single most important attribute of Facebook is not what is new about it, but the degree to which it seems to help us return to the kind of involvement in social networks that we believe we have lost.[32]

But he also illustrates that Facebook is massively culturally variable in terms of its modes of use. In Trinidad, Facebook is used in quite different ways from in the UK, giving the lie to the more exaggerated accounts of globalization which are determined to see a flat world without borders.

Objects and practices, therefore, are simultaneously about creating differentiated social networks, as the study of different forms of globalizing practice and the lessons of global history amply show, and about gradually furnishing complete worlds of interaction, 'spheres' which have their own special 'atmospheres' of belonging based on common rhythms and spaces, not so much a pattern of order projected onto objects as a set of effective propositions about globality which are always agitated feelings of expanse.[33]

Global Elites

Over the last twenty years, there has been a considerable growth of that group of people who are able to use globalization in order to produce untold-of

---

[32] Daniel Miller, *Tales from Facebook* (Cambridge: Polity Press, 2011): 217.
[33] Peter Sloterdijk, *Neither Sun Nor Death*, trans. Steve Corcoran (Los Angeles: Seminotext(e), 2011).

wealth. This global elite has been able to achieve its power and influence by using various kinds of practices replete with their own object worlds in order to build an empire of wealth and influence which is often outwith the control of individual nation states. These practices are not necessarily the obvious ones, like obsessive business travel or inhabiting just a few global cities with the infrastructures to support their distinctive ecologies. There are other practices involved too. Janine Wedel names four: personalizing bureaucracy; producing shared conviction and action; juggling roles and representations in order to produce a new pool of resources and information; and finessing, circumventing, or rewriting rules (some of these themes are explored by her in this volume).[34] In other words, elites are able to create their own forms of habitat which allow them to reorganize or suborn governing processes and bureaucracies to suit their own purposes. For example, these elites have gradually built the capacity to intervene in the process of policy formation in flexible and opportunistic ways which often require remarkably little in the way of bureaucratic infrastructure. They rarely have to wait, a practice all too familiar to those who are involved in globalization from below. And they are able to talk about objects as possessions in ways which are not ironic. None of this is to argue that this global elite is completely immune from governmental influence, as exemplified by the power of the Russian state to defenestrate wayward oligarchs, but this is the exception rather than the rule.

Obviously, maintaining this kind of loosely interacting and highly flexible network depends upon its own ecology of objects and practices. In particular, it requires an ability to travel when needed, an ability to deploy resources rapidly, and an ability to build a network of contacts which cuts across most areas of life.

One of the elements that elites have to reproduce is a habitat of sociability.[35] This can take a number of forms. One of them is the siting of a constellation of cultural practices and places which are associated with 'worth'—financial, moral, and epistemic. For example, it is clear that certain restaurants, clubs, and places of entertainment require significant social and economic resource to access and themselves confer status through their consumption. But elites have gradually gathered other mechanisms of adhesion to themselves. Perhaps the most obvious example of these mechanisms is the modern conference and workshop.

It would no doubt be possible to spend a large amount of time at these conferences, but the more critical issue is understanding which are actually important. So far as global elites are concerned, the acme may be the World Economic Forum, held annually at Davos, or perhaps the annual meeting of

---

[34] Janine R. Wedel, *Shadow Elite: How the World's New Power Brokers Undermine Democracy, Government, and the Free Market* (New York: Basic, 2009).

[35] Mike Savage and Karel Williams, eds, *Remembering Elites* (Oxford: Blackwell-Wiley, 2008).

bankers held at Jackson Hole in Wyoming, but there are many other meetings that are less well known but probably as or more influential in that they provide much more concentrated interaction in a less visible environment. Critical for the global elite is that leading political figures feel compelled to participate and often kowtow, as in the case, at least until recently, of the annual News International meeting in Australia.

Another example is the ability to create the conditions to allow elite wealth and influence to expand and multiply. That involves a battery of practices such as personal banking, gaining favourable access to various investment opportunities, specific kinds of credit card, tax arbitrage, and the ability to own many domiciles at once. When they coalesce, they produce a state of permanent advantage.

Globalization from Below

Globalization does not just involve the practices of multinational corporations, global elites, and government diktats. There is also a constant hum of other kinds of activity which depend on practices very different from those at the 'high end'. In particular, it is possible to talk about 'low-end globalization'. In his meticulous ethnography of Chungking Mansions in Hong Kong, a dilapidated set of buildings that simultaneously is a guest house, a location for high-end Cantonese restaurants, a zone packed with illegal working, and an entrepôt for small-scale traders from around the world, Gordon Matthews shows how the site embodies a low-end transnational flow of people—in his count 129 different nationalities are represented—and goods involving relatively small amounts of capital.[36] Chungking Mansions is a node for informal transactions that allow lower- and middle-class consumer markets to interact.

Just like global elites, globalization from below has its own objects and practices, whether these be informal money-transfer systems, increasingly including networks of traders, organizers of undocumented labour, or landlords willing to be flexible about terms and leases. When these objects and practices are put together, they provide a perfectly viable system of trade and opportunity which incorporates many millions of people. Not all such examples make for comfortable reading, as the sheer size of international trade in illegal recreational drugs would suggest. There is also growing evidence that much of the 'foreign' direct investment driving Indian economic growth is, in fact, money recycled by corrupt politicians and bureaucrats but also that, paradoxically,

---

[36] Gordon Matthews, *Ghetto at the Center of the World: Chungking Mansions, Hong Kong* (Chicago: University of Chicago Press, 2011).

the endemic nature of corruption in India means that this is one of the few forms of capital that can be mobilized rapidly.[37]

Possibly the most potent example of globalization from below, however, is the growth of the mobile phone as a means of producing a low-cost economic ecosystem. Indeed, in certain areas of the world, like sub-Saharan Africa, the mobile phone has become the key infrastructural moment in allowing low-end markets to form, prices to be set, money to be transmitted, and accumulation to be registered. In 1998, there were fewer than four million mobiles on the continent. Today, there are more than 500 million. This growth has had obvious effects, as Killian Fox reported in the *Observer*:

The most dramatic example of this is mobile banking. Four years ago, in…Kenya, the mobile network Safaricom introduced a service called M-Pesa which allows users to store money on their mobiles. If you want to pay a utilities bill or send money to a friend, you simply dispatch the amount by text and the recipient converts it into cash at their local M-Pesa office. It is cheap, easy to use and, for millions of Africans unable to access a bank account or afford the hefty charges of using one, nothing short of revolutionary.[38]

The Book

In the rest of this book we want to take up these five themes in the round by concentrating on the objects and practices that go to make up the current phase of globalization. These objects and practices are diverse, and between them they add up to a necessarily incomplete approach to what globalization currently is. In the future, new objects and practices will come into existence which will gradually reconstitute and recondition actually existing globalization. But, for now, these are some of the key focal points of how and why globalization matters.

In sum, then, this book takes as its starting point the fact that too often globalization continues to be depicted as a set of extraterrestrial forces with no real physical manifestation, except as effects. This book takes a rather different tack. It explores the mundane means by which globalization has been achieved and concentrates on the everyday life of capitalism, the not-so-'little' things that keep the 'large' forces of globalization ticking over.

This is at once an empirical and a theoretical project. With its eye on the objects of globalization, the book demonstrates that a series of everyday, mundane and—consequently—all but invisible formations critically facilitate and

---

[37] Rana Dasgupta, 'India's Revolt Against the Undeserving Rich', *Financial Times*, 21 August 2011.
[38] Killan Fox, 'Africa's Mobile Economic Revolution', *Observer*, The New Review, 24 July 2011, 20.

create the conditions under which globalization has been able to flourish. The emphasis, in other words, is on concrete moments in the conduct of globalization when new physical means of regular reproduction were invented and deployed. It is on the use and enactment of mundane arrangements in practice, the nitty-gritty operation of the machine. Only by understanding these everyday infrastructures and passage points, or so we argue, can we understand the dynamics of globalization.

Each of the following essays reflects upon the ways that everyday social and/or physical infrastructures are embedded within apparently footloose globalizing tendencies and, indeed, enable these tendencies to be mobile. In the main, the essays each work from concrete examples to make a general point. Together, they aim decisively to demonstrate the value of an approach which allows the 'little things' their space. This volume thus hopefully makes a distinctive contribution to debates around globalization which have become caricatured and sometimes rather predictable.

Organizationally, our editorial approach in this volume has, reflecting the necessarily partial nature of globalization, been itself partial. We have not tried to produce an exhaustive survey of those objects and practices that constitute globalization. Rather, we have picked out some of the main passage points and some of the residuals which are revealing of how globalization proceeds. But we have followed two principles. First, we have tried to emphasize the point that 'globalization' occurs in relation to a vast, myriad array of ordinary objects, devices, and practices. Hence, the volume is designed around a large number of relatively short contributions on very diverse topics. Second, we want to make clear how globalization is made manifest, brought into being, and sustained in and through the most unlikely and ordinary things: bananas, bar codes, the game of rounders; and how apparently global phenomena—news services, CCTV, Bollywood—depend on intricate and detailed assemblage work to give their apparent transcendence. However, we would encourage readers to avoid a linear approach when reading this volume and encourage you to dip and skim and, consequently, come across unexpected entries and make new connections.

Part I
Travel, Tourism, and Mobility

1 Airports

Peter Adey

The airport is a paradox of movement. It is both mobile and incredibly immobile; it is marked by stasis and fluidity. People stop and people go, they shop and they drop. This continual tension of mobility and immobility, I will suggest, constitutes the humdrum nitty-gritty workings of the airport and facilitates the process of what we know as globalization.

Of course, the airport itself is a grand facilitator in the global networks of mobility. Airports permit movement by shuttling people, wealth, and goods across the globe. They do this not in spite of but because of their fixity. Whilst they offer extensive movement to the aeromobile vectors of aircraft, these mobilities are rigidly channelled and fixed. Airports are the obligatory points of passage, the nodes on the network of the global and the local, they are corridors of movement that one simply cannot avoid.[1] As Heidegger tells us, they are sites that we must continually depart from and return to—the fixed form of the airport runway 'stands in reserve' for aircraft to leave from and land on time and again.[2]

Even as the dynamics of moving and going rely upon the stasis of the airport-as-node, what John Urry borrowing from Henri Lefebvre has described as a 'mooring,'[3] if we drop down a scale and look more closely at the airport this pattern repeats itself endlessly. It may even resemble the never-ending iterations of a fractal pattern. But more importantly, without this logic the airport would simply not work.

Let us imagine that we could take the roof off an airport terminal as if it were a toy model. Peering inside you would see the maze-like labyrinth of partition walls, barriers, and bollards reminiscent of an IKEA superstore. For airport designers the intention is to resemble an exhibition space where 'nothing is set in stone'. When traversing an airport you may catch a glimpse through the gaps in a partition, an open doorway, or a window to the other side. In IKEA, a sign on the door might say 'Staff Only' which some of us might choose to ignore. On the other hand, in an airport there is likely a card entry system or a guard armed with a large gun blocking your way and you are forced always on.

---

[1] Claus Lassen, 'Aeromobility and Work', *Environment and Planning A* 38, 2 (2006): 301–12.

[2] Martin Heidegger, *The Question Concerning Technology, and Other Essays* (New York: Harper and Row, 1977).

[3] John Urry, *Global Complexity* (Cambridge: Polity, 2003).

If one spends long enough at an airport you will apprehend the temporality of these structures as shops move and go, rooms are rebuilt, walls are pulled down, repainted, and refurbished, bollards, ropes, and barriers are placed and removed. The airport is continually unmade and un-built.[4] Stuart Brand tells us that this is because many buildings learn and adapt.[5] But they are not necessarily experienced by the general public in this way. The relative fixity, or the synchronicity, of these fairly temporary structures with the passenger creates a tension of moving and staying. In the airport, the wall stays and you move on. Well, that's not the whole truth, for with effort you can remove fixtures and fittings, but only if you don't mind breaking the common airport by-law of 'displacement' which makes it a crime to move or 'displace' those very fixtures and fittings. Such social and legal codes hold the building together and allow it to endure.

The consequence of this is that the airport's relative fixity permits a sense of persistence and hardness to its structure. This infrastructural stickiness creates corridors of passages and thoroughfares where we are exposed to the airport's governing logic of consumer capitalism.[6] Our micro-bodily movements have been planned by prediction and calculation. Likewise, the relative fixities of the terminal are achieved through careful coordination. Everyday practices of shelf stacking and restocking mean that consumables such as the millions of cups of coffee, tea, snacks, and magazines synchronize perfectly with our mobility. Bacon butties and beer meet travelling football fans, while supplies of newspapers and fresh coffee coincide with the morning business-traveller rush. Some structures, of course, are stickier than others. Ageing escalators, elevators, and other expensive infrastructural elements speak volumes about the immobilizing weight of their replacement cost and the 'sunk' capital that they embody.[7]

Having said that, even while we may go and the materials of the terminal are left behind, there are times in the airport when we must be stopped, when our fluidity must be contained or ordered by a sequential system of processing.[8] It is in this sense that one's mobility interferes with itself. I don't mean to get all quantum on you, but at the airport one's immobility simultaneously permits one's mobility, just not at the same time. Your future or virtual movement is

---

[4] Anique Hommels, *Unbuilding Cities; Obduracy in Urban Socio-technical Change* (Cambridge, MA: MIT Press, 2005).

[5] Stuart Brand, *How Buildings Learn: What Happens After They're Built* (New York: Viking, 1994).

[6] Gillian Fuller and Ross Harley, *Aviopolis: A Book About Airports* (London: Blackdog, 2004).

[7] Stephen Graham and Simon Marvin, *Splintering Urbanism: Networked Infrastructures, Technological Mobilites and the Urban Condition* (London: Routledge, 2001). David Harvey, *Justice, Nature and the Geography of Difference* (Cambridge, MA: Blackwell Publishers, 1996).

[8] Jorg Bechmann, 'Ambivalent Spaces of Restlessness: Ordering (Im)mobilities at Airports', in *Space Odysseys: Spatiality and Social Relations in the 21st Century*, ed. J. O. Baerenholdt and K. Simonsen (Ashgate: Aldershot, 2005).

only possible if you wait in the check-in queue so that the airline may process your details, if you spend time in the airside departure lounge so that you may synchronize with your plane. The practice of the airport is a process of storing and holding passengers at various stages through the space. Without these dynamics the operational arm of the airport system would not work. The fact that many airports provide demarcated prayer rooms may be an example of this tension being a real human need: to be still in order to make a later movement possible, or to ease the stress of a prior one.

In other areas of the airport one's mobility is becoming increasingly dependent upon another's. Airport security must differentiate and sort wanted or suspicious from less risky passengers. To do this they are beginning to 'trust' or register passengers. Those deemed to be trustworthy may move at greater velocities and in more comfort through security and immigration spaces. Those 'of risk' may toil in lengthy queues subjected to pat-down searches, lengthy questioning, interrogation, or worse. These mobilities are connected. The dialectic between mobility and immobility means that staffing levels, resources, and increased scrutiny are applied to the less trusted so that registered travellers may actually move at the expense of non-registered.

As internationalizing relationships and free-trade agreements open up borders to people and goods they simultaneously shut them down to others.[9] This is not just the process of liberalization but also that of bifurcation and, indeed, it is a bifurcation with connection.[10] It is a differential relationship of moving and going, 'storing and forwarding',[11] mobility and immobility. In ending this essay I think we can move beyond the airport to consider the thought that maybe the airport's macro and micro practices of mobility and immobility do not just add up to or comprise the processes of globalization, but they actually capture its logic, and with some precision.

---

[9] Ginette Verstraete, 'Technological Frontiers and the Politics of Mobilities', *New Formations* 43 (2001): 26–43.

[10] Matthew B. Sparke, 'A Neoliberal Nexus: Economy, Security and the Bioplitics of Citizenship on the Border', *Political Geography* 25, 2 (February 2006): 151–80.

[11] Fuller and Harley, *Avioplois*.

2 Backpacking

Nick Clarke

'[I]t was not just her body but her whole life that was shattered when she sat only a few feet away from suicide bomber Shehzad Tanweer as he detonated the explosives in his backpack on July 7 last year.'

Guardian, 24 April 2006, page 4

On the London Underground, at least, we may never look at backpacks in the same way again. But then maybe we should have always viewed backpacks with more curiosity and concern than traditionally we have done. Backpacks allow people to walk (or run, or paddle, or ski) while carrying a heavy load. They have existed in one form or another for as long as people have needed to carry heavy loads in this way. But what most of us would recognize as the modern backpack was probably invented in Norway by Ole F. Bergan in 1908, and then developed in partnership with the Norwegian army during the early twentieth century. Indeed, military requirements and programmes played a key role in the development of backpacks and related technologies throughout much of the twentieth century. The kinds of food carried in backpacks, for example—from processed cheese to freeze-dried coffee—mostly began life as projects at the US Department of Defense Combat Feeding Program in Natick, Massachusetts.

For some, backpacking describes a combination of hiking and camping, often in 'remote' or 'wilderness' areas. But for many, increasingly, backpacking describes a certain mode of travel that was born in the late 1960s and has grown and changed almost beyond recognition over the last 40 or so years. Erik Cohen was there at the birth, where he met what he later called 'the drifters'—a handful of Western youths apparently alienated from modern society in the wake of the Vietnam War and the perceived failure of May 1968, travelling, often alone, in places chosen for their otherness—their drugs, their religions—such as Morocco and India.[1]

Today, among other things, backpacking is an object of study and a market niche. A collection of papers edited by Greg Richards and Julie Wilson

---

[1] Erik Cohen, 'Nomads From Affluence: Notes on the Phenomenon of Drifter-Tourism', *International Journal of Comparative Sociology* 14, 1–2 (1973): 89–103.

gives us a sense of what tourism scholars and practitioners have in mind when they use the term backpacking.[2] First, they have certain people in mind: citizens of certain countries such as Australia, New Zealand, Canada, the UK, Germany, the Netherlands, Sweden, Norway, Denmark, Israel, and Japan; people generally in their late teens or twenties; and people with certain 'preferences'—for budget accommodation, meeting other travellers, independently organized and flexible schedules, longer holidays, participatory activities such as white-water rafting, and 'authentic experiences'. Second, they have certain spaces in mind—an established 'circuit' of well-worn 'trails' between 'enclaves' such as Khao San in Bangkok, Ubud in Bali, and Kings Cross in Sydney. Third, they have certain practices, objects, and stories in mind, from video-watching and banana pancakes to narratives of risk and danger (through which, according to Erik Cohen, today's backpackers attempt to bridge the gap between the haunting ideology of drifting and their increasingly recreational practices[3]).

If backpacking describes this mode of travel, then a series of governmental technologies makes backpacking (im)possible, from passports to visa programmes such as Australia's Working Holiday Programme. And a stock of historically, geographically, socially, and culturally specific stories make backpacking (un)desirable, from the stories found in essays, paintings, poems, and novels by artists as similar and different as Keats and Kerouac, to the stories found in biographies of characters as similar and different as tramps, Grand Tourists, and colonialists. And a series of developments make backpacking relatively easy. Travel guides and agents enable backpackers to plan their trips. Relatively cheap flights, public transport, and backpacks enable backpackers to move along trails. Hostels, management companies, recruitment agents, letting agents, takeaway food outlets, laundrettes, vaccinations, insect repellent, and sunscreen enable backpackers to dwell comfortably within enclaves. Credit cards, phone cards, mobile phones, MP3 players, Internet cafes, satellite television services, DVDs, photographs, and curricula vitae enable backpackers to 'take themselves with them' and thus to maintain relationships and a certain continuity across space and through time.[4]

Each of these technologies, stories, and developments has its own unique history. Youth hostels, for example, date back to a variety of movements centred on youth, walking, and nature in late nineteenth- and early twentieth-century Europe. In particular, they date back to 1909 when a German schoolteacher, Richard Shirrmann, arranged walking tours for pupils through the hill

---

[2] Greg Richards and Julie Wilson, eds, *The Global Nomad: Backpacker Travel in Theory and Practice* (Clevedon: Channel View Publications, 2004).

[3] Erik Cohen, 'Backpacking: Diversity and Change', in *The Global Nomad: Backpacker Travel in Theory and Practice*, ed. Greg Richards and Julie Wilson (Clevedon: Channel View Publications, 2004).

[4] Nick Clarke, 'Detailing transnational lives of the middle: British working holidaymakers in Australia', *Journal of Ethnic and Migration Studies* 31, 2 (2005): 307–22.

country bordering the Rhine using schools along the route as accommodation. Shirrmann opened his first purpose-built hostel in 1910. Founding principles referred to education, health, sun, fresh air, and nature—a reaction to the dirty, overcrowded, poorly ventilated industrial towns of the Ruhr. The movement grew and with time further principles were added, referring to environmental conservation, personal development, friendship, and understanding of others and the world. By 1932, when the first meeting of the International Youth Hostel Federation was held in Amsterdam, 2,123 youth hostels were in operation. Today, around 4,500 hostels exist across 60 or so countries.

Moreover, backpacking is one of the many things—again, each with its own unique history—that come together in the achievement and reproduction of what we call globalization. As they move from place to place, backpackers carry things with them, and not just items of material culture such as football shirts or sarongs—though these have their own importance. The explicit aims of Australia's Working Holiday Programme include to foster the transfer of work-based ideas and practices, and to foster the establishment of long-term trade and business links between Australia and elsewhere. Backpackers carry desires and demands too, in the name of which places get remade. So desires for commodities help produce commercialized places. Demands for connectedness help produce networked places. And once places become commercialized and networked, backpackers move on to other places—attempting to bridge that gap between the radical ideology and conservative practice of backpacking—helping to 'switch on' these other places...and so on to 'the four corners of the earth'.

In addition, backpackers bring things home, from souvenirs to photographs, from journals to address books, from old ideas to new habits. They bring home stories from which to construct identities. They bring home skills for life on the move. Ironically, then, backpackers leave home to escape modern life (so they say, at least for a while), but return home prepared for exactly that—a point not lost in subsequent job interviews.[5]

So we should view backpacks with more curiosity and concern than traditionally we have done. Backpacking may not be paid work, and it may not be everyday life, but it has significance nevertheless. And this significance lies beyond the destruction sometimes attributed to backpacking—destruction of so-called 'untouched' societies and environments. Because backpacking is creative. It is creative of differentiation in that backpacking is not available to everyone. It is creative of immobility in that backpackers fix people and places through their representations. And it is creative of networked places and flow-ready subjects, as demonstrated in the paragraphs above. So what you think of backpacking may well depend on what you think of globalization...which in turn may depend on your situation...such as the seat you choose or find available to you on the London Underground.

---

[5] Nick Clarke, 'Free independent travellers? British working holidaymakers in Australia', *Transactions of the Institute of British Geographers* 29, 4 (2004): 499–509.

3 Walking

Tim Ingold

In a classic article on the evolution of the peculiarly human capacity for bipedal locomotion, the physical anthropologist John Napier asserted that the very essence of bipedalism—'the criterion by which the evolutionary status of a hominid walker must be judged'—lies in what he called the striding gait.[1] The stride comprises a rigidly mechanical, straight-legged oscillation from the hips, with eyes gazing steadfastly forwards, the arms swinging loosely, and the hands with down-turned palms. When we consider the full range of ways in which men and women of all ages—from different backgrounds, and having to negotiate the most diverse environmental conditions—have improvised their ways of getting about on two feet, the stride, far from being the marker of our essential humanity that Napier thought it was, turns out to be very peculiar indeed.[2] How, then, did this strange mode of locomotion come to be enshrined in anthropological orthodoxy as a human universal?

By and large, it is not by striding about that human beings have made their ways in the world. Indeed in most circumstances, the striding gait is dangerously impracticable. With his eyes scanning the horizon rather than the ground, and his legs disciplined to a mechanical oscillation, the strider is quite unable to adjust to any unevenness in the texture of the terrain, or to avoid obstacles that he anyway fails to see. On anything but an artificially paved ground, he would constantly be tripping up. Nor can this gait be sustained for any length of time on such a hard and unyielding surface without injury to the feet, save by encasing them in rigid boots. For the most part, people have opted for ways of walking better suited to their means and circumstances. Far from marching out in heavy boots across the paved surfaces of the world, they have made their way lightly, dexterously, and usually barefoot. Nor have they used their feet exclusively for walking. They could be used, in conjunction with the hands, for creeping, crawling, climbing, and a host of other purposes, taking full advantage of the prehensile powers of the toes when not encased in footwear.[3]

---

[1] John Napier, 'The Antiquity of Human Walking', in *Human Variations and Origins: Readings From the Scientific American*, ed. W. S. Laughlin and R. H. Osborne (San Francisco: Feeman, 1967): 116–26.

[2] Tim Ingold, 'Culture on the Ground: The World Perceived Through the Feet', *Journal of Material Culture* 9, 3 (2004): 315–40.

[3] Hitoshi Watanabe, 'Running, Creeping and Climbing: A New Ecological and Evolutionary Perspective on Human Evolution', *Mankind* 8, 1 (June 1971): 1–13.

The stride enacts a bodily image of colonial occupation, straddling the distance between points of departure and arrival as though one could have a foot in each simultaneously, encompassing both—and all points in between—in a single appropriative movement. For the indigenous inhabitants of a country, by contrast, walking is a practice of *wayfaring*. Inhabitants seek not to straddle the earth, and thereby to connect up its locations into an encompassing grid, but rather to make their ways along circuitous paths without beginning or end, through the country that opens up around them. As they go, their feet mark the earth. But they do not, like the feet of the booted colonist, stamp on it. Footprints are not stamps. They are not impressed on the ground, as a mark of appropriation, but embedded *in* it, as clues to a walker's whereabouts and intentions, and for others to follow. Distinct footprints are registered most clearly not on hard surfaces but on those which, being soft and malleable, are easily impressed, such as of snow, sand, mud, and moss. Yet precisely because soft surfaces do not readily hold their form, footprints tend to be ephemeral. They have a duration bound to the temporal dynamics of the ground to which they belong: to cycles of organic growth and decay, of the weather, and of the seasons.[4]

Characteristic of wayfaring is the intimate coupling of movement and perception.[5] The wayfarer's orientation, pace, and rhythm, along with his or her detailed footwork, continually respond to a close perceptual monitoring of the environment that unfolds along the way. Not all wayfaring, of course, is done on foot. It may, for example, be done on horseback or by boat. Australian Aboriginal people use cars as vehicles of wayfaring when they drive in the outback, and read the tyre tracks as they once read footprints.[6] But conversely, not all pedestrian movement amounts to wayfaring. Where it does not, it takes the peculiar form of the march. This is the walk of colonial occupation. Characteristic of marching is that the body is propelled on a predetermined course by a mechanical movement that is unresponsive to environmental conditions. Soldiers on the march are expected to keep to the steady beat of the drum, but not to look where they are going. Before their unswerving gaze and in their deafened ears the world passes by unnoticed and unheard. Far from laying a circuitous trail, marching is understood as a *progress*.[7] It advances, in strides, from a point of embarkation towards a destination. Moreover the route has been surveyed and surfaced in advance of the movement that takes place along it.

---

[4] Tim Ingold and J. Lee Vergunst, 'Introduction', in *Ways of Walking: Ethnography and Practice on Foot* (Aldershot: Ashgate, 2008).

[5] Tim Ingold, *Lines: A Brief History* (London: Routledge, 2007): 78.

[6] Diana Young, 'The Life and Death of Cars: Private Vehicles on the Pitjantjatjara Lands, South Australia', in *Car Cultures*, ed. Daniel Miller (Oxford: Berg, 2001): 35–57.

[7] Kenneth Olwig, 'Landscape, Place, and the State of Progress', in *Progress: Geographical Essays*, ed. Robert David Sack (Baltimore: Johns Hopkins University Press): 22–60.

According to historian Jan Bremmer, the stride can be traced to the culture of ancient Greece.[8] Its origin lies in an age when every man had to carry arms, and to be ready to fight to protect both reputation and possessions. It was unequivocally masculine. Women were expected to walk with smaller and more nimble steps, with palms upturned and eyes downcast, signifying modesty and submission. Bremmer shows how these gendered ideals of walking were passed from Greek Antiquity to early modern Europe through the works of Cicero, Saint Ambrose, and Erasmus. And from there, they entered the discourse and practice of European military discipline. It was on the parade ground—hard surfaced, levelled, and cleared of obstacles—that the stride evolved into its most extreme and stylized form, namely the goose step. The step has its origins in marching styles developed by the Prussian army in the early eighteenth century, and survived for almost three centuries until the East German Ministry of Defence abolished it in 1990.[9]

But it was in Germany too, that the first systematic studies were undertaken of the mechanics of human locomotion. By the end of the nineteenth century, these studies would feature photographs of more or less naked men pacing a bare floor. The idea was that by stripping the body of all appurtenances and the ground of all features, the universal essence of human walking would be revealed in a form untrammelled by the particularities of environment and culture. Yet as Mary Flesher has shown, the scientific study of human locomotion had its roots in military discipline.[10] Many of the earliest subjects to be roped into laboratory tests were in fact soldiers, already trained in the routines of the drill. Unsurprisingly, when commanded to walk they stepped out as if on parade. Thanks to their obedient performance, the stride entered the discourse of physical anthropology as one of a suite of criteria of essential humanity, linked to a triumphalist evolutionary narrative of increasing uprightness, supremacy over other species, and eventual global domination.

---

[8] Jan Bremmer, 'Walking, Striding and Sitting in Ancient Greek Culture', in *A Cultural History of Gesture*, ed. Jan Bremmer and Herman Roodenbug (Oxford: Polity Press, 1992): 15–35.

[9] Mary M. Flesher, 'Repetitive Order and the Human Walking Apparatus: Prussian Military Science Versus the Webers' Locomotion Research', *Annals of Science* 54, 5 (1997): 463–87.

[10] Ibid.

4 Mobile Phone

Eric Laurier

The telephone used to stay where it was installed. An engineer would arrive, threading out some cable, pinning it, along with a small junction box, to the skirting boards, running it up and over doorframes, and sometimes through walls. The telephone itself either rested on a horizontal surface or was firmly screwed to a wall. Ecologies of telephony grew up around its location: paper for writing messages on, address books, business cards, doorstep directories often years out of date in yellow and white, and, as often, a chair. The latter put there because calls could last a long time and sometimes there were calls where you were asked if you were sitting down first. When you called someone at their number you were also calling them at the address of that number. People had home numbers and work numbers, and, while on holiday, hotel room numbers.

Even though the payphone in the street may be gradually disappearing under posters, advertising, and their ever-present misuse as urinals, the old domestic and office infrastructures of the immobile phone (as it's never called) are still there. The phone line laid by the engineer is busier than ever with broadband. The question I would like to raise is about the new mundane ecologies of the mobile phone. In what ways have our everyday lives been rearranged through and around them? It hardly seems appropriate to say that we have our mobile phones installed. We buy them in the way that we bought that first mobile, the Sony Walkman, in a box. Our device is registered, our batteries are left charging overnight, and our apps, emails, and address books transferred from one to another. In buying them as we would cameras or watches and acquiring them like credit cards, each of whose functions they have infringed upon, we have now come to the slightly peculiar situation in the UK of having a greater population of mobile phones than people.

The mobile phone, if we will risk saying that it is installed at all, is installed in pockets and in handbags. Mine gradually wears a rectangular bleach mark into my jeans. A fair few have cracked screens from being installed in the back pockets of trousers and then having their owner sit on a hard wooden chair. That this new global technology has managed to secure a spot in our pockets is an incredible turn of events. In one sense because at their outset mobile phones were the size of a briefcase themselves and in another more fundamental sense because we are only willing to carry a tiny number of notionally portable items in our pockets. Usually small change, folded wallets, keys, perhaps a pen, cigarettes, or chewing gum. Petite items that have a centrality to our lives that gives them entry to that tiny baggage compartment on our bodies. Once installed in the pocket, mobile phones can summon our attention not only by ringing or playing the first few notes of favourite songs but by touching us. They can vibrate. Few of us will forget the initial oddity and intimacy of those first few summons by vibration. The mobile phone's buzzing touch is now incorporated into the routine ways in which our attention is sought by others through various social media.

Installed in the handbag or rucksack, the mobile phone drifts ever downward, escaping our clutches in the clutter of notebooks, pens, make-up, water, gloves, and other stuff that it is riding with. As a consequence, when calls are anticipated, mobile phones are pulled to the top or placed on tabletops in front of us. Temporary installations. Rucksacks and shoulder bags have been redesigned with pockets acting as sockets for the mobile phone.

While the global cellular infrastructure required to make mobile phones seem infrastructureless is truly massive (just start counting the masts—often camouflaged—as you travel along any road) what is equally amazing is the insinuation of the phone into the maintenance of our daily domestic infrastructures. It is not an accident that the mobile phone's origins as voice- and text-based are linked to distributed workforces maintaining communication networks. Mobile phones are ideal for the sharing out of all manner of jobs. How often do I find myself in a shop phoning home to check whether another member of the household has bought milk already? Or texting an address or phone number for someone to someone else?

Beyond the domestic chores, daily logistics, and accountable absences, the mobile phone has allowed us to rearrange our privacy, private lives, and, indeed, the private sphere in all manner of ways. There are the obvious invasions of this new privacy perpetrated by states spying on citizens through phone tapping, email intercept, locating devices using the cellular network, and the press obtaining recordings of phone calls between the rich and famous by various means. There are the new intrusions where we find ourselves party to a stranger's private life on the train or in a shop. A curious party too, because we only hear one half of what are sometimes painfully intimate topics. If we recall though for a moment the geography of houses and fixed-line phones: the teenage son to trying to arrange a date from the family phone in the hallway with his sister eavesdropping and teasing; more urgently, the wife of an alcoholic husband whispering in hushed tones from her kitchen phone nook fearing that he may come in at any moment and hear her calling for help from her sister.

A question raised early on about the likely uses of mobile phones in private lives was much more straightforward: they made infidelity between cohabiting couples easier. There was no longer the danger that the cheated-on party would pick up the phone when the 'other' woman or man called. But there is a more subtle rearrangement of privacy. From our tightly knit domestic spaces we can turn to friends for advice, counsel, and reassurance via voice, text messaging, Facebook, or Twitter while out doing the shopping or driving home from work in the car or sitting on the train. Thoughts that one would once have dwelt on alone are thoughts we share with our friends, family, and a newly articulated set of public audiences while walking in the street in the rain or sitting having a coffee. Those others that matter to us, majorly and minorly, are with us in a new arrangement of togetherness and care. Who would have thought that the briefcase-sized device dragged around by highly paid business workers and military officers would become just as important to the work of loving and tending to kith and kin.

5 Mobility

Peter Merriman

Mobility and movement could be taken to be watchwords of globalization. Global companies, cultural commentators, and academics stress that we live in a world of incessant movement (the 'annihilation of space by time', the 'shrinking of space', or 'the end of geography') as modern means of communication, high-speed transportation, and logistics appear to facilitate the free and frictionless circulation of people and objects around the world at ever-increasing speeds.[1] Movement and fluidity are seen as more fundamental than fixity or locatedness in today's world and—in the most extreme versions of the future—we are said to be destined (doomed) to live in a world of soul-less, solitary homogeneous 'non-places', in a future where people will resort to taking motionless trips. Reading authorities such as Augé, Virilio, Castells, or Jameson is seductive, and it is easy to get caught up in the globalized hyperbole of globalization-speak, embrace (or critique) the dystopian worlds pictured, lament the purported loss of local character and difference, and despise multinational capital and globalized consumer brands.[2] These assumptions/claims need to be explored: do we really live in a world of free, homogeneous, frictionless movement or of limitless acceleration; are global and globalized mobilities really that new? and what does it mean to call a mobile process or agent global or globalized?[3]

Not everyone benefits from new forms of communication and connection. Processes of 'global shrinkage' or 'time–space compression' have differential

---

[1] All manner of commentators have remarked on the 'annihilation of space by time' and the 'shrinking of distance', from Karl Marx to David Harvey. See Wolfgang Schivelbusch, *The Railway Journey: The Industrialization of Time and Space in the 19th Century* (Leamington Spa: Berg, 1986); David Harvey, *The Condition of Postmodernity* (Oxford: Blackwell, 1990); Nigel Thrift, *Spatial Formations* (London: Sage, 1996).

[2] Marc Augé, *Non-Places: Introduction to an Anthropology of Supermodernity* (London: Verso, 1995); Paul Virilio, *Polar Inertia* (London: Verso, 2000); Frederic Jameson, *Postmodernism, or, the Cultural Logic of Late Capitalism* (London: Verso, 1991); Manuel Castells, *The Rise of the Network Society* (2nd edn, Oxford: Blackwell, 2000); see also Peter Merriman, 'Driving places: Marc Augé, Non-Places, and the Geographies of England's M1 Motorway', *Theory, Culture and Society* 21, 4/5 (2004): 145–67.

[3] Doreen Massey, 'Power-Geometry and a Progressive Sense of Place', in *Mapping the Futures*, ed. Jon Bird, Barry Curtis, Tim Putnam, George Robertson, and Lisa Tickner (London: Routledge, 1993): 59–69; Tim Cresswell, 'The Production of Mobilities', *New Formations* 43 (2001): 11–25; Tim Cresswell, *On the Move* (London: Routledge, 2006); Tim Cresswell, 'Towards a Politics of Mobility', *Environment and Planning D: Society and Space* 28 (2010): 17–31; Peter Merriman, 'Mobility', in *International Encyclopaedia of Human Geography (Volume 7)*, ed. Rob Kitchin and Nigel Thrift (Oxford: Elsevier, 2009): 134–43.

effects for different actors in different places.[4] Trafficked people, refugees, and asylum seekers rarely benefit from the high-speed mobility and ease of border crossing experienced by the kinetic elite of Western nations (see Chapter 1 by Peter Adey and Chapter 41 by Nicholas Gill),[5] while the inhabitants of rural areas rarely have Internet access or mobile telephone coverage that is comparable to larger towns and cities. Global(ized) processes, forces, and agents are enacted and act, they are moved and move, in a multiplicity of different ways, patterning the world in an uneven, patchwork manner. And yet, certain actors—from Western governments and international NGOs, to large transnational and multinational companies—do appear to have a degree of power to influence and shape global flows. Many iconic global brands are associated with technologies of mobility and communication (Microsoft, Apple, Nokia, Ford, Toyota, Boeing, or HSBC to name a few). While computers, mobile telephones, motor vehicles, aeroplanes, bank accounts, and Internet access may be inaccessible to many, ownership of technologies such as the mobile telephone is growing at an exponential rate in less-developed parts of continents such as Africa and Asia, in part aided by global networks of second-hand exchange. And yet, such globalized technologies of mobility are not simply consumed in standard or homogeneous ways. Motor cars, for example, are driven, inhabited, and consumed in very different ways in non-Western cultures, being incorporated into everyday life in inventive and disparate ways.[6]

Globalization is frequently associated with a present where the quality and quantity of movements are changing and there is a 'speed-up' of communications. Indeed, many of the earliest 'grand' theoretical treatises on globalization suggested that 'we' had entered a new phase of global capitalism, accordant with a new era of late modernity, late capitalism, supermodernity, or postmodernity.[7] While there is no doubt that new forms of mobility and communication are emerging, facilitating new geographies of capitalism, exchange, connection, and disconnection, it is questionable whether there was ever a shift, rupture, or turn that gave rise to a 'condition', as there is a long history of globalizing mobilities resulting in experiences of acceleration, disorientation, and placelessness for *some* people.[8] Global migrations and patterns of exploration have a history inseparable from the fundamental *and* mundane materialities

---

[4] Massey, 'Power-geometry and a progressive sense of place'.

[5] Thomas Birtchnell and Javier Caletrío, eds, *Elite Mobilities* (London: Routledge, 2014); Tim Richardson, ed., 'Borders and mobilities' (special issue), *Mobilities* 8 (2013): 1–165.

[6] Daniel Miller, ed., *Car Cultures* (Oxford: Berg, 2001); Peter Merriman, *Driving Spaces* (Oxford: Wiley-Blackwell, 2007); Peter Merriman, 'Automobility and the Geographies of the Car', *Geography Compass* 3 (2009): 586–99.

[7] Augé, *Non-places*; Harvey, *The Condition of Postmodernity*; Anthony Giddens, *The Consequences of Modernity* (Cambridge: Polity Press, 1990); Jameson, *Postmodernism*.

[8] Nigel Thrift, 'A Hyperactive World', in *Geographies of Global Change: Remapping the World*, ed. R. J. Johnston, P. J. Taylor, and M. J. Watts (2nd edn, Oxford: Blackwell, 2002): 29–42; Schivelbusch, *Railway Journey*.

of ships, compasses, sextants, maps, and charts, as well as leg irons, political ideologies, and techniques of racial classification. Technologies of mobility, ranging from ships and railways, to letter writing and motor cars, have helped to weave together empires.[9] Ships, in particular, have been central to European colonial conquests, the trade of slaves, natural resources, and consumer goods, as well as the more-or-less voluntary migrations of millions of people world-wide.[10] Indeed, in the twenty-first century, global mobilities are still shaped by these Atlantic, Pacific, and Indian ocean geographies, especially when it comes to the circulation of commodities and shipping containers—although three-dimensional printing may increasingly offer up alternatives.[11] In previous centuries global mobilities were a precarious, time-consuming, and watery affair, subject to the influences of global sea currents, prevailing winds, storms, wars, and piracy. Today's globalized mobilities continue to operate with a sustained resilience that, while vulnerable to volcanic dust clouds, extreme weather events, power failure, and terrorist attacks, are characterized by their multimodality and their distributed, networked, and multi-centred nature.

What makes movements or mobilities global or globalized? In one sense, processes and agents of mobility of various kinds appear to be *the* agents and processes which enact globalization, but once we consider these mobilities in their agential, linear, vectoral, spatial, and temporal specificities, the image of a globe enwrapped in an all-pervasive, smooth web of relations and presences quickly fades away. Rather, as a broad array of thinkers, from Bruno Latour to Nigel Thrift, have remarked, we live in neither a local nor a global world:

[T]he words 'local' and 'global' offer points of view on networks that are by nature neither local nor global, but are more or less long and more or less connected...So the strength of the error that the modern world makes about itself is now understandable, when the two couples of opposition are paired: in the middle there is nothing think-able—no collective, no network, no mediation...We poor subject-objects, we humble societies-natures, we modest locals-globals, are literally quartered among ontological regions that define each other mutually but no longer resemble our practices.[12]

Following this line of thinking I would suggest that we do not live a glo-balized world, but rather a world of movements and flows of varying dura-tion, intensity, force, and direction. Mobilities connect and conjoin, they pulse and vibrate, and the resulting frictions and turbulences give rise to all manner

---

[9] See e.g. Miles Ogborn, 'Writing Travels: Power, Knowledge and Ritual on the English East India Company's Early Voyages', *Transactions of the Institute of British Geographers* 27 (2002): 155–71.

[10] William Hasty and Kimberley Peters, 'The ship in geography and the geographies of ships', *Geography Compass* 6 (2012): 660–76.

[11] Martin Parker, 'Containerisation: Moving things and boxing ideas', *Mobilities* 8 (2013): 368–87; Thomas Birtchnell and John Urry, 'Fabricating futures and the movement of objects', *Mobilities* 8 (2013): 388–405.

[12] Bruno Latour, *We Have Never Been Modern*, trans. Catherine Porter (Harlow: Pearson, 1993): 122–3; see also Thrift, 'A Hyperactive World'.

of effects—sociologies, geographies, globalities, etc.[13] This is a world of flux, change, and becoming,[14] a world of mobilization (not globalization) in practice. This is also a highly contingent, relational, and personal world, yet these personal experiences and individual mobilities frequently get erased or generalized in much of the globalization literature.

Over the past decade or so, anthropologists, geographers, and sociologists have attempted to remedy the situation by providing more nuanced and messy accounts of how people in different cultures are positioned in relation to these global flows. One influential example from my own discipline (geography) has been Doreen Massey's essay 'A Global Sense of Place'.[15] Here Massey challenges the literature describing time–space compression, homogeneous globalizing forces, and the erosion of place by emphasizing the differential politics of mobility which underpins global connectivity and flow, and the ways in which places are 'in process'. One of her memorable descriptions is of her local London shopping street, Kilburn High Road:

[U]nder the railway bridge the newspaper stand sells papers from every county of what my neighbours, many of whom come from there, still often call the Irish Free State…[T]here's a shop which as long as I can remember has displayed saris in the window…In another newsagent's I chat with the man who keeps it, a Muslim unutterably depressed by events in the Gulf, silently chafing at having to sell the *Sun*.[16]

Massey's article advances a number of important arguments for understanding globalization. One of them is that while Kilburn is globalized in highly distinctive ways through the presence of all manner of things and flows (it is not typical, but neither is it unusual), one could also approach the places I inhabit, you inhabit, and countless others inhabit in similar kinds of ways. People, objects, and information are more-or-less incessantly and intermittently mobilized in countless ways, (re)shaping places on an ongoing basis, and provoking tensions about the impact these very mobilities have on the make-up of places. A focus on *mobilization* rather than *globalization* might enable one to trace the geographies of these emergent, linear, web-like processes without resorting to global or regionalized generalizations about the effects of *globalizing* processes or forces.

---

[13] On friction and turbulence, see Tim Cresswell, 'Friction', in *The Routledge Handbook of Mobilities*, ed. Peter Adey, David Bissell, Kevin Hannam, Peter Merriman, and Mimi Sheller (London: Routledge, 2014): 107–15; Tim Cresswell and Craig Martin, 'On turbulence: entanglements of disorder and order on a Devon beach', *Tijdschrift voor Economische en Sociale Geografie* 103 (2012): 516–29.

[14] E.g. Henri Bergson, *Creative Evolution* (London: Macmillan, 1911); Henri Bergson, *Matter and Memory* (London: George Allen, 1912); Alfred North Whitehead, *Process and Reality* (New York: The Free Press, 1978); Michel Serres, *Hermes: Literature, Science, Philosophy* (London: The Johns Hopkins University Press, 1982); Michel Serres, *The Birth of Physics* (Manchester: Clinamen, 2000); Gilles Deleuze and Félix Guattari, *A Thousand Plateaus* (London: Athlone, 1988); Peter Merriman, *Mobility, Space and Culture* (London: Routledge, 2012).

[15] Doreen Massey, 'A Global Sense of Place', in *Space, Place and Gender*, ed. Doreen Massey (Cambridge: Polity, 1994): 146–56.

[16] Ibid., 152–3.

6 World Maps

Annemarie Mol

A world map evokes the globe by spreading it out flat on a two-dimensional plane.[1] But what is evoked by implying that a globe can be depicted in this way? Once, European world maps celebrated the glory of God. They had Jerusalem in their shining, wood-printed middle. Later they traced sailing routes to spices and other tangible wonders with a high cash return. Maps made travelling possible while at the same time resulting from it—they were cause as well as effect of imperialist expansion.[2] Gradually they began to show the expanse of this, that, or the other empire: Spain, the Dutch Republic, England. Hung up in an office they bore witness to the worldliness and wealth of their owner. Not everyone could afford a demonstrative print from Blaeu, Amsterdam, mapmakers.[3]

Old world maps are still expensive, but new ones are often not. In 1984 I bought one in Sofia, Bulgaria, in a shop that sold them to schoolchildren. Printed on cheap paper, it showed a variant of the so-called Greenwich projection: one vertical meridian drawn as a straight line in the middle, the others bending around it, in an attempt to suggest the earth's spherical shape. However, on my Bulgarian map the straight line did not run through the 0 degree meridian that the English projected through Greenwich. Instead, it went through the 40th degree east. Thus, the visual centre of the map was shifted slightly: to Moscow indeed.[4]

A few years later I bought a world map in San Francisco, USA. It cuts Eurasia into two. The Americas are in the middle, Europe and Africa on the right, Asia on the left. This type of map only became popular in the USA after the Second World War. Before that war, English maps were used. But many Americans, having spent years in classrooms with English maps on their walls, were taken by surprise when the Japanese proved to be able to attack a USA army base. It was so far from America, Japan: on the other side of the world! How had they done it?

My first Chinese map came from Bangkok, Thailand. From across the street, my travel companion and I had recognized the small shop, with cheap paper

---

[1] Thanks to Peter van Lieshout for dragging me around the world; and to John Law for collaborative work on spatialities, and for comments and corrections.

[2] There is a lot of great literature on all of this. See for instance: David Turnbull, *Tricksters and Cartographers: Maps, Science and the State in the Making of a Modern Scientific Knowledge Space* (Amsterdam: Harwood Academic, 2000).

[3] For the context of the art of printing in the Dutch Republic, see: Pamela Smith, *The Body of the Artisan; Art and Experience in the Scientific Revolution* (Chicago: University of Chicago Press, 2004).

[4] For more insight into such visual tricks, see: Mark Monmonier, *How to Lie with Maps* (Chicago: University of Chicago Press, 1991).

stuff in its window, as the one to go for. But the shopkeeper was not eager to sell. No, he said, in English (the triumphant imperialist language we shared) when I pointed to a Chinese world map. No, he did not have maps in English, but I would no doubt find them elsewhere in town. Stubbornly I pointed once more to the map in Chinese and said I wanted to buy it. Such strange people, tourists! What might a white woman who does not even speak Chinese do with an utterly ordinary Chinese map of the world? A great addition to my collection. As you can guess: it has China in the centre.

There are horizontal meridians, too. Where to draw the equator: two-thirds down the page, as Mercator projections do? Recently I even saw a composite photo of the globe (the images shot from satellites on cloudless days) pushed into a Mercator shape. Greenland far larger than India. A deception. The equator belongs in the horizontal middle of the page. Or does it? One may also unfold the globe in other ways. Take the Buckminster Fuller projection.[5] This is made out of triangles. In its visual centre is the North Pole. From there, triangles with bits of the Americas as well as the South Pole are folded out to the right. Others, holding parts of Eurasia, Africa, Australia, and Oceania, are folded out to the left. The land masses thus seem to be an outstretched island floating in an ocean. And the pressure of the north on the south is not repeated, at least not visually. Not again.

The maps I collected in the eighties, however new at the time, are now out of date: their Moscow is in the USSR. But what has also rapidly changed is what it is to depict the world. Take the T-shirt I bought in Philadelphia in 1990. It shows a world map in shiny green with a caption that says: *Go Global*. At the time, that was an ecological message. The T-shirt was meant to encourage everyone to take account of the fact that the effects of their local actions were likely to stretch out far beyond their own horizon. A decade later, the globe was no longer a favourite icon of political radicals. Instead, late capitalism was accused of going global. The term *globalization* took off.

It may well be that popular culture, especially in the form of music, spreads out even more easily than the means of production and goods for consumption.[6] It does not even need a map; it depends on radio waves. Radios could catch them over long distances. Mobile phone networks are more dependent on the irregularities of the land again.

Does capitalism need a map? The film *The Coca-Cola Kid* (Makavejev, 1985),[7] that dates from well before the rise of the term 'globalization', suggested that it might. In the film, an entire wall of the boardroom of an iconized Coca-Cola company is covered with a map that reveals the intensity of Coca-Cola sales in

---

[5] 'R. Buckminster Fuller', Worldtrans, <http://www.worldtrans.org/whole/bucky.html>.

[6] See for this: René Boomkens, *De nieuwe wanorde; Globalisering en het einde van de maakbare samenleving* (Amsterdam: Van Gennep, 2006). And: Marc Schade-Poulsen, 'Which World? On the Diffusion of Algeria raï to the West', in *Siting Culture; The Shifting Anthropological Object*, ed. Karen Fog Olwig and Kirsten Hastrup (London; New York: Routledge, 1997): 59–85.

[7] *The Coca-Cola Kid*, directed by Dusan Makavejev (Sydney: The Australian Film Commission, 1985).

various regions of the world. The shades vary, but the company managers worry most about a single valley in Australia. It shows no colour at all. So far Coca-Cola has failed to get there. The all-American hero of the film is sent out to go, see, and conquer that valley. (Once there, this 'kid' falls in love with the daughter of the old man whose soft drink so far enchanted the locals. Why does Makavejev suggest this boy-meets-girl story to be effortlessly universal? But that is another question.)

World maps do not only map out markets, but also feed present-day imaginations of governance. Until well into the eighties, politics was theorized as a matter of bounded nation states. This has changed. Now, *we are the world*. To convince us, the world map works wonders. An example. The United Nations World Food Programme tries to unite us (in as far as we have Internet access) into a humanist commonality (that includes everyone else) with a website that shows a *World Hunger map*.[8] It presents the world in five colours. In red countries the relevant numbers are extremely high: more than 35 per cent of the population is hungry. In green countries by contrast they are extremely low: less than 2.5 per cent of the population is hungry. In between there are: orange countries (moderately high); yellow countries (moderately low); and light green countries (very low). When you click on a button or two, you are taught what causes hunger and what can be done about it (see Figure 6.1).

Economy and politics (or capitalism and governance?) are both concerned with the world. In the social sciences, meanwhile, the term 'globalization' has all but replaced 'modernization' as the ultimate buzz word.[9] *Modernization* came with a specific form of historicity: it suggested that history has made us, but that, living in an all-pervasive now, we have left its ties behind. *Globalization* evokes other concerns. It links selves to others, makes differences spatial, and rings geographical bells. These days, then, history is no longer the ever-present backdrop of the social sciences. Instead geography is made to call out loud that we live somewhere.[10] We are situated.[11] But where? On a world map? And if so, on which one? On that of *The Coca-Cola Kid*'s company or on that of the UN World Food Programme? Certainly not on one with Moscow in the middle. One in Chinese?

In Google Earth we live.[12] Please situate yourself. Here's a map to dive into and then move through. One that at least does not *entirely* erase the notion of travel—as most other world maps do. No, on Google Earth you are not slowed

[8] 'Hunger Map', United Nations World Food Programme, <http://www.wfp.org/hunger/map>.

[9] For an examplary collection, see: Aihwa Ong and Stepher J. Collier, eds, *Global Assemblages: Technology, Politics, and Ethics as Anthropological Problems* (Malden; Oxford: Blackwell Publishing, 2005).

[10] Geographers have put serious effort into the assertion. See e.g. Edward W. Soja, *Postmodern Geographies: The Reassertion of Space in Critical Theory* (London: Verso, 1989); or Doreen Massey, *For Space* (London: Sage, 2005).

[11] Even our knowledge is no longer universal, but, indeed, situated. See e.g. Donna Haraway, 'Situated Knowledges. The Science Question in Feminism and the Privilege of Partial Perspective', in *Simians, Cyborgs and Women: The Reinvention of Nature* (London: Free Association Books, 199); and John Law and Annemarie Mol, 'Situating Technoscience: An Inquiry into Spatialities', *Environment and Planning D: Society and Space* 19, 5 (2001): 609–21.

[12] Google Earth, <http://earth.google.com>.

Figure 6.1 Hunger map, 2011. For an interactive version, see <http://cdn.wfp.org/hungermap/>

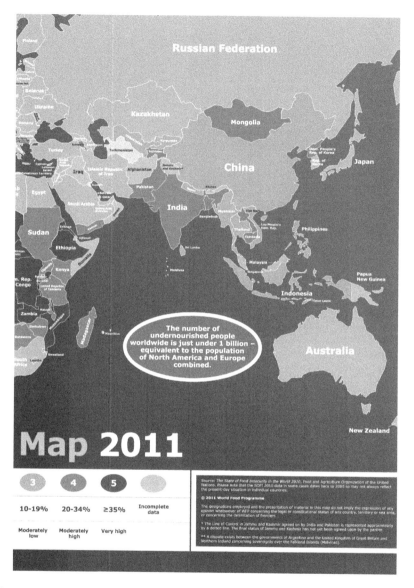

Figure 6.1 (Continued)

Figure 6.2 World maps come in all shapes and political colours. A sample of the author's collection

down by well-policed borders, impenetrable forests, a lack of resources, or other, unexpected boundary makers.[13] But the program requires you to at least move your cursor as you move from one place to the next.

Travel. Indeed. World maps may have resulted from and allow for travel, but they do not show it. Let's look once more at the assembled maps that I keep in my study, Utrecht, The Netherlands (see Figure 6.2). More surprising than the striking differences between these maps is the fact that they are here. How did they get here? How is it that I've actually been able to pick them up in Sofia, San Francisco, Bangkok, Philadelphia, and in other places, too? In the generation of my parents very few people got round to travelling those kinds of distances. These days one can do so quite easily if only one belongs to a privileged enough group in a green country (less than 2.5 per cent of the population hungry) or to the otherwise strikingly rich. But what will happen to such globalization in practice once the earth stops feeding airplanes?

---

[13] On Earth offline, however, many boundaries, made and sustained in various ways, tend to hamper travel. See e.g. John Law and Annemarie Mol, 'Globalisation in Practice: On the Politics of Boiling Pigswill', *Geoforum* 39, 1 (2007): 133–43.

7 Airport Security*

Harvey Molotch

It takes about the same amount of time with the same trials and tribulations to travel by air today as it did dozens of years ago. But there has been big change in one department: the implementation of security, something that alters the whole mood of going by air, with consequences far and wide.

Transportation systems tend to require standardization—like the development of a consistent railway gauge within a continent or minimum runway dimensions at airports.[1] There is also, it seems, a nearly identical repertoire of patter from flight attendants announcing take-offs and landings around the world. Air standardization occurred primarily post the Second World War through a network of bilateral agreements and a series of multilateral conventions that followed. Coordination now officially occurs through an agency of the United Nations that strives, through 15 training centres across the world, to help governments implement security protocols.[2]

Before 1973, when a number of hijacking incidents forced US authorities to take action, people in most countries entered airports as casually as they come and go from department stores. Indeed, air travel had something of a festival nature—the panache of joining the 'jet set'. People saw one another off right at the gate and met those coming in. For at least some (like me and my family and friends), airports were urban attractions—places to go even if neither you nor anyone else was travelling anywhere.

Security transforms this architectural space into a more troubled and troubling zone, a foretaste perhaps of what security angst brings more generally to urban life. To learn something of the degree to which the effect is or is not universal, I accessed passenger critiques of airports posted on websites.[3] I have also tried to closely observe at airports in which I travel and have talked with friends about their experiences. Through the prism of voiced complaints

---

* For further elaboration see: Harvey Molotch, *Against Security: How We Go Wrong at Airports, Subways, and Other Sites of Ambiguous Danger* (Princeton, NJ: Princeton University Press, 2012).

[1] John Braithwaite and Peter Drahos, *Global Business Regulation* (Cambridge: Cambridge University Press, 2000).

[2] This is the International Civil Agency Organization (ICAO). For access to this unit's security branch, go to: <http://www.icao.int/atb/avsec/index.asp>.

[3] For passenger comments on their experiences at airports around the world, go to: <http://www.airlinequality.com/main/forum.htm>.

(and commendations), we can gain familiarity with the intersection of human experience and security systems at the gates of the world.

Privacy Intrusion

The process begins with a check of identification papers at the moment of check-in—with various national intelligence agencies, we now know, having advance information about our travel plans and personal data. In prior times, in North America and Europe at least, security was so 'lax' that people could actually give their tickets away or exchange them with one another—at least if genders were aligned. This could provide quick and easy solutions to life problems that might arise—e.g. 'I can't go to the wedding, so you go.'

Now security agents inspect each of us in situ, first by requesting ID, then by scanning our bodies, sometimes conducting a frisk. Technologies scan the body itself, to discover metallic, ceramic, or chemical substances that may be on one's person. In some versions, recurrently contested, agents see an intimate outline of the human figure. Those who resist on grounds of privacy are allowed (in the USA at least) to 'opt out'. This then initiates a full body pat-down. The security agent reaches inside one's clothing and feels for obtrusive materials. In my personal experience (I often opt out if I think I have enough time before my flight), the agent has not touched my genitals or anus. But others have told me the agents on their case went all the way. Security becomes a meet-up between the zeal to know with the zeal to protect one's most intimate parts. Apparently, it can go either way.

Depending on circumstance, security agents handle the contents of carry-ons as passengers watch. These inspections are more intense in the USA than in most other places, including the requirement that laptops be removed from their cases. Inspectors can and do open, look, and take things out of one's carry-ons. In one instance, a New York colleague reports watching an agent lift his toothbrush out of his personal effects kit, holding it by the brush end. The inspector was wearing plastic gloves, but these gloves had touched many other things besides my colleague's own. He had the quandary of worrying about how to buy a replacement toothbrush at his hotel when arriving late at night.

All this boosts self-consciousness of what one has in one's possession: A prosthetic device? Illicit drugs? Pornography? Materials that are politically incorrect or religiously blasphemous? Bloody underwear? Even for those with 'nothing to hide', tension can grow. There are gender effects: women have more items of their own to deal with (liquids, medicines, make-up), in part because they are carrying paraphernalia for those under their care—children or disabled people.

Distress of Personhood

Quite apart from any anxiety about terrorists, air travel carries built-in emotional baggage, including concern about the journey to the airport, mechanical safety, making connections, arrival times, and seat assignment. An aspect of it all is the anxiety of being dislodged from normal routines of life, including the tools and goods through which to manage those routines. The act of packing is an effort to secure a smooth transition from home base to strange place. Deliberation goes into choosing the right clothes, drugs, and more idiosyncratic paraphernalia that needs to fit within a circumscribed space, a small fraction of one's normal holding capacity. Some people fold carefully, following special tips to avoid creases, crushing of gifts, and damage to important papers.

While significant loss looms large when the suitcase is turned over at check-in, the most crucial materials are held in the carry-ons. Depending on airport and country, elements are disaggregated to go into separate trays and bins. All go beyond one's reach and view as inspectors take custody. They risk being commingled with other passengers' goods. In Hong Kong, if you put small items in a container for the X-ray machine, you are given a number so that you can collect that basket when you've gone through the check.

Non-Design

There are better and worse ways to manage these arrangements. Airport security, both as a system as well as the artefacts that make it up, is crude—particularly in the USA. Despite constituting a market in the billions of dollars, the artefacts are primarily off-the-shelf products, or modified from otherwise standard goods. Hence the trays into which you are to place your laptop, jacket, lunch, and shoes (!) are commercial restaurant gear used for bussing dishes. The tables might be fold-ups of the sort used in school recreation halls. At a time when the design of a routine can opener receives vast attention from focus groups, aesthetic connoisseurs, and ergonomic experts, airport security remains dumb to the issues of design competence.

What would an alternative look like? Start with the bowl where you put your metal stuff. If it had a funnel, coins would return more easily into the hand. If the grey trays (usually they are grey) were transparent, it would be easier to see if they had anything in them. Not only would this help with security, it would make it less likely that a beefy agent would grab a tray without knowing it had a laptop still in it, swing it in the air, and cause the laptop to hit the floor and sail a number of feet (as happened to a different New York colleague). Passengers should be able to place bags at ground level, with a motorized incline taking them up to the screening device.

Disregard of Local Custom

Airport security can be especially antagonistic to notions of comfort and decency among certain groups. Shoe removal forces those from 'sockless' cultures to remove sandals and flip-flops and expose bare feet. Japanese people rarely make direct physical contact between a part of their bodies and a surface that receives outdoor foot traffic—they do not, for example, sit on steps. Compared to men, women (of all groups) are frequently barefooted, or wearing thin stockings rather than socks. So are the young.

Bare feet on airport floors spread fungus. Random objects like paper clips, pens, pencils, wire bits, and tacks fall to the floor where they can pierce the skin. A friend of mine was pierced by the business end of an American flag lapel pin dropped by a patriot who had gone before—who was probably forced to remove it to go through the metal detector. Another type of vulnerability comes from the opposite direction of footwear, heavy shoes with many laces, worn by those with ailing feet or workers in high-tops. Manipulating the footwear while simultaneously holding on to boarding pass and/or passport (sometimes in one's mouth) creates a special anxiety for this traveller niche.

Even within the USA, there is variation from city to city with shoe removal required in only some places (at moment of this writing). Passengers in most of Europe can keep shoes on but not, for example, in Dublin. Other idiosyncrasies occur; a traveller through Abu Dhabi reports security guards deserting their station to go for a smoke; passengers just walked through. At Accra, guards look for a little money to facilitate your passage. Some airports generate consistent complaints of rudeness (Frankfurt), others of friendliness and efficiency (Stockholm). With all the precautions and billions of dollars spent, contraband of all sorts gets through, as evidenced by the repeated failed 'tests' set up by the US Transportation Security Administration.

US Hegemony

US dominance in air travel goes back to the modern jet plane, which is based on Second World War bomber development. This massive initial advantage reinforced US firms' centrality, continuously coordinated with the Department of Defense and the Federal Aviation Authority. US corporate-governmental policies influence aircraft peripherals like gangways, luggage-handling equipment, and even—especially in the contemporary no-knife moment—on-board catering. As with other safety issues, airlines that do not conform are not allowed at US airports—a very high cost for any operator to face.

The US preoccupation with security and its methods for dealing with it radiate out to airlines, equipment producers, and governments as well as to travellers' experience everywhere. Militarism trumps even the market, creating a stark contrast with the behaviours of airline flight crews who become lights at the end of the security tunnel. Security contrasts with the friendly pleasantries of capitalism, oriented as they are toward at least the illusion of friendly skies. Disneyland shows benign ways to move people and their objects through a complex array of pathways and paraphernalia. There could be, and at some airports they come close (Stockholm and Hong Kong, for example), security people who are also *helpers*. They could reassure, lift bags up, hold a stroller, and manage the flow in a supportive way. This might cause them to learn more, not less. Every parent knows that in helping a child 'get ready', you learn a lot about what is going on—an intelligence feature of kindness.

All of the security policies and some of my reactions to them presume that what is being done at the airports actually affects individuals' safety, a dubious assumption. At least in regard to US airport operations and in regard to flights bound for the United States, the vast security apparatus has not stopped a single incident of mayhem – nor even legal charges related to terrorist threat. Instead, plots to do mayhem have been thwarted by spontaneous acts of passengers and flight staff (as in the 'shoe bomber' incident), or by rank incompetence among the plotters. Perhaps, some say, the paucity of incidents is at least partly due to the likelihood of getting caught. But it is a common observation in the security business that in hardening a particular facility against perpetrators, you deflect attack to a more opportune location. For a private individual or firm, it may make sense to take advantage of this fact by shifting threats to another setting— a competing bank or restaurant. With public facilities, it makes no sense at all. In the airport, the pre-screening area often gathers up a denser crowd than will be found on any plane—and before any screening has occurred. This is a graphic display of the deflection predicament. A security apparatus in one place creates security vulnerability in another.

Equipment and processes like those found at airport security have been termed 'security theatre'.[4] Under this scenario, the disregard of difference, of intimate experience, and of aesthetic content is itself a contrivance. Perhaps, some say, authorities create conspicuous control to make people feel they are more secure, with their own inconvenience a way for them to think they have made a personal contribution to the cause. Or it may be a ruse for other ends; since 9/11, at least on US planes, flight attendants announce that passengers are not to use toilets of the higher classes 'for security reasons'. More darkly, the security regime can—through nefarious plot or unintended consequence—reinforce a feeling of vulnerability. This can transfer to deference toward national leaders who can putatively keep us safe by undermining our own liberties, at the gates and elsewhere too.

---

[4] The term now circulates widely but is often associated with Bruce Schneier, *Beyond Fear: Thinking Sensibly About Security in an Uncertain World* (New York: Copernicus Books, 2003).

8 Passports

John Torpey

As nation states—states of and for particular 'peoples' defined as more or less mutually exclusive groups of citizens—modern states have typically been eager to regulate the movements of persons within and across their borders when they wish to do so. Their efforts to implement such regulation have driven them toward the creation of the means uniquely and unambiguously to identify individual persons, whether 'their own' or others. In order to effect this regulation, states and the international state system have been compelled to define who belongs and who does not, who may come and go and who not, and to make these distinctions intelligible and enforceable. Beyond simply enunciating definitions and categories concerning identity, states must give effect to these distinctions, and they require documents in order to do so in individual cases. Although passports are not the only documents that may be used for these purposes, passports have played a decisive role in achieving these aims.

Documents held by individuals as 'ID' correspond to an entire series of files chronicling movements, economic transactions, familial ties, illnesses, and much else besides—the 'power-knowledge' grid in which individuals are processed and constituted as administrative subjects of states. The achievement of this administrative knowledge was a long time in coming, however; state-sponsored identification practices with the aim of extending states' 'embrace' of their populations have evolved significantly over time. Prior to the French Revolution, for example, descriptions of a person's social standing— residence, occupation, family status, etc—were generally regarded as adequate indicators of a person's identity for purposes of internal passport controls in France. Thereafter, the growing preoccupation with surveillance and the progress of modern science combined to render insufficient these earlier, more homespun practices. States wanted to embrace their inhabitants more firmly, and to be able to distinguish them from outsiders more clearly, than was possible with such methods. Achievement of this aim necessitated greater precision in identifying them. Yet at the same time, the rise of liberal ideologies proclaiming individual freedom and the inviolability of the person cast into disfavour older habits of 'writing on the body', such as branding, scarification, and tattooing, as means for identifying persons.

As a result, states with a rising interest in embracing their populations had to develop less invasive means to identify them. The techniques for 'reading off the body' have become more and more sophisticated over time, shifting from unreliable subjective descriptions and anthropometric measurements to photographs (themselves at first often considered unreliable by police), finger-printing, electronically scanned palm prints, DNA fingerprinting, and retina scans. The persistent tinkering with these techniques indicates that states have a powerful interest in identifying persons, both their own subjects and those of other countries, especially when they are in motion.

Clearly, (external) passports and internal passports or 'passes' are not the same thing, although the former probably evolved out of the latter. External or international passports, most familiar today to those from liberal-democratic countries, are documents associated with movement across international boundaries. They ordinarily constitute prima facie evidence of the bearer's nationality. In contrast, internal passports or passes—where they exist—are designed to regulate movements within the jurisdiction of a state.

The legal implications of the differences between 'internal' and 'external' passports are far-reaching. The right to leave and return to one's country is a prerogative that has come to be widely accepted in international human rights law, even if that law may be ignored in practice. In contrast to the widely rec-ognized right to leave and return, the right to move within one's country is a matter of the domestic law of sovereign states, subject only to the relatively weak and largely unenforceable strictures that may be imposed by human rights norms and conventions.

Most familiar to and accepted by people today is the right of states to control entry, a prerogative that has come to be understood as one of the quintessential features of sovereignty. It is important to note, however, that the widespread recognition of this state prerogative is a fairly recent development. A survey of international legal opinion during the period immediately preceding the First World War was unable to muster any consensus for the view that states had an unequivocal right to bar foreigners from entry into their territory.

Still, although they have come to be governed by different bodies of law, passports and passes share the function of controlling the movements of people within and across delimited spaces, thereby affirming states' control over bounded territories and enhancing their embrace of populations.

The State Monopolization of the Legitimate 'Means of Movement'

Following the rhetoric used by Marx and Weber, one might say that modern states, and the international state system of which they are a part, have expro-priated from individuals and private entities the legitimate right to movement, particularly, though by no means exclusively, across international boundaries. The result of this process has been to deprive people of the freedom to move across certain spaces and to render them dependent on states and the state system for the authorization to do so—an authority widely held in private hands theretofore.

States have sought to monopolize the capacity to authorize the movements of persons—and unambiguously to establish their identities in order to enforce this authority—for a great variety of reasons that reflect the ambiguous nature of modern states, which are at once sheltering and dominating. These include such objectives as the extraction of military service, taxes, and labour; the facilitation of law enforcement; the control of 'brain drain' (that is, the limitation of departure in order to forestall the loss of workers with valued skills); the restriction of access to areas deemed 'off limits' by the state, whether for 'security' reasons or to protect people from unexpected or unacknowledged harm; the exclusion, surveillance, and containment of 'undesirable elements', whether these are of an ethnic, national, racial, economic, religious, ideological, or medical character; and the supervision of the growth, spatial distribution, and social composition of populations within their territories.

States' efforts to monopolize the legitimate means of movement have involved a number of mutually reinforcing aspects: the (gradual) definition of states everywhere—at least from the point of view of the international system—as 'national' (that is, as 'nation states' comprised of members understood as nationals); the codification of laws establishing which types of persons may move within or cross their borders, and determining how, when, and where they may do so; the stimulation of the worldwide development of techniques for uniquely and unambiguously identifying each and every person on the face of the globe, from birth to death; the construction of bureaucracies and related arrangements designed to implement this regime of identification and to scrutinize persons and documents in order to verify identities; and the creation of a body of legal norms designed to help adjudicate claims by individuals to entry into particular spaces and territories.

Things have not always been this way. The great migrations that populated many of the world's inhabited regions would otherwise have been greatly hampered, if not rendered impossible. Where the right to authorize movement was controlled by particular social groups before the coalescence of the modern state system (and indeed until well after it had come into being), these groups were as often private entities as constituted political authorities. Indentured servants' right to move, for example, was under the control of their masters. Under serfdom, the serfs' legal capacity to move lay in the hands of their landlords, who had jurisdiction over them. Slaveholders held the power to grant their slaves the right to move. As modern states advanced and systems of forced labour such as slavery and serfdom declined, however, states and the international state system stripped private entities of the power to authorize and forbid movement and gathered that power unto themselves. In doing so, they were responding to a considerable extent to the imperatives of territorial rule characteristic of modern states. The transition from private to state control over movement was an essential aspect of the transition from feudalism to capitalism.

The process through which states monopolized the legitimate means of movement thus took hundreds of years to come to fruition. It followed the shift of orientations from the local to the 'national' level that accompanied the development of 'national' states out of the panoply of empires and smaller city states and principalities that dotted the map of early modern Europe. The process also paralleled the rationalization and nationalization of poor relief, for communal obligations to provide such relief had been an important source of the desire for controls on movement. As European states declined in number, grew in size, and fostered large-scale markets for wage labour outside the reach of landowners and against the traditional constraints imposed by localities, the provision of poor relief also moved from the local to the national arena. These processes, in turn, helped to expand 'outward' to the 'national' borders the areas in which persons could expect to move freely and without authorization. Eventually, the principal boundaries that counted were those not of municipalities, but of nation states.

The process took place unevenly in different places, following the line where modern states replaced non-territorial forms of political organization and 'free' wage labour replaced various forms of servitude. Then, as people from all levels of society came to find themselves in a more nearly equal position relative to the state, state controls on movement among local spaces within their domains subsided and were replaced by restrictions that concerned the outer 'national' boundaries of states. Where pronounced state controls on movement operate within a state today, especially when these are to the detriment of particular 'negatively privileged' groups, we can reliably expect to find an authoritarian state (or worse). The cases of the Soviet Union, Nazi Germany, apartheid-era South Africa, and contemporary China (where a 'floating population' of perhaps 100 million people lives without proper papers in jurisdictions other than those where they have a right to live) bear witness to this generalization.

Ultimately, the authority to regulate movement came to be primarily a property of the international system as a whole—that is, of nation states acting in concert to enforce their interests in controlling who comes and goes. The creation of the modern passport system and the use of similar systems in the interior of a variety of countries—the product of centuries-long labours of slow, painstaking bureaucratic construction—thus signalled the dawn of a new era in human affairs, in which individual states and the international state system as a whole successfully monopolized the legitimate authority to permit movement within and across their jurisdictions. The point here is obviously not that there is no unauthorized international migration, but rather that such movement is specifically 'illegal'; that is, we speak of illegal (often, indeed, of 'undocumented') migration as a result of states' monopolization of the legitimate means of movement. What we now think of as 'internal' migration has come to mean movement within national or nation states; the term 'migration' now normally implies international movement because movement within nation states is regarded as unexceptionable.

None of this is to say that private actors now play no role in the regulation of movement—far from it. Yet private entities have been reduced to the capacity of 'sheriff's deputies' who participate in the regulation of movement at the behest of states. Since the development of commercial air travel, for example, airline companies have been required to establish that persons are who they say they are and to regulate their movement on behalf of the government. Both shipping enterprises and air carriers have frequently resisted carrying out the sheriff's deputy function, mainly because they fear that their participation in such quasi-governmental activities will hurt their profitability. Not wanting to appear guilty of mere cupidity, however, what they are likely to say instead is that they regard the regulation of movement as the proper province of the state—and so it is.

9 Sex Workers

Jackie West

In July and August 2006, police in Washington, USA, arrested four women in connection with offering commercial sexual services advertised on a popular 'classifieds' website. The women, from as far as California, had arranged several weeks' appointments in advance of their visit to hotels near the international airport in Baltimore. The Web is increasingly facilitating mobility in the sex industry, in this case the movement of both sex workers and their clients, yet its global reach is no absolute guarantee of protection from local regulation. In summer 2006, the growth of online gaming was also interrupted by the arrest of company chief executives when they entered US jurisdiction, though here prompted less by moral outrage than the threat posed by illegal gambling markets to the profits of land-based casinos and horse-race betting.

But if the Internet's capacity to evade state surveillance is both conditional and in process, it is nevertheless reinventing modes of organization and regulation within the entertainment industry, with both negative and positive effects. Commercial sex is no exception. Indeed it is pornography that many regard as a driving force in the very development of digital technologies, and the global proliferation of images is held to be linked to increased sexual exploitation of children. But the Internet, at least, has a more mundane and progressive role in transforming the sex industry. Teela Sanders, who interviewed both website managers and sex workers and undertook content analysis of communications within 350 sites, as well as in-depth observation of the most established site in the UK, highlights the potential for increased safety and self-regulation, as well as new forms of marketing.[1] Examples include the use of message boards, databases, and emails to screen, monitor, and record clients. There is a clearer separation for sex workers between their work and private life, between online and offline identities. And the Web is helping to create 'entrepreneurial networks', enhancing the possibilities of self-employment and real prospects of autonomy.

Online communities of clients are also mushrooming, with websites providing feedback on experiences, prices, laws, and policing in locales across the globe. Additionally, Sanders reminds us, they enhance awareness of sexual health, although they are more likely to be viewed as symptomatic of the

---

[1] Teela Sanders, 'Researching the On-Line Sex Work Community', in *Virtual Methods: Issues in Social Research on the Internet*, ed. Christine Berg (Oxford: Berg, 2005).

salacious demand from Western tourists for sex with racialized 'exotic' bodies. The supply of such bodies is rooted in the poverty of rural hinterlands and urban barrios in many developing economies, which propels young women, men, and children, especially those with poor education and prospects, into the informal economy.

But sex tourism has been actively promoted too by governments and mainstream business. Its roots in Thailand, for example, were in legislation in the 1960s that ostensibly banned prostitution but allowed 'special services' in the entertainment sector. It was subsequently boosted by treaties with the USA to secure 'rest and recreation leave' for its military servicemen in South-east Asia and also by IMF pressure to expand tourism as an earner of foreign exchange.[2] Once facilitated by small and medium capital, sex tourism has been increasingly mediated through hotel chains, package holiday firms, and airlines, as well as tour agents, local police, hoteliers, and restaurateurs.

Transnational migration for sex work is also growing. Estimates of the numbers of migrants in prostitution are frequently unreliable, but those produced by TAMPEP,[3] which works to advance the civil rights of sex workers rather than seeking the abolition of prostitution, are well grounded in the experience of outreach health and social projects. In 2008 it was thought that around 60 per cent of sex workers in France and the Netherlands, for example, were of foreign origin, two-thirds in Germany and Denmark, as much as 90 per cent in Spain and Italy, though only around 40 per cent in the Czech Republic and the UK (if not London). But the proportion of migrants alters over time, as do their countries of origin. In the past decade migrants to—and increasingly within—the EU have come predominantly from Central and Eastern Europe, Central Asia, Africa, Latin America, and Asia-Pacific. These origins reflect—in common with migration flows in general of which they are an integral part—proximity, past colonial connections, levels of poverty and unemployment, political upheaval, and social transition. Migrants may have experienced family violence, sexual abuse, or homophobia, but above all they are seeking economic and personal independence. Sex work is but one of the employment strategies deployed to achieve these goals.[4] Considerable numbers are undocumented, as are migrants in other destinations.

The dominant political paradigm for understanding prostitution is abolitionist and focused on violence, aided by radical feminist groups such as the

---

[2] Lin Lean Lim, ed., *The Sex Sector: The Economic and Social Bases of Prostitution in Southeast Asia* (Geneva: International Labour Office, 1998).

[3] TAMPEP (European Network for HIV/STI Prevention and Heath Promotion Among Migrant Sex Workers), *Sex Work in Europe: A mapping of prostitution in 25 European countries* and *Outreach in Indoor Work Settings* (<http://www.tampep.eu>, 2009 and 2012).

[4] Laura María Agustín, *Sex at the Margins: Migration, Markets and the Rescue Industry* (London: Zed Books, 2007); Nick Mai, 'Non-heteronormative Migrants Working in the UK Sex Industry', *Sexualities*, vol.15, no.5/6, 2012.

Coalition Against Trafficking in Women. These have very successfully influenced policy at supranational level, notably the 2000 UN Protocol to Suppress Trafficking and a variety of EU policing instruments. Their growing influence at national level is also evident. Examples include Sweden, which criminalized the purchase of sex in 1999, as did Norway and Iceland in 2009 (though its effects are much debated). Similar approaches are gaining ground elsewhere in Europe. [5] In the UK, concern with trafficking and abuse overdetermines government strategy that seeks to disrupt all markets in sex.[6] Suggestions that commercial sex be accepted let alone normalized are rejected in favour of measures to promote exit and reduce victimization.

Routes into sex work are nevertheless diverse. Restrictions on migration and punitive policies against prostitution exacerbate illegal entry and greater reliance more generally on third parties. Most anti-trafficking policies are framed by assumptions that all migrants in sex work are unwilling victims and by government interests in controlling immigration and crime. Yet force, deception, and enslavement are less common than other forms of indebtedness—and intentional, voluntary migration.[7]

Migrants may seek sponsorship from family or moneylenders, may need the active assistance of smuggling networks, and be correspondingly at higher risk of abusive treatment. Control over employment and earnings is greater where vulnerabilities can be exploited—fear of deportation, racial, ethnic, or linguistic differences, for example. The legality or otherwise of sex work is a further factor. The Dutch law of 2000 allowed municipalities to regulate brothels and sought to improve conditions for those working in consensual prostitution. But non-EU migrants are excluded from the legal sector (work permits are denied for sex work) so they remain vulnerable to agents and less likely to access health and social services. And everywhere there are additional difficulties for those whose sex work is related to drug dependency or transgender identity. However, employment relations vary and some sex workers, including migrants, are relatively autonomous, able to move between settings in response to working conditions and local demand. The pressures they face, to sustain the good life, to support dependants, to seek personal freedom, are not dissimilar from those facing other workers in the informal sector—except that their trade exacerbates their marginalization and social exclusion.

A border zone between Germany and the Czech Republic became in 2002 the focus of an exhibition, Warte Mal!, at the prestigious Hayward Gallery in London and associated panel discussions featuring the artist, cultural

[5] Prostitution Policies in Europe, *Sexuality Research and Social Policy*, special issue, vol.9, no.3, 2012.

[6] Home Office, Provisions in the Policing and Crime Act 2009 that relate to prostitution (<https://www.gov.uk>, 2010).

[7] Julia O'Connell Davidson, 'Men, Middlemen and Migrants: The Demand Side of "Sex Trafficking"' (<http://www.eurozine.com>, 2006); Rutvica Andrijasevic, *Migration, Agency and Citizenship in Sex Trafficking* (Basingstoke: Palgrave Macmillan, 2010).

critics, and academics. One of these included a representative from the Central European campaign group La Strada, and the audiences included a number of sex-work activists. The exhibition itself foregrounded issues of transition and degradation, themes featured in a publicity article in the gallery's magazine on just these themes. Voyeurism might even have been encouraged by the principal display, a video installation with extended footage of women in bars, soliciting custom on highways from passing truck drivers, and individual interviews projected in booth-like 'windows'. Yet the stories of the various protagonists—women, pimps, police, hotel and bar staff—were often nuanced and complex. And this was reinforced by a room of material artefacts including a wide variety of research publications, the artist's own textual documentation in the form of her diary, and interview transcripts and web-based resources of La Strada and activist groups.[8]

This exhibition was testimony, then, not only to transnational prostitution itself, but also to its contemporary cultural presence and political campaigns. It expressed the tensions, albeit very unevenly, between degradation and stigma and the possibilities of agency and resistance. Campaigns orchestrated by those wanting to abolish prostitution have been ascendant in the past three decades, but activists seeking to advance the right to practise sex work with dignity and respect are also organized at global and local levels. They include the Kolkata collective DMSC, representing 10,000 sex workers, and the Argentine trade union AMMAR, which has seen the repeal of some laws penalizing sex workers.

Some collectives have worked with government health departments and other stakeholders to secure decriminalization, most notably the New Zealand Prostitutes Collective. The 2003 New Zealand law reform is, importantly, more enabling than that developed in the Netherlands, Germany, or even in some Australian states: it endorses rights to refuse unwanted clients or sexual practices and exploitative conditions, and it provides more support for independent cooperative working.[9] But political outcomes depend on specific national and local agendas, the politics of migration, and local markets. And the wider economic, gender, and racial inequalities that underpin migration in sex work can only be addressed by concerted local and global action.

---

[8] Ann-Sophie Siden, *Warte Mal! Prostitution After the Velvet Revolution* (London: Hayward Gallery, 2002).

[9] Gillian Abel, Lisa Fitzgerald, Catherine Healy, Aline Taylor, eds, *Taking the Crime out of Sex Work: New Zealand Sex Workers' Fight for Decriminalisation* (Bristol: Policy Press, 2010); Barbara Sullivan, 'When (Some) Prostitution is Legal: the Impact of Law Reform on Sex Work in Australia', *Journal of Law and Society*, vol.37, no.1, 2010.

10 The Gap Year
Alexandra Woolgar

Globalization all too often connotes uniformity, the flattening and dissolution of difference between places and cultures. This makes it easy to forget how vivid are the experiences of difference and how much can be learned from them. Here we present excerpts from newsletters written home by an 18-year-old on her 12-month gap-year project in the Dominican Republic.

Newsletter 1

There are things I have come to expect. For instance, I find myself automatically hoping that water will come out of the tap when I go to switch it on, and knowing that '4 pm' means 6 pm and 'tomorrow' could mean never. I understand that my white skin automatically labels me as American (I'm actually British), rich, and naïve, and that taxi drivers and street vendors will rip me off if I demonstrate my naïveté by asking the price—just pay and pretend you know! I am even becoming accustomed to the constant shouts of 'Americana', 'Rubia' (blonde), and 'Linda' (beautiful!!) in the streets, and the fact that 'la gente' (the people) are so desperate to help that they'll gladly direct you to the post office, despite having absolutely no idea where it is. I also expect the second question after 'Where are you from?' to be 'Aren't you thinking of getting married?' either because everyone gets married and has kids young here, or because they're looking for a visa, depending on who's doing the asking. They aren't even always subtle either—we were approached by a *guagua* (minibus) driver whose first line was 'Do you speak Spanish—I want to marry an American!'

Julie and I have just about conquered the public transport system—if you can call it that. Heralded by the *Rough Guide* as 'a study in successful anarchy', this is an informal system of packed *guaguas* and *carros publicos* (public cars), which cover the city and can get you everywhere if you know what you are doing—or ask enough questions! There are no delays—there are in fact, no timetables, let alone tickets. *Carros publicos* are a sort of taxi, identified by the lack of doors, wing mirrors, speedometer, and other unimportant parts (although the horn is always in good order), which run set routes. You get everywhere by asking where they are going, and for five pesos you can go two minutes down the road or half an hour across the city. The capacity of these tumbledown cars is six plus the driver: four in the back and two in the front passenger seat; plus kids, who don't count. They are hailed basically by jumping out in front of a likely-looking car, and, so long as you are in the know about where to go to catch another to your destination, and you don't mind if the driver pulls over to a street bar to order a beer, or pulls into a garage along the way to be fitted with an exhaust pipe, you really can get around!

Music is an essential part of life here. *Merengue* and *bachata* threaten to deafen you in the *guaguas*, and beat constantly from the *colmados* (small shops) on every street—the one across the road from us plays music at full volume 24 hours a day. (And no, there's no glass in the windows here, but what would be the point of glass when you'd only have the windows open all the time anyway?) All the bars and nightclubs play *merengue, bachata*, and salsa, and all the dancing is in pairs, and with rules! I am beginning to think dancing ability is innate here, because even the smallest kids in the school I teach at dance—and well. It makes me laugh so much to see 6-year-olds wiggle their hips to 'La bomba'.

I really can't believe I have actually spent three months in this incredible place! I have learnt so much, I can't even begin to tell. I have learnt about the culture and about living and working with incredible people with learning disabilities. About cooking in a kitchen where you have to light the oven with a match and it takes two to three hours to bake a cake depending on the gas supply, where there's no such thing as a frying pan with a handle, and where everything from juice to tomato sauce to garlic butter has to be made from scratch. About doing my washing where the water is cold, if running, and of course, I have learnt a huge amount of Spanish in a place where almost no one speaks English. More than that I have learnt so much about trust, kindness, and patience, and to appreciate my many blessings so much more.

Newsletter 2

Without any official increase in hours, Yessica and I are now working even harder than before—and I feel more needed here than ever. I am included in meetings and decisions made concerning the *hogar* (home) I'm working in, and I am trusted with many more responsibilities. At no moment in the day do I feel like an outsider looking in on a world, or even like a temporary visitor, although I will in fact leave in six months' time.

Since I last wrote, I was glad to have the chance to see how Christmas is celebrated here. In some ways it was very different: Christmas dinner is on the evening of the 24th of December, and there is no present exchanging on the 25th. The traditional Christmas dinner includes pasta, rice, potato salad, apples, and grapes! The *muchachos* (residents) received many presents from members of the *consejo* (board) and other friends of the community long before Christmas, and they opened them immediately. It would apparently be an insult to save a present to open on the 25th, because it would mean that you weren't excited about it! It was wonderful to see how thrilled the folks were with everything they received. They seemed not to distinguish between large and small presents, and had no appreciation of cost. Lorena was so pleased with her pack of five carbon pencils, she barely noticed that they had also given her curling irons! The closest thing to Father Christmas is the *Dia de los Reyes Magos*, on the 6th of January, where all the kids receive toys. I was delighted to see that in the *barrio* (local area) literally all the kids in the streets were playing with new brightly coloured toys of various descriptions, instead of the sticks and bottle tops that serve them for baseball the rest of the year.

In January I also experienced the baseball mania that came with the conclusion of the national baseball tournament. This was something like the British fascination with the World Cup in football, only done Dominican style! On one particular night Julie and I were awake for hours listening to the progress of the game from the 'commentary' of the streets. From miles around you could here the cheering as Licey (the team from Santo Domingo) scored. And not just cheering. With every score, Dominicans all, mothers, young children, and grandparents, came screaming out of their houses (where the game was played on every TV station), banging pots and pans, screaming, jumping up and down, blowing whistles, tooting horns, and even running through the streets dragging large pieces of corrugated metal roofing to make as much noise as possible!

Also adding to the noise of the streets is the build-up to the election next month. Propaganda is in the form of huge vans carrying impressive sound systems driving slowly through the streets blaring *merengue* at an unbearable volume, pausing only occasionally to shout the name of the candidate—whom it seems you should vote for if you like his music! As the time draws nearer this is happening with more intensity. Sometimes huge processions of such vans with flags and people dressed all in red with whistles and horns drive past, preventing any sort of verbal communication for several minutes! Oxford is going to seem very silent when I get back home.

Newsletter 3

With only a few weeks left of my year in Santo Domingo in the Dominican Republic, the end seems to be hurtling towards me at a frightening speed.

My life in England seems so far away, I have almost forgotten what it is like to expect hot water to come out of the shower or to consider eating by candlelight a luxury!

Nine months down the line, people seem impressed when Julie and I mark ourselves out from tourists, saying how long we've been here. I love it when people say my Spanish sounds Dominican, or that I know my way around the *guaguas*! I have learnt so much about the Dominican culture that I can now respect and admire it beyond the frustrations of the Dominican work ethic etc., which were more quickly apparent. At the same time I think I could never be completely accepted in the streets of Santo Domingo, because of the sort of reverse racism towards white people. While it is attractive to be white, because it marks you further away from the Haitians, it sometimes seems to make you automatically intimidating, and also stereotypes you as having money and opportunity. Despite this I have experienced little or no resentment. Perhaps this is surprising because I can't understand how Dominicans could not resent us, given what they think about the 'heaven' we come from and the opportunities we have. As it happens, on the issue of being charged more than Dominicans, I have begun to really see where they are coming from with the idea—sometimes I feel that tourists should pay more because we have more! So important in the culture here is the attitude of always helping one another out—on the *guagua*, in the *carro publico*, in the street: 'We're all in the same boat.' I can't help feeling that as a white person I'll never quite be inside that boat.

Semana Santa (Easter Week) is a major holiday here, and so much so that we were all paid in advance for the occasion! This makes perfect Dominican sense: 'because everyone spends money at Easter'. I was glad to be around during *Semana Santa* because it was really interesting to see how Easter was celebrated in the complete absence of bunnies or chocolate eggs! In the *barrio* the *semanalistas* sung mass in the streets before dawn, passing under our window with candle and guitar just as we were getting up about 6 am—a much preferred alternative to the evangelical shouts over loudspeaker, which was our wake-up call during Lent! In the community we had several celebrations including *Santacruxis*, which involved parading around the streets with candles at dusk commemorating Jesus's journey to the cross, reading bible passages and chanting 'Hail Mary' and the Lord's prayer, before all meeting to re-enact the Last Supper. This was really nice because the two *hogares* (homes) were together, joined by friends of the community and Father Adrian, who later washed all of our feet.

After supper we all piled into the community *guagua* for the traditional visit to the churches in the colonial zone of the city. As it turned out, this isn't just a tradition in our community—we were joined by hundreds of Dominicans doing the rounds! The churches were open late and decorated especially for the evening. The atmosphere was amazing, as if everyone already knew each other, the same spontaneous camaraderie as forms between people on public transport! Someone in the crowd would start a rosary and everyone would reply. In one church a group of youths pushed their way to the front with a guitar and everyone joined in the song, a lovely experience. Back in the community we also had a *vigilia*—loosely a pyjama party with a religious edge. It was really nice as it brought the house together, and was good fun lying around on our mattresses on the floor by candlelight talking, singing, and drinking root tea!

The most surprising part of *Semana Santa* was the silence that befell the city. This is the noisiest place I have ever experienced, but on Good Friday I was shocked to be able, for the first time, to hear the crickets! Large numbers of people left the city, and even the *colmados* had a day off blasting *meringue*! I was told later that it is in fact illegal to play music on this day. I don't know if this is true or just a way of explaining the inexplicable, but given how easy it is to get arrested here (often without doing anything if the policeman is 'hungry'), I can see why nobody wanted to risk it!

As much I am looking forward to coming home and spending time with my friends and family, I wouldn't be anywhere else in the world right now. I know that I will never be able to tell everything that I have seen, experienced, and learnt this year, but I hope that this has given some small insight.

Part II
Infrastructure and Transport

11 Pipelines*

Andrew Barry

While proponents of the idea of globalization talk of the decline of the importance of location, the existence of pipelines reminds us that natural resources such as oil and gas are only found in certain locations, and that their construction may be necessary if those resources are to be exported to global markets. It is not surprising that pipelines are often simply drawn as lines on a map, connecting resource-rich regions with regions that are high in their demand for energy. In this context, the politics of pipelines could simply be understood in terms of their wider geopolitical or geoeconomic significance, linking certain states and markets, while bypassing others. But such a view fails to notice that pipelines have become routes for information flows as well as for the flow of hydrocarbons, and their politics has come to revolve around the production of knowledge as well as the transportation of energy.

The case of the Georgian village of Dgvari in the period 2003 to 2006 is a good illustration of this point. At this time, the village, located close to the route of the Baku–Tbilisi–Ceyhan (BTC) oil pipeline and near to the borders of the Borjomi national park, came to be the site of a transnational controversy. Although its population probably numbered no more than 250, it attracted an extraordinary number and range of visitors, including consultants, government officials and scientists, specialists from an international financial institution, environmental activists, lawyers, journalists and film-makers, and myself. Why should so many be interested in finding out what was happening in one remote Georgian village?

To answer this question we need to understand more about the relations between the village and the pipeline. How did the pipeline come to pass near Dgvari in the first place? Quite simply, the choice of route of the BTC pipeline was broadly determined by geopolitical and security considerations. For in the aftermath of the collapse of the Soviet Union the independence of Georgia opened up a way of exporting oil from the Caspian Sea to the West along a path that avoided passing through Russia or Armenia or Iran. One of the reasons why the pipeline came to pass near Dgvari and Borjomi, in particular, was that the route was also forced to skirt around the major area of Armenian population in southern Georgia, which was poorly controlled by the Tbilisi

* An expanded and substantially revised version of this chapter is published in A. Barry, *Material Politics: Disputes along the Pipeline* (Oxford: Wiley-Blackwell, 2013).

Figure 11.1 Pipeline construction in the region of Dgvari, Georgia, 2004

government and, during the period of BTC's construction, also hosted a Russian military base. Although the more southerly route was considered preferable to the Borjomi route on environmental grounds, the security risks of passing through Armenian areas were judged to be too great by President Shevardnadze. The president's decision, taken less than a year before the Rose Revolution of 2003 that led to his downfall, was heavily criticized in Georgia, including by his own Minister for the Environment.

But neither the proximity of the village to the pipeline nor the political and environmental sensitivity of the Borjomi route, in themselves, can account for the level of global interest in Dgvari. After all, the pipeline was planned to follow a route approximately 1 km away from the village on the other side of the valley nearer to the neighbouring village of Tadzrisi and, in any case, the problems of Dgvari predated the arrival of the oil company in the region, for the village was subject to frequent landslides, which are all too common in the mountains of the Lesser Caucasus. Indeed, scientists from the Georgian state department of geology had completed an initial assessment of the civil engineering and geo-dynamics of Dgvari in 2003 and it was acknowledged by the Georgian government that, given the threat of landslides, the population needed to be resettled. The residents of the village were certainly facing an environmental catastrophe, but this did not necessarily have anything to do with the construction of the oil pipeline on the other side of the valley, although one dissenting Georgian scientist argued that even if the construction of the pipeline would not cause landslides, landslides did pose a threat to the pipeline itself.

But if the problems of Dgvari were partly due to the occurrence of landslides, their prevalence can hardly account for the sudden influx of foreign visitors to the village in the mid 2000s. Perhaps it was the movement of pipes and lorries that had greater short-term impact on the village than the movement of earth. Certainly, both villagers and the Georgian environmentalists, Green Alternative, argued that construction work might precipitate further landslides and, moreover, that the oil company had failed both to carry out any social and environmental impact assessment on the village and to consult its residents prior to the pipeline's construction. One of my informants explained away the concerns of the Dgvari villagers and environmentalists simply in terms of their desire to gain compensation from the company. In his view, the huge cracks in Dgvari's houses (see Figure 11.2) that were routinely shown to visitors had nothing to do with the construction of the pipeline and might have been exacerbated by logging on the hillside above the village. In light of this observation, the problems of Dgvari could be understood as local matters for the Georgian government to solve, symptoms perhaps of the wider decimation of the rural economy that had followed the collapse of the Soviet Union; they had little directly to do with the construction of the pipeline, and were not just geological problems either.

To answer the question of why Dgvari came to be a matter of such global concern, we also have to understand the specific manner in which the BTC company, led by BP, accepted responsibility for the social and environmental impact of the pipeline. This was not straightforward, for any acceptance of responsibility in principle also implied the need to generate assessments of potential impacts for which the company could be held responsible. At the same time, the International Finance Corporation (IFC) and the European Bank for Reconstruction and Development (EBRD) had provided finance for the project and their guidelines governed the extent of the oil company's responsibilities in relation to a whole series of issues, establishing mechanisms, moreover, through which affected communities could make complaints about the conduct of the company. In addition, in accordance with the Åarhus Convention,[1] as well as BP's public commitment to the principle

---

[1] *The UNECE Convention on Access to Information, Public Participation in Decision-making and Access to Justice in Environmental Matters* (Åarhus: United Nations, 1998).

Figure 11.2 Damage to houses in the village of Dgvari, Georgia caused by landslides, 2010

of transparency, a vast quantity of documentation concerning such matters as environmental impacts, compensation rates, and community investment were made available on the Internet. In short, the development of the BTC pipeline involved much more than the construction of the physical structure. It entailed the creation of an extraordinary and growing archive by BP, an information infrastructure that contained the reports of consultants, company managers, and scientists, updated as the project progressed.

What was the publication of the archive intended to achieve? On the one hand, it was expected to render the operations of the company visible to both global and local audiences, in accordance with the norms of corporate social responsibility and transparency that had been adopted by BP. The creation of the archive was a manifestation of globalization in practice. On the other hand, while the archive documented, in some detail, the potential environmental and social impact of the pipeline in a narrow corridor along its length, it had little to say about the impact of pipeline construction beyond this corridor. The village of Dgvari lay near to the borders of the pipeline corridor and should have been consulted prior to the start of construction work, on account of its location, but it was not. This led to a complaint by the residents of Dgvari to the IFC ombudsman. The intensity of interest in the village was driven not just by the prevalence of landslides nor by the physical presence of the pipeline in themselves, but also by the question of why the village and its concerns were not adequately represented in the public archive according to international guidelines. Responding to the residents' complaint, the IFC ombudsman's office considered it unlikely that the construction of the pipeline would increase the risk of landslides; but it noted that 'early consultation [with the village] would have provided an opportunity for villagers to voice their concerns'.[2] Earlier, the BTC company had commissioned consultant geoscientists to investigate the problems of the landslides more thoroughly. However, the consultants' report, which documented the relation between the landslide system and the villagers' houses in remarkable detail, was not placed by BP in its public archive, reflecting the oil company's view of the formal limits of its responsibility. The report was also criticized by Green Alternative for merely proving what was already known about the occurrence of landslides, while failing to address the impact of the pipeline on the village. In effect, it was both ambiguous and disputed whether Dgvari should be placed inside or outside the corridor within which the global norms of transparency and corporate social responsibility applied.

Yet, whatever its direct environmental impact, the construction of the pipeline did affect the village profoundly, in the guise of the circulation of information and knowledge. First, as the IFC ombudsman noted, the village mistrusted the BTC-commissioned study. Second, many residents of the neighbouring village of Tadzrisi were to receive substantial compensation, particularly those who owned land through which the pipe itself passed. In a region in which the rural population is largely reliant on subsistence farming for survival, the villagers of Dgvari were no doubt aware that their neighbours' financial difficulties would be solved, whereas their evidently greater environmental problems would not. Indeed, the story of how the villagers of Tadzrisi anticipated the arrival of the pipeline to the valley, and the possibility of both environmental catastrophe and compensation that it might bring, attracted the interest of the Georgian documentary film-maker, Nino Kirtadze. The social impact of the pipeline on Dgvari therefore derived, in part, from its impact elsewhere (in Tadzrisi); yet the possibility of this second-order effect was not the object of assessment.

In thinking about the politics of Dgvari in 2003–6, it is helpful to conceive of the village not so much as a location on a map, or even as a point on the route of the pipeline, but as an event, the dimensions and constituent elements of which were in flux. For a period it became the nexus of a series of

---

[2] International Finance Corporation, Office of the Compliance Advisor/Ombudsman, *Assessment Report: Seven Complaints regarding the Baku–Tbilisi–Ceyhan (BTC) Pipeline Project Bashkovi, Dgvari, Rustavi, Sgrasheni, Tetriskaro and Tsikhisjvari, Georgia* (September 2004).

different but coexistent dynamics: those of the post-Soviet rural economy, of intra-village politics, of building materials and land, and of the evolving global practices of corporate social responsibility and environmental activism. At the same time, this very particular conjunction of elements generated unexpected consequences elsewhere, at a distance, drawing in the attention of journalists, scientists, international experts, and film-makers, who themselves contributed to the event, creating feedback, increasing the intensity of interest. We cannot isolate any one cause of the event of Dgvari in 2003–6, nor can we say that the controversy that raged in and in relation to the village was about one specific issue or problem. Dgvari was a political situation in which the question of what the situation was about was itself in question. Whether the case should or should not have implications beyond the borders of Georgia and whether the impact of the pipeline stretched across Dgvari were contested.

Many of the features of the event of Dgvari are unique, to be sure. And although disputes occurred in many other villages in Georgia along the route of the BTC pipeline, none attracted the remarkable level of interest that came to be shown in Dgvari. Yet, despite its specificity, the case does tells us something more about pipelines, as well as about the developing global practices of corporate social responsibility and transparency. Pipelines have become immaterial as well as material infrastructures, the boundaries of which stretch well beyond the steel of the pipe itself. In these circumstances, the global politics of pipelines may come to revolve not just around questions of geopolitics, but also the politics of knowledge.

12 Pipes and Wires

Stephen J. Collier and Nino Kemoklidze

In January 2006, a dispute between Ukraine and Russia exploded into the international media. It stemmed from a deal that the two countries concluded in 2001. As an in-kind payment for transporting Russian gas to Europe, the parties agreed that Ukraine would divert a certain volume of Russian gas for domestic use. The amount diverted—a bit less than 20 per cent of Ukrainian consumption—established an implicit rate of exchange between gas and transport. Over time, however, rising world gas prices made these terms increasingly disadvantageous for Russia. The situation became particularly unpalatable from the Russian perspective in the wake of Ukraine's Orange Revolution in 2004. The victory of a Kremlin-backed presidential candidate—Viktor Yanukovych—was met by massive protests against what was widely assumed to be a fraudulent election. The Ukrainian Supreme Court annulled the result and Yanukovych lost a revote to one of the Orange Revolution's leaders, Viktor Yushchenko. In the event, the Russians were not inclined to continue providing former 'Soyuzniki' with cheap gas.

Russia demanded that, beginning on 1 January 2006, Ukraine pay higher rates. Ukraine initially refused. In response, Russia cut off Ukraine's gas supply. Although the two sides offered different accounts of what happened next, most observers agreed that Ukraine then diverted gas destined for Western Europe running through Ukrainian pipelines that, at the time, carried the vast majority of Russian gas exports. The event precipitated a crisis, as Western European countries were faced with gas shortages in the middle of winter. Pressure from European leaders rapidly mounted, and new tariffs were established.

But this passing spat was only a prelude to much bigger crises. In January 2009 another dispute between Moscow and Kiev left 18 countries in Europe without gas for weeks. A deal to end the crisis, which tied the price Ukraine paid Russia for gas to the global price of oil, was brokered by Prime Minister Yulia Tymoshenko, another leader of the Orange Revolution who in the 1990s had become one of the richest people in Ukraine through her dealings in the energy sector. After narrowly losing a run-off election for the presidency in 2010 (to her long-time nemesis Yanukovych), Tymoshenko's government fell. The General Prosecutor brought a series of criminal charges against her, based in part on allegations that she abused her office in concluding the 2009 gas deal, which, her political opponents claimed, had been ruinous for the Ukrainian economy, given rising oil prices. The Russian Foreign Ministry proclaimed that the charges against the former leader of the Orange Revolution had an 'anti-Russian undertone'; the Ukrainian government quickly assured the Russians that the trial's outcome would not be a factor in future negotiations about the price or transport of gas. But this agreement, too, fell apart. In early 2014 protests erupted in Kiev following Yanukovych's decision to abandon plans to sign an Association Agreement with the European Union in favour of deepening ties with Russia. Amid the deterioration of relations between the two countries that followed Yanukovych's eventual ouster—and the seizure of the Crimean Peninsula by Russian forces—Gazprom Chief Executive Alexei Miller announced an increase in the price Ukraine was charged for Russian gas and demanded payment of gas debts. Russian President Vladimir Putin insisted, implausibly, that the decision had 'nothing to do with the situation in Ukraine'. The renewed struggles about gas provoked fears about disruptions in global energy markets. But as of early February Russian gas continued to flow through Ukrainian pipelines and into Western Europe.[1]

Behind these flare-ups over gas lies a more enduring structural—or, better, infrastructural—story. In the Soviet period a system of pipes was constructed to deliver Russian gas to Western Europe. These pipes began in the massive deposits of north-west Siberia, passed over the Ural Mountains, through European Russia, into Ukraine, and from there to distribution networks in Western Europe. During the Cold War this system provided a reliable connection between adversaries. With Soviet break-up, political borders changed and economic systems—to one degree or another—were transformed. But the pipes' material set-up and geographic pattern persisted, of course, and, for better or for worse, producers, consumers, and transshippers were stuck with each other. Russia could not easily reroute its gas exports to avoid its neighbours when disputes arose. The Europeans could not simply buy their gas elsewhere when these disputes resulted in interruptions. For Ukraine, notwithstanding the conflicts that emerged around it, the pipeline initially appeared as a happy accident, offering the country leverage and revenue it would not have under other circumstances.

Conventional portrayals of globalization are filled with footloose commodities and geographically untethered corporations that set up shop in one locale only to zip off to another, choosing those economic interactions and national milieus that best fit a calculus of cost and benefit. But globalization in practice is also shaped by intransigencies, blockages, and points of friction. These often take the form of material structures—such as pipes and wires—that shape political and economic developments in surprising ways.

One useful economic term for thinking about the role of these intransigent features of the global economy is 'substitutability'. Substitutability concerns the extent to which an economic agent can replace one set of exchange

---

[1] Rushton, Katherine, 'Russia cancels Ukraine's gas discounts and demands $1.5bn', *The Telegraph*, 4 March, 2014.

relationships, geographical locales, or methods and instruments of economic production for another. An example of high substitutability—or high elasticity of substitution—is the remarkable capacity of global apparel manufacturers to change production locales in pursuit of lower costs. In other areas substitution is inelastic. Many forms of energy production, distribution, and consumption depend on capital-intensive and spatially fixed infrastructures. Relationships in this sector, thus, tend to be sticky, and less responsive to changing costs, whether these costs take the form of increased prices or political conflicts.

Even here, however, there is significant variation. Global oil production, distribution, and consumption are organized through relatively flexible relations of exchange, thanks to efficient tanker shipping and the energetic efforts of major powers to establish and maintain a liquid market in oil.[2] Most natural gas, by contrast, is delivered through fixed networks of pipes that lock in relationships between suppliers, transporters, and consumers. There is not a single global market for natural gas. Price levels, thus, are determined not only by supply and demand but also by bargaining, coercion, or the simple inertial weight of existing agreements or material relationships. Thus, low elasticity of substitution often means high politics, particularly given the amount of money involved.[3]

The examples are innumerable, and the political conflicts that take shape around these intransigencies of infrastructure are not always resolved in ways that allow free commodity flow across borders or advance the general tendency of economic globalization as usually understood. Take, for example, the case of post-Soviet Georgia. In 1992, immediately after the collapse of the Soviet Union, Russia cut off gas supplies to Georgia due to non-payment. As a consequence, the centralized gas-fired boilers that once delivered heat to households in Georgian cities went idle. The heating infrastructure was looted and sold for scrap. Georgians were left to find other means to heat their houses, using wood-burning stoves, often dangerous gas stoves (a leak from one allegedly killed then-Prime Minister Zurab Zhvania in 2005), or expensive electric heaters.

But these substitutes—particularly electricity—bear their own problems. During the 1990s, the Georgian electricity system spiralled into decline. A string of suspicious accidents at key facilities left the country with a significant supply deficit and increasingly dependent on imports from Russia and Armenia. These problems were compounded by rampant non-payment and corruption—much of the imported electricity was allegedly stolen by

---

[2] See Thomas W. O'Donnell, 'The Political Economy of Oil in the U.S.–Iran Crisis: U.S. Globalized Oil Interests vs. Iranian Regional Interests', GPIA Working Paper 2009-05 (New York: New School Graduate Program in International Affairs, 2009).

[3] See Daniel Freifeld, 'The Great Pipeline Opera', *Foreign Policy*, September/October 2009.

dispatchers and re-exported to electricity-starved Turkey, Georgia's neighbour to the south. By the end of the decade, Georgia's electricity system was in tatters.[4]

In the late 1990s Western donors began to pour money into Georgia to rehabilitate the electricity system—hoping, in part, to establish Georgia as a beachhead of influence in a Russian-dominated region, and to forge new energy geographies that would bypass Russia.[5] The most famous example—recounted in the 2003 documentary *Power Trip*—is the adventures of the American firm, AES, which in 1998 purchased the distribution network in the Georgian capital, Tbilisi, as well as some generation capacity in Georgia. The company planned a multi-pronged approach to reform. It would raise consumer rates, invest in the city distribution system to increase reliability, and import electricity from power plants it had acquired in Central Asia. Its efforts were backed by the United States Agency for International Development, which paid for subsidies to provide free electricity for poor households in Tbilisi (the subsidies, of course, went directly to the Tbilisi affiliate of AES).

But the stubborn materiality of infrastructure and the inconvenient facts of local and regional politics tripped up the company's plans. Reform efforts collided with Georgian citizens' deeply held expectations about government provision of electricity as a basic public good. Thus, notwithstanding substantial progress in the reliability of supply and in cost recovery—and alongside problems with corruption and bureaucratic entanglements—AES's managers were soon grappling with well-organized protests over the rate hikes and widespread efforts to physically bypass the electricity meters that the company installed throughout the city. AES's problems had an international dimension as well. The long-distance transmission wires that connected AES's Central Asian generation facilities to Tbilisi ran through Russia, then over the Caucasus and into Georgia. But AES did not control the transmission of electricity, and power it purchased for import was allegedly diverted by dispatchers.[6]

In 2003, after investing—and losing—hundreds of millions of dollars in Georgia (and after the murder of its chief financial officer Niko Lominadze), AES gave up and sold its shares in the Tbilisi grid.[7] The buyer was RAO-UES, the state-controlled Russian electricity giant, which was purchasing electricity

---

[4] For background see Transparency International Georgia, 'Georgia's State Policy in the Electricity Sector: Brief History and Ongoing Processes', (February 2008), <http://www.investmentguide.ge/files/160_158_615717_TIGeorgia-GovernmentEnergyPolicyandStrategy-3rdreport.pdf>.

[5] For an overview see Jim Nichol, 'Armenia, Azerbaijan, and Georgia: Political Developments and Implications for U.S. Interests' (Washington, DC: Congressional Research Service, 2011).

[6] The World Bank, Operations Evaluation Department, 'Project Performance Assessment Report: Georgia', (Washington, DC: The World Bank, 2003), <http://lnweb90.worldbank.org/oed/oed-doclib.nsf/DocUNIDViewForJavaSearch/8E64AA33C4E92B3785256D900073CA80/$file/Georgia_PPAR_26439_light.pdf>.

[7] The rationale for the sale was called into question by some observers, who claimed AES's Georgian operation was on the cusp of profitability ('Georgia's State Policy', 4).

system assets in Georgia at a remarkable pace. The sale was met with protests in Tbilisi (one resident asked: 'Would we have died fighting in the [1992–3] war in Abkhazia…if we'd known they were going to sell Georgia back to Russia?'[8]). But the infrastructural connection between Georgia and Russia only expanded and stabilized in subsequent years, even amidst explosive political and military conflict. During the 2008 Georgia–Russian war, electricity supplies from Russia to Georgia were not cut off; and only months after the war RAO concluded a deal with the Georgian government to operate its largest electricity-generating facility, the Enguri hydropower plant. Today, RAO 'dominates the Georgia electricity market, from generation to end user'.[9]

The Georgian case is hardly atypical. Many European or American efforts to reshape energy politics in the region have been stymied by stubborn facts of geography, the intransigent materiality of infrastructure, and the weight of recent history. And over the first decade of the twenty-first century, RAO-UES has succeeded in reconsolidating its control over energy assets in the former Soviet republics. Indeed, this private Russian company (with intimate ties to the Russian government) is now close to realizing a 'long dreamed-of goal of Soviet planners' by creating a synchronized electricity grid across what is now *post*-Soviet space.[10]

Nothing is forever, of course. If in the electricity sector old relationships are being re-established, and Soviet dreams of an integrated regional system are being realized, new ties are also being forged. For example, RAO aims to link the consolidating regional grid with other desirable markets[11] (a new high-voltage transmission line through Georgia to strengthen this grid is currently planned). In the gas sector, meanwhile, the landscape is unsettled and shifting, and the region is teeming with plans for new pipelines. In 2011 Russia and Germany completed the first pipeline of the Nord Stream, which connects the two countries via the Baltic Sea, and Russia has been working with Turkey to build a South Stream pipeline in Turkish waters of the Black Sea. Meanwhile, competing plans to supply Europe with gas from other sources abound: the Nabucco pipeline, to supply European markets with gas from the Caspian region via Georgia, Turkey, Bulgaria, and Romania; a Turkey–Greece–Italy line to supply Europe with Azerbaijani gas; a trans-Adriatic pipeline that would cross Greece, Albania, the Adriatic Sea and reach the rest of Europe via Italy; and a trans-Anatolian pipeline that is currently favoured by the Turkish government. These plans reflect the complex dance of countries

---

[8] Quoted in Dima bit-Suleiman (2003) 'Georgia: Russian Hands on the Switches'. *Transitions Online*, 11 August 2003, <http://www.tol.cz> (accessed 23 February 2012).

[9] See Courtney Doggart (2009) 'Russian Investment in Georgia's Electricity Sector', USAEE Working Paper 09-035, p. 16.

[10] See Theresa Sabonis-Helf (2007) 'Unified Energy Systems of Russia (RAO-UES) in Central Asia and the Caucasus: Nets of Interdependence', *Demokratizatsia* 15(4): 429–44.

[11] Sabonis-Helf, p. 431.

with different relationships to production, shipment, and supply. Russia has been working to lock in major consumers while avoiding problems with intermediaries, in part by bypassing them, and in part by buying up their energy assets. Countries along a long arc from the Caucasus to the Baltics are jostling to position themselves as attractive routes for transshipment while avoiding the snare of Russian influence. Western European countries, finally, are playing a delicate double game: seeking to ensure that Russian gas is reliably delivered while diversifying sources of supply.

But building such structures takes a long time (witness the fact that over two decades after Soviet break-up a new pipeline geography is still taking shape). They involve monstrously complex political and economic arrangements (as often as not they simply collapse, as now seems to be the fate of the Nabucco line). And even completed lines that solve today's problems of geography, economics, and politics may well be at the root of tomorrow's. In practice, then, we can expect that globalization will continue to be shaped by struggles over the intransigent paths of pipes and wires.

13 Automated Repair and Backup Systems

Stephen Graham

In the summer of 2004 a vast, squat, and anonymous building was completed next to Highway 71 on the edge of the unprepossessing mid-western US town of Jane, Missouri. Apart from the compete lack of the usual corporate signage and iconography, this 133,000-square-foot structure was indistinguishable from the countless other suburban distribution centres that now spring up in the vague margins between urbanity and rurality that encircle the world's towns and cities.

'There is nothing about the building to give even a hint that Wal-Mart owns it,' writes Max McCoy for the *Joplin Globe*. 'Despite the glimpses through the fence of manicured grass and carefully-placed trees, the overall impression is that this is a secure site that could withstand just about anything.' The centre is deliberately placed on solid bedrock and is designed to withstand powerful local thunderstorms, earthquakes, and terrorist attacks. 'Earth is packed against the sides,' continues McCoy. 'The green roof—meant, perhaps, to blend into the surrounding Ozarks hills—bristles with dish antennae. On one of the heavy steel gates at the guardhouse is a notice that visitors must use the intercom for assistance.'

Rather than being concerned with orchestrating continuous streams of physically transported goods and products, this centre is at the heart of an equally vital but much more invisible complex: the orchestration of continuous digital data flow. For the Highway 71 complex is the epicentre of Wal-Mart's global architecture of data traffic—an assemblage developed specifically to make sure that the 100 million or so apparently mundane digital transactions, communications, and surveillance events that sustain the world's biggest retailer each day carry on, relentlessly, no matter what extreme events, malfunctions, or acts of political violence effect the firm's operations.

The centre concentrates, and backs up, all data captured across the firm's stores and transactions, worldwide. This process allows sophisticated data-mining software to predict market trends, so allowing the global chains of production and distribution to synchronize as near as possible with changing market geographies as they play out.

As Hurricane Frances bore down on Florida in the summer of 2004, for example, Wal-Mart's data-mining centre quickly analysed changing consumption patterns from previous events. It was predicted that local stores would need a range of certain products in large quantities beyond the obvious torches and candles. 'We didn't know in the past that strawberry Pop-Tarts increase in sales, like seven times their normal sales rate, ahead of a hurricane,' Ms Dillman, Wal-Mart's chief information officer, said in a *New York Times* interview at the time. 'And the pre-hurricane top-selling item was beer.' Thanks to those analyses, large loads of these items were soon speeding down towards Wal-Mart stores in the path of the hurricane.

Wal-Mart's is only the largest and most spectacular of a whole new field of stealth data-centre architecture—what London architecture critic Martin Pawley called 'terminal architecture' in a book of the same name.

Such buildings are springing up in the most unlikely locations, presenting a whole incipient geography of backup and repair spread across the world. Around the hearts of global finance centres such as London and New York, for example, bunker-like business continuity centres cluster, ready to go into operation to support corporate data flows and archives whenever the main corporate headquarters and electronic trading floors face disruptions of any kind. Districts adjacent to the main corporate and financial downtowns, such as London Docklands or New Jersey, are now chock full of such fortified centres, and the specialized firms that operate them now constitute an important economic sector in their own right.

In the downtown cores, meanwhile, disused and obsolescent modernist tower blocks have had their windows blacked out as they are converted into so-called 'telecom hotels'. Such complexes house web servers and major digital switching systems and connect directly to the planet's optic fibre grids. They allow the world's major communications providers to serve the world's major metropolitan markets cheaply, efficiently, and with minimum vulnerability to disruption.

Far away from the world's main metropolitan hubs, meanwhile, the world's nooks and crannies—from disused ballistic missile silos to closed-down salt mines and rusting anti-aircraft forts—are being turned into data backup and storage centres. Such spaces offer ultra-secure data archiving and backup facilities, using the accumulated regolith of military architecture abandoned since the end of the twentieth century.

To this list we should also add, of course, the burgeoning data and surveillance centres of national security states, emboldened by the rapidly extending 'national security' capabilities as a result of the 'war on terror'. In such complexes, the commercial innovations of data mining, communication tracking, and profiling are now mutating into new assemblages for (attempted) social and political control. Often, such operations blur troublingly with operations like Wal-Mart's. For the very commercial firms who specialize in such tasks for corporate clients are taking up the mantle of national security data mining, as they colonize the contracting opportunities left by privatized and neoliberal states.

Finally, all of the world's major telecommunications operators now operate their own large-scale bunker complexes. These are designed to allow for the automatic or near-automatic repair of the world's data and communications networks, in the event of catastrophic events such as the 9/11 attacks on Manhattan, or the devastation of New Orleans by Hurricane Katrina. With their room-size digital world maps displaying real-time events, and tiered ranks of operators, such bunkers are reminiscent of the Cold War nuclear weapons control rooms portrayed so memorably in classic Cold War films such as Stanley Kubrick's *Dr Strangelove*, rather than sites to manage the more mundane threats of teller machines, mobile phones, supermarket checkouts, gas pumps, or Internet computers displaying 'network unavailable' signs.

In a digitized, globalized, and 24-hour economy, the absolute imperative, amidst all others, is continuity of digital connection and service. For e-commerce firms, digital financial service corporations, global logistics and transport systems, call centres, and international information and consumer data companies, continuous digital data flow and archiving are, very literally, the only possible means of operation. The costs when such digital flows are disrupted because of technical malfunction, 'natural' catastrophes, or political violence quickly lead to the very erasure of these firms. Neil Stephenson, CEO of the Onyx Group—a major provider of business continuity centres—commented in 2006 that, according to statistics produced by the UK Office of the Deputy Prime Minister, '[Eighty] per cent of businesses affected by a major incident [which disrupts their digital operations or erases their database archives] close within 18 months.'

It is not surprising, then, that in the world's interstitial economic geographies, and the remote or bunkered nooks and crannies left abandoned after the Cold War, a new brand of stealthy yet anonymous architecture is mushrooming. So anonymous are such buildings that they remain far from visible—unknown to all but a few hackers, urban explorers, hardened enthusiasts, or researchers or the urban esoteric.

But such built architectures of data backup and digital repair remain much more manifest than their vital, digital shadow. For such centres and buildings do an even more powerful job of hiding the data infrastructures of fibres, servers, and software that link them together. Most invisible of all is a growing universe of software that automatically detects, diagnoses, and attempts to repair interruptions to flow and connectivity within transnational data systems, routing traffic away from failing nodes within the Internet's famous 'packet-switching' architecture, and backing up data records in the most secure sites on transnational networks of data centres.

Not to be forgotten, also, are the massive electrical and air conditioning systems—usually with one or two backups in case of power failures—which sustain both the built data centres and the power-hungry server architectures that they house.

Together, these built and digital spaces and systems constitute what we might call the global assemblage of digital flow. Here we confront perhaps the most crucial infrastructure of globalization: the pervasive digital skein of communications systems that continuously works to bring the global digital economy, and its physical mobilities and flows, into apparently magical being.

And yet, like all true infrastructures, the invisibility of global data systems in everyday life means that they are only really noticed—and then fleetingly—when they cease to function. At such moments, the constant calculative background sustaining global digital capitalism, is momentarily interrupted until the reinstatement occurs and the digital assemblages can sink back into the background.

Such a perspective has clear analytical implications. It means that it is best to see the so-called 'network' or 'information society' not as some extraterrestrial impactor magically transforming cities and societies in its wake—as if from outer space. Rather, our perspective should stress that such transformations are the result of new systems, built spaces, digital architectures, and practices being brought into being and sunk anonymously, and often invisibly, into the places of the world.

If we were to pay more attention to the mundane infrastructures, landscapes, and assemblages involved, and the ways in which they quite literally surround and sustain our everyday lives, we might be less likely to wrap these transformations in the hype of utopia, or dystopia, with all the unhelpful gloss that emerges when this happens.

14 Road Safety and Traffic Management

Daniel Neyland and Steve Woolgar

Introduction

Road safety and traffic management have long been concerns for authorities, road users, and campaigners. The last have engaged in different ways in different countries of the world in campaigns both for and against road safety measures. Indeed, over the last hundred years it is clear that what counts as a road safety issue for one individual or group in one part of the world is also likely to be seen by others as an infringement of liberty, unnecessary meddling by the authorities, or unlikely to work. One should not leap too quickly to assume that road safety and traffic management have always been about the car. Prior to the internal combustion engine, speed limits were applied to steam-powered traction engines (to prevent them travelling at dangerously excessive speeds beyond 4 mph) and bicycles were subject to regulation to guard against what in the UK was termed scorching (riding recklessly through built-up areas at excessive speed[1]). And just as these regulations and limits were discussed, so they were disputed as an unnecessary limit on the individual's freedom and an unnecessary intrusion by the authorities. This cycle of lengthy discussion and debate, the production of a limitation, and anxiety focused on the limitation (as too much and/or not enough of a limitation) has been repeated for a hundred years in most countries of the world.

Speed Limits

The importance, necessity, and apparent reasonableness of speed limits for cars in particular have never reached a comfortable consensus. There has never been a globally standardized speed limit (although there have been attempts

---

[1] Clive Elmsley, "'Mother, What Did Policemen do When There Weren't Any Motors?' The Law, the Police and the Regulation of Motor Traffic in England, 1900–1939', *The Historical Journal* 36, 2 (1993): 357–81.

to standardize signage). Indeed, the motivations for having a speed limit have altered across different times and locations: the oil crisis in the 1970s provided one motivation for introducing a nationally standardized speed limit across the USA (subsequently scrapped in 1995); the 1934 UK speed limit was introduced as a road safety measure (although it was in effect a reintroduction after the previous limit had been removed in 1930); the absence of a speed limit on German autobahns was regarded as a citizen's right; and the French speed limit in the early 1900s was seen in the UK as being just the peculiar kind of thing the French did. It is also a myth that one needs to be exceeding a speed limit in order to be stopped, prosecuted, and fined. In the UK, for example, if a driver is considered to be driving in a manner unreasonable for the conditions (based on a notional test of what most reasonable people would do), then they can be fined (similar principles apply in the USA and were taken to an extreme in the state of Montana which had a speed limit from 1995 to 1999 based on reasonableness rather than numerical speed).

In terms of justifying speed limits as a road safety measure, arguments continue over the level of danger posed by cars and the appropriate focus of responsibility for ensuring road safety. Clive Elmsley quotes figures that show that in 1913, 209,000 vehicles on the road in Britain were involved in 44,643 accidents, of which 2,099 proved fatal.[2] This suggests a high percentage of vehicles were involved in accidents. However, we have no way of knowing whether this was a few drivers having many accidents while the majority drove safely, the potential importance of the lack of driving lessons and tests for this level of accidents, and the extent to which an early speed limit helped prevent accidents. These kinds of arguments over the level of danger posed by cars being driven at some speed continue today. In 2005, for example, an accident in Oxford, England, involving a car carrying several children, led to the imposition of a 50 mph (from 70 mph) speed limit on the city's ring road.[3] One interpretation of this measure would be to say that the whole city now has to drive 20 mph slower as a result of one driver's reckless actions and that recklessness is assumed to be the default characteristic of all drivers and cars in Oxford. Similar arguments about the level of danger and the need for speed limits are played out around the world. Examples include recent moves in Austria to encourage drivers to recognize that road safety and Godliness are one and the same[4] and attempts in Ghana to get drivers to slow down so that doctors can fulfil obligations other than just treating road accident victims.[5]

---

[2] BBC Oxford, 'Fatal Crash Probe to Study Cars', *BBC News*, 31 May 2005, <http://news.bbc.co.uk/1/hi/england/oxfordshire/4593273.stm>.

[3] Ibid.

[4] Colin Coyle, 'Dublin Pushes the Speed Limits', *Times Online*, 14 February 2010, <http://www.timesonline.co.uk/tol/news/world/ireland/article7026237.ece>.

[5] IRIN Africa, 'Ghana: Road Crash Casualties Hit Maternal Health Efforts', *IRIN*, 12 June 2009, <http://www.irinnews.org/report.aspx?ReportID=84828>.

Responsibility and Accountability

A key feature of determinations of the level of danger posed by cars/drivers is arguments about responsibility and accountability. Who or what should take responsibility, in what form, for road safety? Who or what can be held to account? Globally, there are two lines of argument that play out slightly differently in different places. The first line of argument is that enforcement of road safety (via speed limits) should not be left entirely in the hands of drivers. Various delegates are called upon in different parts of the world to manage road safety, remind drivers of the speed limit, and enforce the speed limit through the use of technology, the police, or retraining schemes.

The UK has gone the furthest in developing technological means of keeping drivers aware of the speed limits and punishing lack of compliance. The UK speed camera network currently includes around 6,000 cameras that sit by the side of the road, reminding drivers of the need to adhere to the speed limit and issuing penalty notices to those who do not. The assumed need for, and value of, technical delegates to do this work on behalf of drivers is nationally specific. In the USA and Australia, for example, speed cameras have been developed to a lesser extent, been met with strong opposition, and there have been far fewer stories of the positive benefits of such cameras in comparison to the UK.

In the USA and Australia, technological delegates are vastly outnumbered by human delegates in the form of police officers. In the UK, replacing police officers with cameras has been promoted as a way of allowing the police to focus on cutting other crime. However, in Australia and the USA, a large proportion of police time is still devoted to speed limit enforcement.

The UK has also led the world in combining the enforcement of speed limits with driver retraining ('speed awareness') schemes. These schemes are offered as an alternative to a fine and with the express intention of encouraging drivers to take responsibility for road safety and for knowing and abiding by speed limits. They thereby shade over into the second line of argument over who or what ought to take responsibility for road safety and speed limits. This second line of argument clearly places an emphasis on driver responsibility, rather than delegated responsibility to technology, police officers, or retraining schemes. The German autobahn absence of speed limits has been a notable historical example of this responsibilization. In place of a focus on reminding drivers via, for example, speed cameras, that they ought to slow down comes a constant focus on drivers taking responsibility for their actions.

Further in this line of thought are shared-space initiatives. These are said to have origins in experiments carried out in Draachten in the Netherlands. The basic assumptions of shared-space initiatives are that by removing distinctions between road and pavement/sidewalk, by removing clear road markings, signs, and lines, all road users (drivers, pedestrians, cyclists) are forced to accept responsibilities for using the space and to pay attention to other users of the space. This mode of responsibilization is designed to do away with the need for enforcement and reminders of speed limits. One of the most curious shared-space experiments is proposed in the UK town of Southend-on-Sea.[6] This is called the shared-space triangabout. It is proposed that a major roundabout, busy with cars, pedestrians, cyclists, and buses, will be replaced by a triangular shared-space scheme. Advocates hail this as a victory for pedestrians who, it is said, will now be in a position to reclaim the space. Local residents have tended to respond to the proposal with more scepticism, particularly given the large number of young teenage drivers in customized cars who have a reputation for driving recklessly through the town for their own entertainment (a modern-day version of scorching).

However, this brief overview of the history and contemporary approaches to road safety and speed limits in the UK, Australia, the USA, Germany, and France is by no means a global picture. The rationales for, ideas about, and the operation of road safety and speed limits are very locally specific. Various countries of the world are said to have speed limits, but little enforcement (particularly developing countries, which account for around 90 per cent of road traffic fatalities each year), the Isle of Man uses its complete lack of speed limits to try and attract tourists, and 'road safety' appears to be an alien concept in many places.[7] The operation and enforcement of speed limits can also vary considerably within national boundaries. Thus, for example, the level (speed) at which 'safety cameras' are set to trigger, the numbers of speed cameras containing film, and the resources devoted to the pursuit of prosecutions have all been shown to vary markedly between different regional authorities within the UK.[8] Furthermore, the delegation of road safety to technological means in, for example, the UK assumes that those technological delegates are able to perform their roles consistently. However, breakdowns of road safety technology, for example when traffic lights stop working or the suspension of speed camera operation due to cutbacks in local council budgets, are fairly frequent. When this happens, responsibility seems to shift back to drivers, at least temporarily. Whether or not the absence of road safety technology actually gives rise to improved traffic flow is much contested.

[6] Echo, 'Work Starts on £7m Victoria Gateway Scheme in Southend', *Echo News*, 15 January 2010, <http://www.echo-news.co.uk/news/4848786._7million_plan_to_change_the_face_of_Southend_town_centre/>.

[7] Adnan Hyder, 'Road Safety: A Major Killer in Developing Countries Like India', *Bulletin of the World Health Organization* 82 (2004): 240.

[8] Steve Woolgar and Daniel Neyland, *Mundane Governance: Ontology and Accountability* (Oxford: Oxford University Press, 2013).

Conclusion

To what extent are road safety and traffic management a global phenomenon? Driving through different countries of the world one comes into contact with a variety of signs, technologies, forms of enforcement, and speed limits (or their absence). What counts as safety and what counts as appropriate enforcement varies enormously. Yet efforts are being made to introduce a more standardized experience of road safety. For example, in an attempt to alleviate the burden of a high number and high percentage of fatalities in road traffic accidents in developing countries, the UK-based Transport Research Laboratory has actively considered exporting UK road safety initiatives. Clearly, however, a key prior issue is whether and to what extent these UK initiatives can be said to work. As already hinted, the answer is uncertain. The BBC has questioned whether or not cameras actually cut accidents.[9] Others claim that speed cameras have actually caused 28,000 accidents in ten years.[10] The UK government (Department for Transport) claims to have achieved a year-on-year improvement in road safety conditions in the UK and a reduction in minor and major accidents since the inception of the national speed camera network in the UK in 2000. Yet at the same time, parts of the UK are beginning to remove speed cameras. If efforts at globalizing road safety and traffic management are to succeed they will have to do so despite the enormous variation in what counts as safety, and despite considerable uncertainty and controversy about whether or not attempts at enforcement actually work.

---

[9] BBC Oxford, 'Fatal Crash Study to Probe Cars'.
[10] 'Speed Cameras Have Caused 28,000 Accidents in a Decade', *Mail Online*, 6 August 2010, <http://www.dailymail.co.uk/news/article-1300830/Speed-cameras-caused-28-000-accidents-decade.html?ito=feeds-newsxml>.

15 Containers

Susan M. Roberts

Even if you live miles from the ocean, you have seen shipping containers. They are the big steel boxes seen on the back of truck trailers, travelling on rail cars, and stacked at terminals and depots. Sometimes rusting containers can be found turned into temporary storage facilities behind shopping malls, at the edges of school playgrounds, and on construction sites. All around the world containers can be spotted, adapted, and transformed into everything from movable barracks ('battle boxes') and prison blocks to houses and stores.

The genius of the container, though, lies in its original purpose: as a standardized, multimodal shipping box. Containers are either 20 or 40 feet long, 8 feet wide and 8½ or 9½ feet tall ('high cube'). Each standard container can hold about 20 tons in weight and can withstand having five full containers stacked on top of it. Most containers are 'dry boxes'—just empty steel boxes with a wooden floor lining and double doors at the back. Others are temperature controlled ('reefer' boxes) or are designed to hold liquids in tanks, but all can be stacked on top of one another and be moved by the same equipment. Over 80 per cent of all containers are manufactured in China.

If you live in the global north, the chances are that nearly every manufactured thing you buy (and each of its components) has seen the inside of a shipping container. Over 90 per cent of international non-bulk trade travels in containers, and even items that were previously considered not suitable for containerization (such as metal ingots) increasingly are containerized. World trade is growing faster than world output, and world container traffic is growing much faster than world trade. It is estimated that there are about 30 million containers in circulation globally.

This simple and unassuming box has had a complex and very dramatic role in changing the world we live in: it has propelled globalization, altered the global geography of trade, restructured labour relations, and changed the face of cities.

The shipping container made its first appearance on the world stage just over 50 years ago, when the *Ideal X*, an old tanker with decks converted to hold a few dozen containers, sailed from Newark, New Jersey, down the east coast of the USA and around to the port of Houston, Texas, in 1956. (See also Helen Sampson's discussion of seafarers and changing global labour markets in Chapter 17.) Now there are over 3,000 specialized container ships, or 'box boats', sailing the world's oceans (see Figures 15.1 and 15.2). Some of the newest and biggest box boats can hold over 10,000 20-foot containers (or

Figure 15.1 Container Ship Maersk Kleven being loaded at the Port of Felixstowe, United Kingdom (the Maesrk Kleven, launched in 1996, has a capacity of 7,908 TEUs)

Figure 15.2 Container Ships at the Port of Felixstowe, United Kingdom (the Gunvor Maersk, in foreground, was launched in 2005 and has a capacity of 9,000 TEUs)

TEUs—'twenty-foot equivalent units') each. Before 1970 only the New York Port Authority, with the creation of the Port Elizabeth Marine Terminal next door to the Port of Newark in New Jersey, and the ports in Rotterdam and Singapore had invested in building specialized container terminals. Today there are more than 50 ports with facilities to each handle over two million TEUs per year. Ten ports (nine of them in East Asia) have throughputs in excess of 12 million TEUs a year.

Vast investments in physical infrastructure, from dredged deep-water channels to quays to cranes to feeder highways and rail lines, have propelled some port cities, such as Singapore, to global status, whereas many ports unable to muster the investments have been bypassed by container traffic. The once-busy piers and quays of Brooklyn, Hoboken, and Manhattan fell quiet as Newark and Port Elizabeth took over the job of handling the increasingly containerized trade of the north-eastern USA. Because containers are predominantly moved by machines, not men, once-powerful port labour organizations such as the longshoremen of New York have seen their clout diminish.

The story of the container is often told as the story of Malcom McLean, a self-made trucking company owner from North Carolina. It was he who had the *Ideal X* refitted and designed the wheel-less truck trailer containers that were stacked on its decks. McLean was not the first to see the possibilities for intermodal traffic based on a standardized freight container, but he did determinedly take advantage of every opportunity and pushed to make it happen, in the process building his Sea-Land company.

The Vietnam War, it turned out, was a major opportunity for McLean. In 1965, the US military was embarrassed by its inability to organize the speedy offloading of much-needed military equipment at the harbours in Vietnam. Ships would wait for days to be painstakingly unloaded by hand and, once unloaded, equipment often sat on the docks for weeks without being sent on to the battlefield. Malcom McLean lobbied hard to persuade the US military to change from using smaller steel boxes (so-called Conex or Container Express boxes) to transport equipment, to adopting the larger container format. Sea-Land soon won the US military shipping contracts to Japan, the Philippines, and Vietnam, operating a largely containerized supply chain on those routes from 1967 on. As its Pacific business grew, Sea-Land looked for loads to carry on the return trip to the USA and began bringing containers full of Japanese-made goods back across the Pacific to consumers in the USA.

For the potential of containerization to be unleashed there needed to be agreement on basic issues such as the dimensions of the container. Like time zones and railroad gauges, it took some time for one set of standards to prevail. The 1960s were a time of intense jockeying among railroad, trucking, and shipping companies, sometimes in national coalitions, as the International Organization for Standardization (ISO) debated the pros and cons of various sizes of container and different types of construction. Even the fastening mechanisms at the corners of the boxes, allowing containers to be fixed to different chassis and to each other, were the subject of fierce battles. Eventually ISO standards were established, such that by 1970 there was emerging convergence among manufacturers and users on the 20- and 40-foot lengths. With the standards in place, ports authorities and freight corporations felt secure investing in containerization. Before that, no one had wanted to potentially be stuck with the Betamax version of containers and container-handling equipment.

What has containerization done? First it has tremendously lowered transportation costs. Freight costs now make up only a fraction of the overall cost of many products, from phones to shoes, which travel immense distances from producer to consumer. Costs are lower for a variety of reasons: there is less pilfering when goods are containerized; labour costs are lower at ports, on ships, and at warehouses and depots; far-away production locations have become more substitutable, and the industry has tended to exploit possible economies of scale at every point.

The latest class of so-called post-Panamax (too big to fit through the Panama Canal) container ships can carry 11,000 to 15,500 TEUs, depending on their weight, and a Korean shipbuilder is building the first of a new ('Triple E') class of container vessel that will have a capacity of 18,000 TEUs. Such enormous ships transport containers across oceans very cheaply. However, the tremendous economies of scale they embody have had some curious effects. They have tended to lock in some ports and exclude others. The very biggest of the box boats can only call at a few of the world's ports whose facilities can handle such large vessels and the logistical challenges entailed in unloading, loading, and sorting thousands of containers in as few hours as possible. A train carrying a post-Panamax load of containers would be at least 71 kilometres (44 miles) long, so you can imagine the logistical problems a port could face in managing and sending such a quantity of boxes on their way. The potential for 'traffic jams' at the largest container terminals and the way the network tends to bypass many world regions (notably much of Africa) open the possibility for there to be a niche for specialized players (shippers and terminal operators) who serve smaller ports, or who might be able to promise greater speed or some custom handling.

However, the major site of innovation in the container business these days is information technology. Shipping companies and container-leasing companies can see the efficiencies and thus the profit that can be squeezed from better managing the host of small and big logistical challenges faced in keeping vast numbers of containers on the move—what one analyst called 'an exercise in mass synchronicity'. Such technologies can also be tailored to mesh with tracking systems that, much like those offered by parcel delivery services, can be used by customers to more exactly coordinate their logistic chains. Not coincidentally, such technologies can be mobilized to somewhat counter security concerns aroused by the opaque and ubiquitous container.

16 Resisting the Global
Paul Routledge

Dhaka Gathering

May 2004. In the grounds of the Institute of Social Science on the semi-rural outskirts of Dhaka, Bangladesh, a week-long conference has been organized by People's Global Action (Asia) (PGA Asia), a network of peasant movements from various struggles in South and South-east Asia. One hundred and fifty activists have gathered to share testimonies of one another's struggles, to discuss the common problems and opponents that they face, and to plan collective strategies to confront these. Workshops and meetings are held, documentary films are shown, meals are eaten together, as people begin to develop interpersonal ties, friendships, alliances. For many activists, it is the first time that they have travelled out of their home districts and countries to meet people from different struggles and cultures. The conference provides an opportunity for poor peasants to learn about other struggles in other countries, decrease their sense of isolation, and generate a sense of solidarity with others. It is a product of 'grassroots globalization'[1]—attempts by marginalized groups and social movements representing different terrains of struggle to forge wider alliances in protest at their growing exclusion from global neoliberal economic decision making.

Grassroots Globalization

Grassroots globalization involves the creation of networks: of communication, solidarity, information sharing, and mutual support. The core function of networks is the production, exchange, and strategic use of information which can enhance the resources available to geographically and/or socially distant actors in their particular struggles.[2] They enable the articulation of a critique

---

[1] Arjun Appadurai, 'Grassroots Globalization and the Research Imagination', *Public Culture* 12, 1 (Winter 2000): 1–19.
[2] Margaret E. Keck and Kathryn Sikkink, *Activists Beyond Borders: Advocacy Networks in International Politics* (Ithaca: Cornell University Press, 1998).

of neoliberalism and a vision of an alternative politics (that asserts the importance of cultural/indigenous integrity and autonomy, and the reclamation of commonly owned resources such as water, land, and forests).

In order to materialize collective struggle, grassroots globalization networks attempt to prosecute transnational collective political action, exemplified by global days of action against international institutions such as the World Bank and key state actors such as the G8. Such protests have brought together political actors from different countries within a particular place (e.g. Seattle 1999 against the WTO) while also witnessing solidarity actions in many other places around the world. For example, during the demonstrations against the World Bank and IMF in Prague in 2000, solidarity actions took place in over 40 countries around the world.

Many social movements, although engaged in grassroots globalization networks, nevertheless remain locally or nationally based, since this is where individual movement identities are formed and nurtured. However, when locally based struggles develop, or become part of, geographically flexible networks, they become embedded in different places at a variety of spatial scales. These different geographic scales (global, regional, national, local) are mutually constitutive parts, becoming links of various lengths in the network.[3]

Grassroots globalization involves a variety of political actors as well as strategic foci. For example, in PGA Asia, there are peasant movements, trades unions, NGOs, and indigenous people's movements. They articulate a range of different (place-specific) goals (concerning the forms of social change), ideologies (e.g. concerning gender, class, and ethnicity), and strategies (e.g. violent and non-violent forms of protest). However, they all, in different ways, link their place-based struggles to broader networks and communities of support and solidarity.[4]

The Global in the Local: Resisting Dams

For example, the Narmada Bachao Andolan (Save Narmada Movement, NBA) is a participant movement in PGA Asia. Since 1985, the NBA has been coordinating the resistance against the state- and multinational corporation-financed Narmada river valley project in central India. This project envisages the construction of 30 major dams along the Narmada and its tributaries, as well as

---

[3] Peter Dicken, Philip F. Kelly, Kris Olds, Henry Wai-Chung Yeung, 'Chains and Networks, Territories and Scales: Towards a Relational Framework for Analysing the Global Economy', *Global Networks* 1, 2 (2001): 89–112.

[4] Paul Routledge, 'Convergence Space: Process Geographies of Grassroots Globalization Networks', *Transactions of the Institute of British Geographers* 28, 3 (2003): 333–49.

an additional 135 medium-sized and 3,000 minor dams. When completed, the project is expected to displace up to 15 million people from their homes and lands.

The NBA is a social movement that comprises—in the Narmada valley— cash-cropping and tribal peasants and rich farmers, organized by a core group of activists, who originate mostly from outside the valley. The movement is also a network as it has constantly attempted to forge an associational politics consisting of individuals, NGOs, and other social movements that have pro-secuted conflict on a variety of multi-scalar terrains that include both material places and virtual spaces. In so doing, the NBA has also participated in trans-national networks such as PGA Asia. The collective visions shared by all actors within this network are those of resistance to the construction of mega-dams, and their desire for development processes that are socially just and economi-cally and environmentally sustainable.

The NBA's living fabric of struggle includes the sites of resistance camps such as those at the tribal villages of Domkhedi and Jalsindhi where people refuse to move from their homes despite the risk of submergence by flood-ing of the river, the ongoing arrival and departure from these sites of activ-ists from all over India and indeed the world, relaying their own messages, linking up with other activists, exchanging information, planning strategies of support and solidarity. They also participate in various demonstrations and rallies while in the valley, lending a transnational character to these events. Domkhedi and Jalsindhi are symbolic sites for the movement since they are imminently threatened with submergence by the construction of the dams. When they act as the places for the resistance camps, these villages become 'articulated moments' in the enactment of networks such as the NBA where opposition to the dams and alternative visions are articulated.

The NBA has conducted its resistance simultaneously across multiple scales. It has grounded its struggle against the dams in the villages along the Narmada valley, mobilizing tribal peasants, cash-cropping peasants, and rich farmers to resist displacement. The NBA has been able to use their local knowledge of the valley to facilitate communication between disparate communities, and to mobilize, at times, tens of thousands of peasants to resist the dams. The NBA has also taken its struggle to non-local terrains, including the national and international levels. Nationally, the NBA has served writ petitions to the Supreme Court of India, and has established, and participated as a con-vener in, the National Alliance of People's Movements—a coalition of differ-ent social movements in India collectively organizing to resist the effects of liberalization on the Indian economy. Internationally, the NBA has forged operational links with various groups outside India, such as the International Rivers Network (IRN), and the broad alliance of international NGOs, the International Narmada Campaign. International solidarity work has been conducted by groups such as IRN, Environmental Defence Fund, Friends of the Earth; human and indigenous rights groups such as Survival International; development organizations such as the Association for India's Development; and groups formed explicitly around the Narmada issue such as the Narmada Solidarity Coalition of New York. These in turn are also part of larger networks such as the Narmada Action Committee and Friends of River Narmada which are mainly US-based collectives of South Asian, development, and environmentalist activists which have developed links with other groups through flows of common experience, writings, and materials such as documentaries.

As part of a broader transnational network, the NBA has been actively involved with the PGA network since the latter's formation in Geneva in 1998 and has attended the World Social Forum. NBA activists have participated in the global days of action in Seattle 1999 and Prague 2000, while still others have mounted concurrent protests within India. By stressing the importance of connection, diversity, and solidarity, such convergences as the NBA and PGA Asia and the struggles which they comprise are engaging in prefigurative action, i.e. embodying visions of transformation as if they are already achieved, thereby calling them into being, and forging the notion of mutual solidarity between place-based struggles—constructing the grievances and aspirations of geographically and culturally different people as interlinked.[5]

---

[5] Thomas Olesen, *International Zapatismo: The Construction of Solidarity in the Age of Globalization* (London: Zed Books, 2005).

17 The Globalization of a Labour Market: The Case of Seafarers

Helen Sampson

Most of us buy our fruit and veg, our cars, our furniture, our domestic appliances without too much thought for the ship that transported them to our 'backyard'. Yet shipping is an essential cog in the wheel of international trade (as discussed by Susan M. Roberts in Chapter 15) and it is essential in driving growth in the global economy via the maintenance of cheap freight rates: allowing us to buy bananas in temperate climates (as discussed by Mimi Sheller in Chapter 40), and asparagus all year round. This is not new, and shipping has long since been the backbone of international trade, but in recent decades ships have changed, and the industry, so long international, has become highly globalized.

In the early twentieth century ships tended to be owned and flagged (registered) in the same country. The German-owned fleet was predominantly flagged in Germany, the UK-owned fleet was mainly flagged in the UK, etc. This assumption of a link between ownership and 'flag' no longer holds, however. A financial crisis hit shipping in the 1970s, when vessel owners were knocked by rising oil prices and a slump in world trade. Many ships were tied up, some, in the Mediterranean, left to rust and rot. Not all tonnage was abandoned, however, and some owners looked for alternative strategies for survival. Many made the decision to 'flag out', registering their vessels in countries offering tax breaks, slack regulation, and, critically, the opportunity to employ seafarers of any nationality on whatever terms and conditions could be negotiated by the parties concerned (see Figure 17.1). Flagging out allowed owners to slash labour costs and in many cases made the difference between bankruptcy and survival at a time when the industry was being tightly squeezed. This trend of flagging out continued and at the present time approximately 57 per cent of world tonnage is flagged with 'open registers' of which Panama, Liberia, Bahamas, Malta, Cyprus, and Bermuda are the most significant.[1] Such

---

[1] Regina Asariotis et al., *Review of Maritime Transport 2012* (New York and Geneva: United Nations), http://unctad.org/en/PublicationsLibrary/rmt2012_en.pdf >.

Figure 17.1 Modern cargo vessels operate in a complicated ownership environment and are often crewed by ethnically diverse seafarers in poorly regulated conditions

registers compete with each other for tonnage and in doing so work at being as attractive as possible to shipowners: perhaps offering easy registration with few preconditions, little regulation, and few restrictions (for example with regard to the approval of minimum crewing levels over which flag states have oversight, etc).

This break in the link between vessel ownership and vessel registration represents the point in the development of the industry at which it is possible to talk of shipping becoming globalized, as opposed to internationalized. As a consequence of flagging out, the labour market for seafarers has also become globalized. On board open-registry vessels, seafarers are no longer employed on terms and conditions mediated by the governments[2] and trade unions of the countries where vessels are owned but are employed in an open, relatively unregulated, and unrestricted, global labour market. Employers today are able to scour the world for the cheapest seafaring labour and when a new cheap

---

[2] Here the Philippines may be regarded as something of an exception.

source comes to their attention they are able to switch sources rapidly and often at little cost.

However it is no longer necessary to 'flag out' to benefit from the introduction of non-traditional labour on board a ship. National registers, reluctant to lose their fleets entirely, have reduced, and often entirely removed, the conditions that formerly attached to registration in terms of the employment of nationals aboard vessels. Seafarer numbers in traditional maritime labour supply countries have consequently plummeted and in many cases national collective bargaining agreements are no longer negotiated for national seafarers, being replaced to some extent by case-by-case employer agreements (for example in the UK).

The new global labour market for seafarers largely centres on developing countries in the East (for example, Philippines, India, China) and on former USSR states such as Ukraine and Russia. Seafarers are recruited from a variety of socio-economic backgrounds and with varying levels of education and training. The least-skilled seafarers, occupying the lowest-ranking positions on board, are vulnerable workers, some of whom become involved in corrupt deals to access employment on board. Knowing little of the industry and in a position to do little more than 'hope for the best', some such workers, in India for example, have found themselves in vicious debt spirals. For a fee, they may be 'placed' on board vessels where conditions are poor and 'their' ship may be scrapped under their feet, as it were, leaving them with only a month or so of salary rather than the eight to ten months they were anticipating. These unfortunate individuals find it difficult, and sometimes impossible, to earn the money they require to get them out of debt to the 'agents' who found on-board employment for them. The money that can, potentially, be earned at sea generally represents their only hope of repaying their debts, as land-based jobs pay nothing by comparison and would never enable them to come close to paying off their creditors. However, for these unskilled seafarers, jobs are very hard to come by and they are frequently forced to return to their creditors and once again take a 'loan' to get a place on board, hoping for better luck next time. There are other examples of exploitation that the global labour market has created: seafarers who work unpaid in agency offices in countries such as the Philippines for periods of up to two years on the 'promise' of a place on board a ship; seafarers who sign away rights to trade union representation prior to joining a vessel; seafarers, in China for example, who pay a 'deposit' to agencies which is only returned to them on completion of a voyage with 'good behaviour', i.e. no complaints to the International Transport Workers Federation, to management, and so on.[3]

---

[3] Effective enforcement of the Maritime Labour Convention 2006 (which came into force in August 2013) would drive out some of these practices. However, whether or not the convention is successfully enforced remains to be seen.

The global labour market provides a tremendous space for exploitation and many ship operators are happy to make use of this to drive down the costs of labour and maximize returns. Seafarers are under pressure as a consequence and are conscious of the threat to their 'national' labour market position deriving from newly emerging labour supply sources. Such competitive pressures are evident to them when they sail aboard ships with crews comprised of many nationalities. Generally, seafarers working within multinational crews are paid at different rates, according to their nationality, and experience different terms and conditions in relation to leave-pay, length of contract, overtime payments, and general benefits. This applies to all ranks on board and yet it rarely generates open conflict although it may provoke disquiet and a general discontentment.

However, just as there are many negatives associated with the global labour market for seafarers, so too are there some positives. Seafarers today frequently sail in multinational groups and whilst there are documented instances of ethnically based prejudice and discrimination on board some vessels, there are also examples of crews that sail together relatively harmoniously in terms of ethnic integration. Seafarers frequently express a preference for working in mixed-nationality crews, explaining that they perceive such crews to be less prone to conflict. In many respects the space of the ship has the potential to be a more cosmopolitan one than the space available to migrant workers based in 'host' societies. A genuinely multinational ship (as opposed to a bi-national vessel) is rarely identified as 'belonging' to a particular national group but is nevertheless closely controlled by senior officers. Where such individuals are relatively benign, marginalization may be less prevalent than in multi-ethnic communities ashore. Many seafarers describe pleasure in meeting and working with other nationalities and taking home with them new cultural practices and norms. The partners of seafarers, particularly those who have had the opportunity to sail on board alongside their spouses, may also have a very positive take on the experience of their partners working as part of a multinational workforce.

The change in the labour market can be seen to be one of mixed fortune in relation to the different constituent interests. For ship operators, the advantages of a globalized labour market relate to cost, and the advantages of flagging out relate more generally to deregulation (not only of labour markets). For seafarers and their families, there may be many disadvantages to employment in a global labour market, including an erosion of working terms and conditions, and increasing vulnerability in the context of precarious employment prospects and little worker representation or protection. Seafarers from regions such as Ghana and Cape Verde who chased jobs to Europe where they boarded 'European-flagged' vessels on nationally agreed terms and conditions (including unemployment benefit, etc.) find two or more decades later that such employment possibilities have dried up and they are stranded in foreign countries with little prospect of future work. However, there are positives too and this is what drives the growth and development of the global labour market: the dollars that can be earned on board considerably outstrip the wages that can be earned by workers ashore in many states. As employers have shifted recruitment into such countries the overall deterioration in the terms and conditions they are offering to seafarers has been obscured. Remittances are not only craved by individuals but by states too which do their best both to promote their local workforce on the global labour market and to put pressure on the workers to be acquiescent and meek in relation to their rights, terms, and conditions. Such workers are reminded of the vulnerability of their labour market position and often they become complicit in the drive to lower wages and 'compete' more effectively with other labour supply states. In this respect, they actively engage with the global labour market and actively 'fight' to retain access to it. Thus the global labour market thrives and extends. As a result, the pears from Argentina that we see on the supermarket shelf are most likely to have been transported there by multinational crews, labouring on ships flagged with open registers, over which little effective regulation (particularly with regard to labour standards) is exercised. Food for thought?

18 Banal Globalization: The Deep Structure of Oil and Gas

Michael J. Watts

> Oil is fluid and fugitive.
>
> > A petro-geologist, cited in *Variant*, 28, 2007.
>
> Oil is a fungible global commodity.
>
> > *Oil Shockwave*, Robert Gates et al., 2005.

We can begin with President George Bush's 2006 State of the Union speech. America, he said, is 'addicted to oil, which is often imported from unstable parts of the world'. As a former oilman and alcoholic, he should know addiction when he sees it. He was not alone in his particular line of thinking. Ian Rutledge has written a very good book, which bears the title *Addicted to Oil*, and *New York Times* columnist Thomas Friedmann has a documentary by the same name. They are part of what is now a small army of oil commentators—by my rough estimation at least one hundred books have been published on oil and oil security in the last couple of years—who are, well, addicted to the idea of oil addiction. In the search-engine world, to Google 'oil addiction' produces over 500,000 online sources. Perhaps inevitably there is a 'Twelve Step' recovery programme. It all sounds rather like an AA session for oil executives.

There are more or less productive reasons for thinking about oil and gas use—hydrocarbon capitalism in short—in terms of addiction. One useful reason is that it compels us to think systemically and globally. Addiction is, of course, systemic, that is to say individual addiction cannot be grasped outside a system or structure of addiction: the crack addict needs the dealer, the trafficker the producer: each is embedded in an immense illicit empire of shady government officials, mules, cartel acolytes, peasant coca growers, and a vast shadow world of drug barons, security forces, and the corrupt governments that characterize the supplier states such as Afghanistan, Laos, or Colombia. To be addicted to oil is necessarily to see a larger oil system, an immense trillion-dollar commodity system or assemblage—the oil and gas 'global value chain' in the language of the oil business—which has its own traffickers, cartels, barons, and oligarchs, and its own massive infrastructure (there are over 500,000 oil wells in the USA alone) to explore, produce, move, and refine oil and gas.

There is another utility of the term, rooted perhaps in some rather questionable organic analogies. Addiction is typically defined as a chronic, neurobiological disease, with genetic, psychosocial, and environmental factors influencing its development and manifestations. Does the global political and cultural economy of oil consumption best, or even usefully, resemble a disease process characterized by the continued use of a specific psychoactive substance despite physical, psychological, or social harm? Here one might productively turn to two great theorists of addiction: Gregory Bateson and William Burroughs.[1] For Bateson the heart of addiction was a problem (a pathology) of maladaptation rooted in epistemology and ontology—what often is inadequately glossed as his critique of Western values. For Burroughs addiction resides in the deadly solicitations of the state and in the constitution of the addict as, to deploy the useful language of Timothy Melley, 'the ultimate capitalist consumer' (consumption without limits).[2] Each points to a larger frame in which oil's universalism and globality—its civilizational properties—are deeply enmeshed in contemporary forms of rule and identity. Thinking about oil and addiction is not to map the SUV or American automobility onto a landscape of disease as much as it is to see it as one expression of the contemporary global relations between humans and things, in short as a form of biopolitics, with its own deep infrastructure.[3]

Linking oil to biopower (and, it needs to be said, gas too because the shale gas revolution has made liquefied natural gas now the hydrocarbon du jour) is to trace the work of oil and gas infrastructure—social, technological, political, institutional—as a technology of rule: in the way that the pipeline, the oil tanker, or the submersible fulfil a similar function to the census, the map, the survey, or the sewer system.[4] Viewed expansively, the infrastructure of oil would necessarily include, for example, the low-cost motorized American way of life that it provisions, what Campbell brilliantly describes as automobility:

---

[1] Gregory Bateson, *Steps to an Ecology of Mind* (New York: Ballantine, 1972); William Burroughs, *Naked Lunch* (New York: Harper, 1986 [1965]).

[2] Timothy Melley, 'A Terminal Case', in *High Anxieties: Cultural Studies in Addiction*, eds Janet F. Brodie and Marc Redfield (Berkeley: University of California Press, 2002).

[3] Michel Foucault, *Society Must Be Defended* (London: Allen Lane, 2003); David Campbell, 'The Biopolitics of Security: Oil, Empire, and the Sports Utility Vehicle', *American Quarterly* 57, 3 (2005): 943–71.

[4] Benedict Anderson, *Imagined Communities: Reflections on the Origin and Spread of Nationalism* (London: Verso, 1983); Patrick Joyce, *The Rule of Freedom: Liberalism and the Modern City* (London: Verso, 2003).

The concept of automobility—or that of the 'auto social formation' or 'car culture'—calls attention to the hybrid assemblage or machinic complex that the apparently autonomous entities of car and driver compose. In the 'automobilized time–space' of contemporary society we can observe a networked, sociotechnical infrastructure that is in process, an infrastructure in which there is the ceaseless and mobile interplay between many different scales, from the body to the globe.[5]

As Kevin Philips writes in *American Theocracy*, oil stands at the summit of American politics: 'an oil, automobile, and national-security coalition has taken the driver's seat'.[6]

To understand the infrastructural question is to start at least with its deep history and geography. More than 150 million years ago, massive blooms of microscopic marine plants formed in the seas, creating a huge blanket of organic material on the sea floor. In some locations sediments built up, creating sufficient pressure to convert—to cook—the unoxidized carbon in the organic material into oil. The oil that did not leak into the sea or onto land was trapped in reservoirs of great diversity, size, and geologic complexity. A second phase of oil formation also occurred 90 million years ago.[7] Most of this oil stayed put until about a century ago. With the 'discovery' of oil in 1859 in Pennsylvania—several millennia after its first use in China—and the invention of the gas-fuelled automobile in 1901, Black Gold became, as it were, the drug of choice: its ascent marked the coming of the age of Big Oil. Eighty years later, 90 per cent of all of our transportation is fuelled by oil; 90 per cent of all goods in our shops involve oil in some way; 95 per cent of food products require oil (to grow and deliver one cow to market requires over 250 gallons of oil).[8] Globally the world consumes over 89 million barrels of oil each day, of which the USA alone accounts for over one-quarter. Virtually everyone on the planet consumes oil in some form or other; it has become a basic need. According to most industry expectations, by 2025 global oil consumption will have increased by over 50 per cent. Quite where this oil will come from is unclear: as the industry puts it, 'the easy oil is gone'.

To what geographical lengths does the petro-addict pursue the object of his addiction, and by what means? The answer is to the ends of the earth, or more properly a mad pursuit to the bottom of the ocean. Deep-water exploration is the new Holy Grail, propelled by oil addiction's ceaseless territorial imperative to locate new fields, with deep-water offshore growing by 78 per cent between 2007 and 2011. On 2 August 2007, a Russian submarine with two

[5] Campbell, 'The Biopolitics of Security: Oil, Empire and the Sports Utility Vehicle', 965.

[6] Kevin Philips, *American Theocracy: The Peril and Politics of Radical Religion, Oil, and Borrowed Money in the 21st Century* (New York: Knopf, 2004).

[7] Jeremy Leggett, *The Empty Tank: Oil, Gas, Hot Air, and the Coming Global Financial Catastrophe* (New York: Random House, 2005).

[8] Ian Rutledge, *Addicted to Oil: America's Relentless Drive for Energy Security* (London: I. B. Taurus, 2006).

parliamentarians on board planted a titanium flag two miles down under the North Pole. At stake were the lucrative new oil and gas fields—by some estimations 10 billion tons of oil equivalent—on the Arctic sea floor. Two weeks later, it was announced that the Northwest Passage was navigable, facilitating the opening up of a new oil frontier the ecological preconditions of which— global warming—were the product of Big Oil. In short, environmental crisis (the second contradiction of capital) creates the conditions for another round of capitalist investment and a new (and spectacular) capitalist frontier (recursive primitive accumulation). Sub-zero temperatures and almost year-round darkness present no obstacles to the purveyors of what has become dubbed as 'hard' or 'unconventional' oil. In late 2006, a consortium of oil companies discovered oil at a staggering depth 150 miles into the floor of the Gulf of Mexico. The test well, Jack-2, delves through 7,000 feet of water and 20,000 feet of sea floor to tap oil in tertiary rock laid down 60 million years ago. The drill ships—and the production platforms—required to undertake such are massive floating structures, much larger than the largest aircraft carriers and more expensive, costing well over a half billion dollars (and close to a million dollars a day to rent). In 2007 the vast new Tupi field in Brazilian coastal waters was discovered in 2,000 metres of water below a massive (5,000-metre-thick) layer of salt in hugely inhospitable geological conditions. One test well cost over $250 million. The cost of a deep-water exploratory and production rig

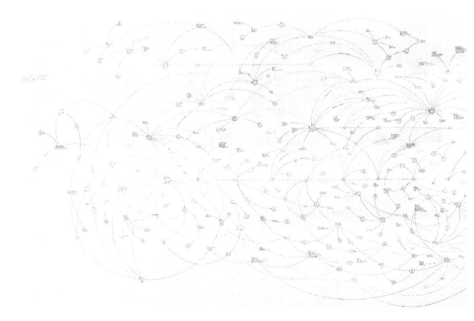

Figure 18.1 Mark Lombardi's map of the global illicit economy

operating in ultra-deep waters over 7,000 feet today is averaging over $500,000 per day, with other deep-water rigs operating in less than 7,000 feet, commanding from $300,000 to $400,000 per day. In short, what is on offer is a great deep-water land grab in train: primitive accumulation at 7,000 metres.

The global oil and gas infrastructure is nothing short of gargantuan. To say that the value of the industry now totals over $4,000 billion says everything and nothing. Close to one million producing oil wells puncture the surface of the earth (77,000 were drilled in 2007, 4,000 offshore); 3,300 are subsea. More than two million kms of pipelines blanket the globe in a massive trunk network: 75,000 kms move oil and gas along the sea floor; another 156,000 kms were completed between 2008 and 2012. There are 6,000 fixed platforms, and 635 offshore drilling rigs (the international rig total for December 2013 is 3,478 according to Baker Hughes). Currently $17 billion is spent annually on offshore drilling. Every year, 4,295 oil tankers (vessels of 1,000 long tons or more deadweight) move 2.42 billion tons of oil and oil products, 30 per cent of global seaborne trade. Crude oil is processed by 717 refineries, and over 80 massive floating production and storage vessels have been installed in the last five years.

As we speak, oil prices have fallen from a high in July 2007 of $150 a barrel to $103 a barrel. As the world recovers slowly from a massive global recession, demand (even in China and South Asia) has been stable since 2007, and

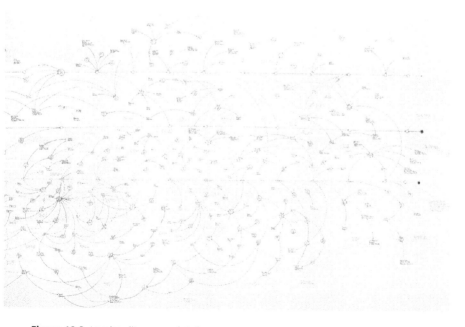

Figure 18.2 Lombardi's map—detail

oil output (propelled forward by the prospect of future super profits and by over-investment in cheap gas due to the shale revolution) is now searching for a market. In the heart of the global recession in 2009, oil companies and oil suppliers were busily filling up much of the world oil tanker capacity to store oil since much of the world's oil storage capacity is already at the limit. Tankers are customarily deployed floating storage devices, waiting for a market.

Addiction, I suppose a universal addiction in the case of oil and gas, has produced a colossal infrastructure, a global network reminiscent of Mark Lombardi's extraordinary atlas of the 'uses and abuses of power in the global political economy'.[9] Like the drug and money-laundering networks that so intrigued Lombardi in his attempts to map the black sites and blank spaces of the map of the global illicit economy (see Figures 18.1 and 18.2), the world of Big Oil is, in spite of its formal market character, an industry shrouded in secrecy, a world of smoke and mirrors in which even the most basic statistics can be meaningless. The hubs, spokes, flows, and nodes that make up the oil, drug, or financial networks led David Campbell to see them as capsular in form: 'capsules are enclaves and envelopes that function as nodes, hubs, and termini in the various networks and contain a multitude of spaces and scales'.[10] Oilrigs, floating storage vessels, flow stations, refineries, gas stations, and, of course, cars, are all capsules within the global oil and gas network. The oil zone is a quite peculiar space of economic and political calculation that can also only be understood as a form of violent economy; oilfields are deeply securitized, military enclaves often with their own mafias, insurgents, paramilitaries, and forms of organized crime.

The oil infrastructure feeds a gargantuan appetite that is perhaps best understood as the very embodiment of 'pure' capitalism. William Burroughs's book *Naked Lunch* brilliantly explores this purity, a 'junk economy' in which the 'junk virus' is a sort of parasitic organism that invades and controls increasingly compliant subjects. The pusher does not sell the drug to the consumer but rather the consumer to the product. Burroughs's bleak depiction, says Timothy Melley, is of a terminal capitalist world, a world of crystalline and unadulterated capitalist desire: the deadly deceits of the market and big business, state control, and technological terror, and the mass production of mindless subjects all rolled into one.[11] It is a dark, dystopian vision but one that speaks directly of the realities that surround us: chronic dependency, demand without limits, violent acquisition, and addictive control. The human body, under siege from a 'vast hungry host of parasites' is reduced to, as Burroughs put it, a 'soft machine'. The global oil infrastructure—the vast oil network

---

[9] Mark Lombardi, *Mark Lombardi: Global Networks* (New York: Independent Curators, 2003): 19.

[10] Campbell, 'The Biopolitics of Security', 951.

[11] Melley, 'A Terminal Case'.

of capillaries, enclaves, bases, pipes, stations, hubs, and mobiles—is in the business, one might say, of producing petrolic versions of Burroughs's soft machines.

Of course, in its current form, petro-modernity also contributes to collective extermination and death. Global climate change is its particular vehicle. Oil addiction points to what Marx once called 'the contradictory form of capital...[that] produces the real conditions of its own termination'. In this sense, the linking of addiction with hydrocarbon modernity has the advantage of pointing toward what Gregory Bateson would have called the global double-bind of capitalism: if it stops producing (where the goal of production is simply more production) it will self-destruct, yet if it goes on producing it will destroy everyone.

19 Putting Standards to Work: Water and the Taste and Smell of Globalization

Ragna Zeiss

Over 2,000 years ago waters from dew, rain, snowmelt, ponds, lakes, muddy-bottomed rivers, and rocky-bottomed rivers were distinguished by their medical effects and purities. Although fewer sources of drinking water are distinguished today (surface water, groundwater), the waters from these sources have different characteristics due to the surrounding soil, animals, industries, temperature, amount of rainfall, etc. Despite these differences, the World Health Organization has set drinking water quality standards that have been accepted by the European Union and national governments. But can local waters (with different characteristics) be made globally comparable? Five examples of routine practices in the (English) water industry where local–global relations play a role will help us to answer this question.

Routine Practice 1—Treating the Water, a Local Practice?

LOCATION: TREATMENT PLANT

When surface water or groundwater is going to be turned into drinking water, it first needs to pass through a treatment plant. There it meets a vast number of treatment technologies. Some scrape off the sludge blanket floating on the surface after compressed air has attached itself to floc particles, others add chemicals to remove (other) 'impurities'. The treatment plant is designed to treat the water that comes in, that is, if water is high in nitrate or colour, the plant is designed in such a way that it can remove or bring down these parameters or characteristics. It is in the treatment plant that the water loses the impurities it carries and even some of its (local) characteristics such as colour. It is no longer surface water or groundwater, but it is not yet drinking water. The water and the treatment plant thus mutually shape each other. The treatment plant needs to take into account the (local) characteristics of the water it is treating (and can therefore not be fully standardized) and the water undergoes a process of transformation in the treatment plant and becomes less local. Local practices, or so it seems.

Routine Practice 2—from Global to Local Standards and Compliance through Technologies

LOCATION: TREATMENT PLANT

The water that comes out of the treatment plant needs to comply with the nationalized, European, and even global regulations and guidelines. In order to ensure this, local standards are developed for each part of the treatment process. These standards include safety standards (which are stricter than the regulatory standards) to ensure that the water can be corrected before it is compared with the regulatory standard and lest the final water should fail the standard. A number of technologies are set up to prevent the water from failing the standard. The smell bell, an instrument that heats up the water and magnifies the odour by a thousand times, is used by having a smell every two hours to identify unusual, unexpected, and unknown substances in the water which are not regularly measured. Checks targeted at specific (regulatory) substances are performed by an automatic sampling process at several points in the treatment plant. Every ten to 15 minutes the results appear on the computer screen of the office manager, who can then identify whether any abnormalities have occurred. There are also other warning systems. Some essential treatment technologies are equipped with alarms—they prewarn of possible failures—and in some plants the water would automatically be stopped from going into supply if, for example, disinfection fails. The global standards have thus been translated into local ones, the compliance with which is largely controlled by technologies.

Routine Practice 3—Taking a Sample and Accommodating (Local) Materiality

LOCATION: FIELD

The water has now been treated in such a way that it will probably make its way through the distribution network unharmed; through e.g. chlorine it will be able to deal with the contamination it encounters on its way to the customer's tap where many of the regulatory samples have to be taken. The European 1998 Drinking Water Directive is therefore often called the tap water directive.

To be able to analyse samples and measure them against the global standards, samples need to be comparable. Yet it is not possible to take one single sample and measure all the different parameters. During transport the material characteristics of the water—the different parameters to be measured—would interact with each other; some may change or even disappear. Since it is important to get to know the quality of the water at the point the sample is taken (that is, the drinking water), each parameter requires its own sample—the diverse material characteristics of the water need to be preserved by taking different samples in different bottles (glass, plastic) and with different preservatives. These help to stabilize the specific material properties of the water until the water enters the laboratory. For example, pesticide and pH samples are taken in a bottle of amber glass to prevent (sun)light changing the material characteristics of the sample. In order to compare local water with global regulations, the (local) materiality needs to accommodated and standardized at the same time.

Routine Practice 4—Analysing a Sample and the Mutual Shaping of Global and Material Standards

LOCATION: LABORATORY

Once the samples are taken they are transported to the chemistry or microbiology laboratory where they are analysed. Since the samples are standardized by bottles and preservatives, the laboratories can, unlike the treatment plants, also be standardized. Yet, as in the field, also in the laboratory the materiality of the sample needs to be accommodated. In a microbiology laboratory, for example, the time needed to grow a colony of bacteria large enough for purposes of analysis is important. Regulations can set a shorter time frame but then all bacteriological samples would fail. The global regulations thus need to take the local and material into account; the 'regulatory' and the 'material' time frame mutually shape each other.

Routine Practice 5—the Final Transformation: from the Local towards the Global and Universal

LOCATION: LABORATORY

There is more: it is in the laboratories that the sample is transformed into a number on a computer screen and can finally be compared to the global standard. Here the local materiality is lost. Once the sample bottle has been opened, the local characteristics of the water change due to light, the length of time in the bottle, the air that came in when the bottle was opened, etc. The characteristics of that sample taken at a particular point in time cannot be traced back. What is left is a dematerialized number; this can be compared to the global standard and exchanged with other water companies, and with regulatory agencies if desirable. It is now that what was originally water can be truly globalized.

Conclusion

Globalization of drinking water through the application of (originally) global standards is, to some extent, made possible through various global–local interactions which entail (non-)standardization of the water itself and its surroundings such as treatment plants and laboratories. Five stages of the transformation of water from 'raw' water to drinking water have shown different global–local interactions. In order to compare local water with global standards the water needs to be treated, local standards tighter than the regulatory standards need to be set in order to be able to correct the water in time, the materiality of the local water needs to be accommodated in both practice and global regulations and standardized at the same time, and the material characteristics are lost when the sample turns into a number on a computer screen.

These stages can be separated into two processes that each provide us with a different answer to the question of whether local waters can be made globally comparable. First, the water is transformed from raw water into drinking water that comes out of the tap. This water, although it complies with the global standards, maintains a 'local' taste and smell. After all, we may like the water in York but not in London. We can call this 'glocal' water. Second, a water sample is transformed into a number on a computer screen and loses its local characteristics altogether; these cannot be retraced. Here the water can be said to be truly globalized and universalized and globalization can be said to be volatile; if a number were to disappear, the whole globalizing process would evaporate.

Is this something Bert and Ernie from *Sesame Street* would have thought about when Bert asked Ernie if he knew what light was and received the following reply: 'Light comes from a lamp, or from the sun, just like water from a tap.'

Part III
Finance and Business

20 **Flowers**
Alex Hughes

Love, gratitude, sympathy, and celebration are some of the many emotions expressed through the giving and receiving of flowers. Flowers are presented to mark special occasions such as births, marriages, anniversaries, and deaths, they are purchased en masse as part of popular (often religious) festivals, and sometimes they are given impulsively. Flowers, both wild and commercially grown, are also used in practices of adornment, decorating clothes, bodies, homes, gardens, workplaces, and public spaces. Flowers, so often associated with 'nature' and 'natural beauty', have been cultivated by people for many different purposes. As the social anthropologist, Jack Goody, observes, flowers have become a part of everyday life in the following ways:

[Flowers] are used throughout social life, for decoration, for medicine, in cooking and for their scents, but above all in establishing, maintaining and even ending relationships, with the dead as with the living, with divinities as well as humans.[1]

There are all kinds of geographies associated with the incorporation of flowers into cultural life, and with the cultural lives of flowers themselves. Goody has shown, for example, that over time flowers have been culturally more significant in Asia and Europe than in Africa. In the European context, he suggests that the use of flowers as gifts developed in the Netherlands during the Renaissance period. The use of flowers in various practices of display within Europe also has a long and complex history, involving the importation of goods and ideas from the Far East in the sixteenth, seventeenth, and eighteenth centuries. In many parts of Europe and North America today, the cut flower is considered a luxury commodity incorporated into everyday life, mainly through practices of gift giving and decoration. In the late twentieth and early twenty-first centuries, flowers have been increasingly linked to the growing gap between the rich and the poor in global society. In many cases, flowers are now cultivated by low-wage labourers on commercial farms in economically less developed countries and are consumed by comparatively wealthy consumers in advanced capitalist economies. So how are flowers—these symbols of natural beauty that are exchanged as part of meaningful personal relationships—now so tightly woven into the everyday life of globalization?

---

[1] Jack Goody, *The Culture of Flowers* (Cambridge: Cambridge University Press, 1993): 2.

The commercialization of popular festivals and gift-giving rituals, along with the rising popularity of flowers as accessories of interior design, has fuelled the growth of a massive global industry in cut-flower production. Historically, the production of flowers for such display and gift giving, particularly in Europe, took place in the Netherlands. While the Netherlands retains a pivotal role in the cut-flower trade, particularly through the operations of the vast Dutch flower auctions, many flowers bought in Europe and North America today are produced in developing countries such as Colombia, Ecuador, Thailand, Kenya, Zambia, and Zimbabwe. In these countries, the internal market for commercially grown flowers is small and typically confined to urban elites because of their high cost and luxury status. So flowers are produced for export and distributed over long distances. They are kept fresh through temperature-controlled distribution systems and air-freighted thousands of miles to their final market destinations. Development programmes based on export-led growth and privatization, along with improvements in transportation and technology, have made this 'stretching out' of supply chains for flowers possible, resulting in an increasing physical distance between producers and consumers of flowers. For many, this represents an increasing social and cultural distance between producers and consumers too. Such cultural distance and anonymity characterizing the commercial distribution of flowers would seem to contrast starkly with the meaningful practices of gift giving and display that go on when flowers are bought. At first glance, this contrast appears no more than an ironic reflection of the workings of capitalism. However, if we look a little closer it is possible to see that this very paradox— where flowers as meaningful gifts are produced and distributed through rather cold and distanced commercial relations—has created some rather different geographies of the global cut-flower industry. And these geographies see the addition of a further set of emotions to the register already associated with the exchange of flowers.

Kenya is one of the most significant producers and exporters of commercially grown flowers in the world. Flowers are the country's second biggest export crop. While hundreds of small growers exist, it is the large farms, each occupying more than 200 hectares of land and employing several thousand workers, in areas such as Lake Naivasha, that have become most tightly bound in to overseas distribution networks. This would seem to represent a success story for Kenya, but researchers and journalists have been quick to reveal problems, including low wages, environmental and health-related impacts of pesticide use, and the vulnerability of seasonal labourers employed only at times of peak demand. The seasonality of flowers and the fact that demand rises massively during the lead-up to particular festivals such as Valentine's Day place producers and workers under a great deal of pressure to meet the orders of demanding customers. In the words of a supervisor working for Kenya's largest flower farm in Lake Naivasha:

For Valentine's Day, you have to really work hard because you have so many lines. When we reach Valentine's Day, we are ever, ever busy. There is not a single minute that is wasted. We have a lot of flowers. The packers, they never rest. The packing area is full. They really work hard, they really work hard.

Low wages, overtime hours, and temporary employment during these times of peak demand go hand in hand with the supply of flowers to overseas markets from Kenya. Such working conditions for many labourers engender fear, anxiety, uncertainty, and, for some, anger. For campaigning groups, journalists, and civil society organizations too, such conditions have sparked shock and outrage. Flower farms in Kenya, and many others around the world too, have been the focus of a string of media exposés and heated debate between private corporations, development organizations, trade unions, and workers' representatives. In media exposés, the juxtaposition of worker vulnerability with the symbols of love so often represented by flowers has proved to be a critical strategy in capturing the imaginations of ethically minded consumers. For campaigning groups and worker activists, passionate endeavours to create greater social justice in supply chains have fuelled attempts to raise labour and environmental standards in the commercial flower industry. As a result, modest improvements in pay and conditions are continually being made and negotiated. For a number of flower farms, some of their products are now being channelled into the supply of fair-trade markets, earning producers a fairer price for their goods and an additional sum of money (a fair-trade premium) that is channelled into various community development projects, including educational programmes, improvements in water supply, and childcare facilities, from which many workers and their families are able to benefit. There remains much room for improvement, as low wages are a persistent feature of export production, but trading relations are slowly changing. The cultural relations that link producers and consumers are also changing, albeit in small ways. And the small ways in which they are changing are very definitely influenced by the meanings that for centuries have been associated with flowers as gifts and objects of display. Love, gratitude, sympathy, and celebration continue to be emotions bound up in the giving and receiving of flowers in everyday life. And as flowers have become an increasing part of the everyday life of globalization, these sentiments have been joined also by feelings of fear, anxiety, anger, and, for some, hope.

21 **The Bureau de Change**

Michael Levi

Transnational money flows are a key part of the global economy, both for business and for individuals. Here, we focus on transfers involving individuals. These are essentially driven by two trends: tourism; and economic migration that preserves links between countries of origin, families, and diasporas. A third aspect—income to individuals from illicit trade in prohibited and in tax-evaded commodities—is also important. These activities would generate money flows even if we all had the same currency, but differences in currencies create the need for places where one can swop one for another. The bureau de change is one such place.

Global migration is not just a product of late modernity: colonialism and slavery generated substantial flows of both people and some international currencies (such as sterling), and their after effects include extended transcontinental family connections that generate travel and both licit and illicit business networks. Informal mechanisms—now often stigmatized as 'underground banking'—preceded banking as ways of making available funds for merchants and other travellers who otherwise might be robbed on their way to glory and/or riches. Clearly, banks can transfer funds and exchange currencies, but they are located only in places where there are many customers and where coverage is profitable, and sometimes at a heavy minimum transaction cost for small sums. Besides, currency exchange existed in early imperial times, long before modern banking, for a price. As it is stated in the New Testament (Matthew ch. 21: 12, 13):

Cleansing the Temple

12 And Jesus entered the temple and...overturned the tables of the money changers....13 And He said to them, 'It is written, "My house shall be called a house of prayer"; but you are making it a robbers' den.'

Money changers could in principle be located anywhere, since they are people with a function. What is needed is a place where people will routinely go and expect to be able to exchange one currency for another: there is no point in having any business, whether legal or illegal, if no one knows it is there!

In many (mainly developing) countries where there are exchange controls on the amounts that can be transferred, a black market arises in which currency is exchanged for a radically different (and, for tourists, better) rate from the official government-set one. Such illicit business activities are unlikely to have fixed locations, though there may be some fixed establishments that are tolerated (through social connections and/or payment of bribes), at least provided they stick to the retail level. Before the collapse of the Soviet Union, and still in many developing countries, international travellers would be approached on arrival to buy local currency at better than official exchange prices. At some point, however, fixed stores for currency exchanges can be established, and these are termed, at least in Europe and in francophone countries, *bureaux de change*. The phrase is widely used throughout Europe, and travellers can easily identify such facilities when abroad. (Though the US and Hispanic-speaking countries would largely see the Spanish word *cambio*.) Bureaux de change are often located inside banks or travel agents, as well as in international travel hubs, and may offer money transmission as well as currency exchange services. They make their profits, and compete—within a usually limited set of options for travellers, since there is an opportunity cost of searching—by manipulating two variables: the exchange rate they use to calculate transactions, and an explicit commission for their service. Sometimes, they advertise themselves as 'commission free', but this means they can make a profit only by offering a poorer exchange rate. They also profit from the margin between the prices at which they buy and sell. There is a trade off-between volume and profit margins, but price elasticity of demand for any particular bureau may be quite modest unless cheapness (or dearness) is well communicated, perhaps within ethnic or national communities.

When the euro replaced many EU currencies in 2002, many bureaux de change reported substantial reductions in profit and closed down. Indeed, they are under threat not just from the homogenization of currencies—Montenegro adopted the euro in 2002, at a time when it had no realistic chance of joining the EU; some countries in Africa, Asia, and Latin America have adopted the US dollar as their currency—but also from globally branded debit and credit cards at ATMs and global pre-paid currency cards from firms such as American Express, Caxton FX, The Post Office, Travelex, many banks, etc that can be topped up before departure. Another source of threat is anti-money laundering (AML) regulations that require them to carry out customer identification, report 'suspicious transactions', and keep better records (at greater cost, which is passed on to consumers). However, illicit transactions may need to use some sort of currency exchange if they involve cash payments for goods and services originating in countries that use a different currency, as well as for expenditure that is less monitored—for tax and AML—than are cash flows going through banks. Mass-marketing or romance scams, for example, often have their victims send money via money service bureaux.

One aspect of globalization that has been better analyzed in recent years has been money flows. The World Bank states that nearly 200 million people live outside their country of birth: remittances to developing countries were estimated at $414 billion in 2013—up $100 billion since 2009 (and unrecorded flows would make them significantly larger, though most estimates of 'money laundering' are indefensibly large, confusing turnover with profits and disregarding lifestyle expenditures). This figure excludes transfer pricing and trade-based money laundering in which value is transferred via mispriced goods and services. Remittances amounted to 1.9 per cent of GDP for all developing countries in 2008, but were nearly three times as important (5.9 per cent of GDP) for the group of low-income countries.[1] In nine countries, remittances constituted at least 20 per cent of GDP in 2012.[2] Reducing the cost of remittance transfers produces significant benefits to the migrants' families. Banks are the most expensive way of sending remittances, and money transfer operators are substantially the cheapest.[3] In addition to raising consumption levels, reliable streams of foreign currency improve a country's creditworthiness for external borrowing. Moreover, unlike foreign aid, it cannot be skimmed by corrupt dictators and their 'rent-seeking' cronies. Whereas investors flee crises, migrants increase their giving during hard times. The money is directed to the poorer sectors. And it is relatively well monitored, by intimates on the recipient or sending end.[4] As migrants become more established, they send less money home, but the financial connections remain.

The top ten remittance recipients include wealthy countries. As a percentage of GDP, however, the top ten remittance recipients were all poor countries. Many of these transfers will be deposited and received in cash.

The largest single official medium for such cash transfers is Western Union, a company that went bust in 1992 continuing to sell telegrams at the dawn of the Internet age, but after purchase by First Data Corporation (and spun off in 2006), now makes some $1 billion a year helping—for a price—migrants across the globe send money home.[5] It has 515,000 agent locations in 200 countries and territories. In 2012, the Western Union Company completed 231 million consumer-to-consumer transactions worldwide, moving $79 billion of principal between consumers, and 432 million business payments (<http://www.westernunion.com>). It has five times as many locations worldwide as

---

[1] See further: 'Migration and Remittances', World Bank, <http://web.worldbank.org/WBSITE/EXTERNAL/NEWS/0,,contentMDK:20648762~menuPK:34480~pagePK:64257043~piPK:437376~theSitePK:4607,00.html>.

[2] 'Migration and Remittance Flows: Recent Trends and Outlook, 2013–2016', Migration and Development Brief 21, World Bank.

[3] 'Remittance Prices Worldwide', World Bank, <https://remittanceprices.worldbank.org/sites/default/files/RPW_Report_Sep2013.pdf >.

[4] 'Migration and Remittances'.

[5] See the *New York Times*, 22 November 2007, and Western Union financial results 2013.

McDonald's, Starbucks, Burger King, and Wal-Mart combined. However, this comes at a price: from roughly 4 to 20 per cent of funds transferred, which costs the company tries to combat with advertising showing family devotion. Many customers of all money transfer firms are unauthorized migrants— around two in five of Latinos in the USA, though this does not represent 40 per cent of the moneys sent. Forecasts of border movements affect the company's stock: showing the ambiguity of capitalist responses to illicit migration, Western Union executives hail migrants as 'heroes' and lobby vigorously for depenalization of immigration laws.

However, a less ambiguous 'dark side of globalization' is the role of bureaux de change in the international drugs trade. This role has been enhanced by the greater measures taken to curb money laundering via financial institutions. Serious criminals can still use corporate vehicles and/or transfer pricing to store and move proceeds of crime. However, both wholly illicit (e.g. drugs) and tax-evaded payments in the informal economy are usually in cash form, and if drugs brought from Afghanistan and Colombia, for example, are to be paid for, the wholesale and middle-market distributors may have to convert the funds into currencies acceptable in their homelands. (Or find ways, such as the 'black peso exchange', of transferring funds to Afghans and Colombians such as businesspeople desirous of accessing the currency, in exchange depositing their own domestic currency into accounts or other 'investment media' controlled by the drugs exporters.) Hence the regular appearance of bureaux de change in analyses and in prosecutions of money laundering. From the late 1990s, investigators in London have monitored as much as £70 million being laundered via one small bureau, and some prosecutions have ensued of a variety of Colombian-, Israeli-, and Arab-run bureaux (demonstrating a certain ecumenicalism as well as evidencing that, just as for the Romans, *pecunia non olet*—money has no smell). Similar sums have been involved in travel agencies acting as informal money transmitters (or *Hawalladars*). In many instances, the exchanged currency is flown out by courier to its destination, and there is little systematic knowledge of what happens thereafter to those funds that are not intercepted.

In the UK, prior to 9/11, anyone could open a bureau and there was no regulation other than via the general criminal law. However, with the concern about terrorist finance and reflecting evidence of the scale of currency exchange for the proceeds of drugs, there has been a tightening. As a compromise—given the cost of regulation to the government (as well as the often disregarded costs to the private sector)—money transmission bureaux are now subject to 'light touch regulation': they are legally obliged to register, may be subject to criminal record checks, and are required to identify customers changing over €15,000 or equivalent and report 'suspicious activities' to the national Financial Intelligence Unit—the National Crime Agency. They are now required to meet the 'fit and proper person' standards, but not to fulfil the elaborate 'Know your customer' requirements of mainstream financial institutions, given that most customers are not 'repeat players'.[6] The UK Money Transmitters Association (UKMTA) represents money service businesses registered with HM Revenue and Customs for the purpose of money transfer. Since 1 November 2009, these companies have also been regulated as payment institutions by the Financial Conduct Authority. It is illegal to operate a payment service business if not FCA regulated or registered with HMRC.

One effect of this tighter surveillance, in the Netherlands as well as the UK, has been to drive some bureaux out of business, but it has also raised the cost of remittances, reducing incomes of poor families in developing countries and (we assume) encouraging remittances via 'underground banking', often trusted members of faith and national communities, very few of whom default since they face 'social death' (and perhaps more material risks!). So long as the UK remains outside the eurozone, the decline of the dollar in favour of the euro makes only a modest difference to the cash market for bureau activity: but if it did join the euro, then this and global cards would imperil the survival of large numbers of bureaux de change, except for persons from outside the eurozone. For if 'normal' trade drops, the illicit trade may be too great a proportion of business to make banks willing to maintain business accounts for the bureaux and risk sanctions from their own regulators (or prosecutions) for having inadequate 'Know your business customer' anti-money laundering systems. Indeed since 2012, both HSBC and Barclays have sought to reduce their own corporate risks from money laundering regulatory and criminal sanctions by exiting their crucial role as bankers to money service bureaux, who would be too difficult and expensive for them to monitor more closely. Somali money service bureaux in particular mounted a strong media and political campaign to ensure the continuation of their vital financial supply line, with an English court requiring Barclays in November 2013 to continue offering account facilities to the largest money service bureau, Dahabshiil, pending a full trial.[7] This highlights both the problems of using terrorism-related material in an open judicial context and the complexities in balancing the self-protection of banks and financing of terrorism control goals against the risk that cutting off money flows may actually increase radicalization as well as increase poverty in the developing world.

---

[6] See, for the UK, *Anti-money laundering guidance for money service businesses*, <www.hmrc.gov.uk/mlr/mlr_msb.pdf.>

[7] <http://www.theguardian.com/global-development/2013/nov/05/somali-remittances-dahabshiil-barclays-ban>.

22 LIBOR*

Donald MacKenzie

Just after 11.00 am every weekday that is not a bank holiday, a calculation is performed at a couple of desks in an unremarkable open-plan office in London's Docklands. Small sets of numbers arrive electronically or—in 2006, when I witnessed the process—by telephone. Discrepancies amongst them are highlighted by error-detection software, and they are also inspected for numbers that simply 'look wrong'. Obvious typing mistakes are corrected. Less clear-cut discrepancies are checked by a telephone call: 'Hello, it's [X]. Just want to check the one-week on the Danish [krone]. You guys are quoting 2.51. You want to keep it around that?' or 'Everyone else is coming in a good bit under that.' Sometimes those who should have provided inputs are telephoned and reminded.

Once half the necessary inputs are in, a simple computerized algorithm begins to be applied. After all inputs have been received and checked, the final results of the algorithm are disseminated via electronic networks. This normally happens by 11.30 am, though when I was watching it was 11.43 before one of the two staff members involved said to his colleague: 'You can publish away.' (It was a Friday, a day on which more reminders seem to be necessary.)

This undramatic process could have been mistaken for the aggregation of sales figures from small shops or the compilation of a sports league table. It was in fact the calculation of British Bankers' Association (BBA) LIBOR, London Interbank Offered Rate: the average interest rate at which major banks can borrow funds from others in the interbank market in a particular currency for a given period. Because, in 2006, BBA LIBOR covered ten currencies and 15 time periods (from overnight to a year), a day's LIBOR was actually 150 rates.

Although its process of calculation was not dramatic, and the scandal surrounding it had yet to erupt, LIBOR's importance could be seen even in 2006 in the arrangements if terrorism or other disruption stopped it being done in the office in which I witnessed it. A nearby, similarly equipped office building was kept in readiness; dedicated lines had been laid into the homes of those responsible for the LIBOR calculation; there was a permanently staffed backup site, over 150 miles away, which could also calculate LIBOR.

* This article draws on D. MacKenzie, 'What's in a Number?', *London Review of Books* (25 September 2008): 11–12. Its updating is part of research funded by the European Research Council (FP7: ERC 291733).

LIBOR matters because it is the dominant interest-rate benchmark. Calculated in London, LIBOR rates are used globally, for example in financial derivatives: contracts or securities whose value depends upon the price of an underlying asset or the level of an index or interest rate (most commonly LIBOR). Data collected by the Bank for International Settlements suggest that derivatives indexed to LIBOR probably total around $440 trillion, the equivalent of over $60,000 for every human being on earth.

In 2006, LIBOR had never been the object of a social-science study; for example, work in economics commonly used LIBOR as an input, but no economist had studied how it is produced. My sources were observation of the BBA LIBOR calculation; interviews with eight people involved in LIBOR (four with its overall design and management or with the calculation itself; four who made, or had recently made, banks' LIBOR inputs); and documents and seminar materials produced by the British Bankers' Association.

Several aspects of LIBOR are of interest. First, BBA LIBOR was part of a gift economy. The banks that made the inputs were not paid; the electronic networks that disseminated LIBOR paid only a small fee; those who use LIBOR to draw up derivatives contracts do so free of charge. (Of course, as all social scientists know, gifts are not arbitrary generosity: for example, being part of a LIBOR Contributor Panel used to be a sign of a bank's standing.) Second, LIBOR shows that it is easy to overstate the death of geography or the flatness of the world.[1] LIBOR was a global fact, and its production involved many international banks (membership of the British Bankers' Association is open to all banks operating in Britain), but it was also recognizably London Interbank Offered Rate. Why that was so—why the benchmark was not, for example, a set of New York rates—was an outcome deeply interwoven with the commercial, cultural, and regulatory history of London. One interviewee even suggested that when the BBA's official interest-rate 'fixing' began in 1985 (before London's leisurely 'gentlemanly capitalism' had succumbed fully to the early mornings of Americanization), 11.00 am was chosen because only by then could one be certain that 'everybody was up and running'.

The most fascinating aspect of LIBOR, however, was that it was a set of facts: until 2008, there was remarkably little dispute about it. A LIBOR input was the rate at which the inputting bank 'could borrow funds ["unsecured" and "governed by the laws of England and Wales"] were it to do so by asking for and then accepting interbank offers in reasonable market size just prior to 11.00' in the currency and for the time period in question.[2] What constitutes 'just prior' or 'reasonable market size' was not defined, and the verb form was

---

[1] Richard O'Brien, *Global Financial Integration: The End of Geography* (London: Pinter, 1991); Thomas L. Friedman, *The World is Flat: A Brief History of the Globalized World in the Twenty-First Century* (London: Allen Lane, 2005).

[2] W. Mason, 'Rate Setting in London', British Bankers' Association, 1999, slides eight and nine.

conditional: 'could borrow…were it to do so'. There was no requirement that money actually be borrowed.

The dealers who made LIBOR inputs seemed most often to do so by adding small experience-based 'spreads' (which are single-digit numbers of basis points: i.e. hundredths of percentage points) to the figures on inter-dealer brokers' screens. One dealer explained:

> [W]ithin, say, the pool of 16 [banks on a LIBOR panel]…you'll probably have three aggressive lenders, so the run-through you get from the broker is where you've going to get the first three lots of money. After that you have to move your price up until it becomes attractive enough for the people that don't want to lend to suddenly think, 'Well, this is becoming attractive enough to do it', and that's where this spread…comes from.…[I]t's not going to be a mid-market rate, it's going to be the point at which you are likely to get the money.

Those who made LIBOR inputs (and no doubt many of those who used LIBOR) were well aware that enormous sums of money hinge on its precise level, sometimes for the particular banks making inputs—an evident source of temptation to manipulate it. However, the core of the 'sociotechnical design' of LIBOR was interlinked mechanisms designed to protect its status as a set of facts. Most important was the LIBOR algorithm, which was not a simple average. Inputs for each currency and time period are rank-ordered, the top and bottom quartiles are ignored, and the mean of the remainder is calculated: that mean is LIBOR. So no single bank could move LIBOR by a wildly high or low input, and it seemed as if the interests of larger groups of banks would vary and under normal circumstances were unlikely to be stable: the same bank will benefit at some times from a higher rate, at other times from a lower.

A single well-chosen input might still move LIBOR marginally, but when making an input a dealer could not see what other banks have done. (The screens employed to make electronic inputs were not originally private, giving rise to the possibility of choosing an input in the light of what others have done.) Furthermore, once a day's LIBOR rates were set, each input—and the name of the bank that made it—was also disseminated electronically, and thus was open to sceptical scrutiny: one interviewee showed me that day's inputs into three-month sterling LIBOR, pointing with suspicion to a bank that had reduced its input—by a single basis point—from the previous day's, while all others had either increased theirs or left them unchanged.

LIBOR was of course a social-kind,[3] performative fact: it *was* the output of the process of calculation described above. Nevertheless, market participants also generally regarded it as a faithful representation, adequately reflecting conditions in the interbank market. The credit crisis did, however, spark controversy over LIBOR, especially in spring 2008. Critics suggested that rates

[3] Barry Barnes, 'Social Life as Bootstrapped Induction', *Sociology* 17, 4 (1983): 524–45.

were being biased downwards because banks feared that reporting that they could borrow only at high rates would spark rumours about their creditworthiness, and central bankers reportedly began to worry that doubts about LIBOR were further unsettling already febrile money markets. Much of the controversy focused on US dollar LIBOR, with some in the USA apparently unhappy that the benchmark dollar rates were being set in London at a time when traders in the USA were only starting to arrive at their desks. However, a potential rival as an interest-rate benchmark, New York Funding Rate, created by brokers Wrightson ICAP in June 2008, actually tended to differ only slightly from LIBOR. The British Bankers' Association created a new subcommittee to vet inputs, which had the power to ask any bank making dubious inputs to justify them, and by late 2008 the controversy seemed to have passed. However, it suddenly returned to the news in March 2011 when it became known that four banks had received subpoenas from regulators investigating inputs in 2006–8 to the calculation of US dollar LIBOR.

Update, November 2013

The outcome of the investigation is now largely known. It has revealed large-scale efforts to manipulate LIBOR, and four banks—Barclays, UBS, the Royal Bank of Scotland, and Rabobank—have so far settled with the authorities and received large fines. Crucially, it seems that in some cases efforts to manipulate LIBOR involved coordinated inputs by traders in several different banks, and brokers—the rates on whose screens are, as noted, important information drawn on by those making LIBOR inputs—were also drawn into the manipulation. These two features meant that the elimination in the LIBOR algorithm of the highest and lowest inputs did not always prevent successful manipulation by ad hoc coalitions of traders in multiple banks and brokers keen for brokerage fees. Both civil actions and criminal investigations are under way, and LIBOR's credibility has indeed been undermined: it is still global, but no longer simply a fact.

Yet LIBOR itself remains, although it has been slimmed down to five currencies (US dollars, euros, yen, Swiss francs, and sterling) and fewer 'tenors' (time periods). Its administration has been taken over by the NYSE Euronext group (which operates the London International Financial Futures Exchange), and LIBOR is now regulated by the UK's Financial Conduct Authority. Manipulating LIBOR is now unequivocally a criminal offence. However, the nature of the inputs and the process of calculation have not been altered fundamentally, although one goal of the slimming down is to restrict LIBOR to currencies and tenors in which there are reasonable numbers of actual transactions against which LIBOR inputs can be compared.

LIBOR's global role in financial derivatives meant it could not easily be discarded. One bank's head trader told *Risk* magazine in November 2012: 'the [derivatives] contracts still exist. Anyone abolishing the fixing would be sued in a big way because that's probably worse than having the rates manipulated, frankly.' Another banker said: 'I hate LIBOR—for many, many reasons—but we need it. It's a consistent fudge factor that allows standardization in the industry.' LIBOR rates are damaged global facts, but essential nonetheless.

23 Taking Note of Export Earnings

Kris Olds

Globalization in Practice clearly signifies the need to be more aware, in a research-analytical sense, of the multifold logics, agendas, networks, and practices that bring globalization to life. This is a valuable stance in general, but even more so when one is researching a phenomenon that is emerging as a major target of developmentalist agendas, albeit in ways that emerge and unfold in geographically and historically specific ways.

Over the last seven years I have been conducting research on one of these phenomena—the globalization of higher education—in a manner that has me engaging with many of the key actors and institutions driving the process forward. They do this via the setting of regulations, the sharing of 'best' (or 'model') practices, the application of traditional and social media to shed light on evolving changes, and the creation and implementation of institutional strategies regarding 'internationalization'. In aggregate what we are seeing is a major realignment of higher education: from mission, to funding frameworks, to scales of operation, to development models, to framing and reference points, higher education is in the process of being globalized, for good and bad.

What follows is a brief practice-oriented analysis of how select actors are attempting to construct higher education into a 'services sector' export so as to generate enhanced revenue for institutions, and nations, especially in the context of declining levels of base state funding for higher education. This analysis is derived from observations of practices unfolding in multiple countries, primarily England, Singapore, Canada, Australia, New Zealand, and the United States. A primer-like logic reinforces my delineation of the steps taken to realign logics, temporal and scalar framings, and regulations, so as to enable higher education to become an export industry. Note, however, that I am not advocating that the export logic take hold, but rather am attempting to shed light on how it is happening.

A practice-oriented approach to the globalization of higher education inevitably brings the analyst 'close to home': by people and units within the nation state, within nationally oriented stakeholder organizations, and within our own universities and colleges. To use the words of Saskia Sassen, this is a prime example of 'denationalization', a process of reorientation from the national and international to the global, though *for* the national.[1] As Sassen notes, in an interview with Magnus Wennerhag:

> With the notion of denationalization I try to capture and make visible a mix of dynamics that is also altering sovereignty but is doing so from the inside out, and on the ground, so to speak—the multiple micro-processes that are reorienting the historic national project towards the new global project. National state policies may still be couched in the language of the national, but at least some of them no longer are: they are now oriented towards building global systems inside the national state. From there, then, the term denationalization.[2]

The denationalization process is thus associated with new policies, the inculcation and valorization of supranational (global) outlooks, norms and subjectivities, and the cultivation of globalizing practices.[3]

The construction of higher education into a services export such as legal services, accountancy services, financial services, and media services is taking place via the following elements that all come together, albeit in unique ways, in different countries.

Element A: Capacity Building re International Student Mobility

A key dynamic in this development process is learning within key stakeholders about the evolving nature of student mobility across borders (e.g. see Figure 23.1). This typically occurs via enhanced awareness of data produced by international organizations (IOs) such as the OECD (e.g. see its annual *Education at a Glance* report), national-scale data collected and profiled by ministries of immigration and ministries of education, and data acquired and profiled by non-governmental organizations such as the International Institute for Education (IIE).

There are two noteworthy impacts generated by the desire for enhanced levels of knowledge about student mobility across national borders. First, IOs are member organizations constituted by nation states. An IO request for such data requires the nation state to produce it, or else provide reasons as to why

[1] Saskia Sassen, *Territory, Authority, Rights: From Medieval to Global Assemblages* (Princeton: Princeton University Press, 2006).

[2] Saskia Sassen and Magnus Wennerhag, 'Denationalized states and global assemblages: An interview with Saskia Sassen', *Fronesis*, 22–23 (2006), <http://www.eurozine.com/articles/2006-11-20-sassen-sv. html>.

[3] Sassen, *Territory, Authority, Rights*.

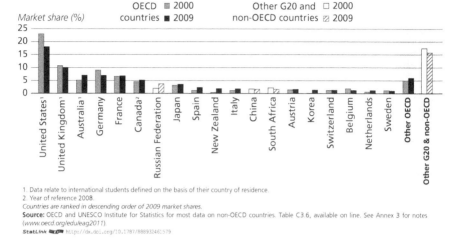

Figure 23.1 Trends in international education market shares (2000, 2009)
Source: OECD (2011) *Education at a Glance*, Paris: OECD.

the data is absent or inadequate. Thus the act of requesting data generates ripple effects to collect and therefore make sense of student mobility data.

Second, knowledge about student mobility enables policy makers at all scales to situate and benchmark their own countries, provinces/states, and institutions, relative to others. This takes place with respect to relative proportions of international students, as well as with respect to tuition fee policy differences (e.g. see Table 23.1).

Element B: Desectoralize Higher Education

The denationalization of higher education goes hand in hand with the desectoralization of higher education. What I mean by this is that the value and impacts of higher education are becoming of increasing interest to arms of the state besides traditional ones (e.g. ministries of education). For example, in this case international student mobility is perceived to be valuable, for these students are viewed as key components of: (a) building a knowledge-based economy, (b) ameliorative solutions to challenging national demographic transitions (e.g. ageing), and (c) a mechanism of 'soft power'. The enhanced interest in higher education, especially by officials representing relatively more powerful arms of the state (e.g. those associated with international trade and/

Table 23.1 Countries offering tertiary programmes in English (2009)

Use of English in instruction	
All or nearly all programmes offered in English	Australia, Canada,[a] Ireland, New Zealand, the United Kingdom, the United States
Many programmes offered in English	Denmark, Finland, the Netherlands, Sweden
Some programmes offered in English	Belgium (Fl.),[b] the Czech Republic, France, Germany, Hungary, Iceland, Japan, Korea, Norway, Poland, Portugal, the Slovak Republic, Switzerland,[c] Turkey
No or nearly no programmes offered in English	Austria, Belgium (Fr.), Brazil, Chile, Greece, Israel, Italy, Luxembourg, Mexico,[c] the Russian Federation, Spain

Note: The extent to which a country offers a few or many programmes in English takes into account the size of the population in the country. Hence France and Germany are classified among countries with comparatively few English programmes, although they have more English programmes than Sweden, in absolute terms.
[a]In Canada, tertiary institutions are either French- (mostly Quebec) or English-.speaking.
[b]Master's programmes.
[c]At the discretion of tertiary education institutions.
Source: OECD, compiled from brochures for prospective international students by OAD (Austria), CITIES and NARIC (Czech Republic), Cirius (Denmark), CIMO (Finland), EduFrance (France), DAAD (Germany), Campus Hungary (Hungary), University of Iceland (Iceland), JPSS (Japan), NIIED (Korea), NUFFIC (Netherlands), MU (Norway), CRASP (Poland), Swedish Institute (Sweden) and Middle-East Technical University (Turkey).

or foreign policy vs education) leads to the application of different development logics regarding higher education. In effect, this multiplies the demands placed on what was previously a sector associated with, for the most part, the responsibility for producing national citizens as guided by cultural-political priorities.

Element C: Contexts of Austerity and Resource Constraint

Enhanced awareness of international student mobility, along with emerging views on the multiple uses of mobile students, is then typically linked to two key debates: (a) declining levels of state support for higher education, which generates fiscal stress on higher education institutions, and (b) regional and national debates about economic development, including the need to generate new streams of revenue for national economies and/or the diversification of the services-related sector of the economy.

It is no accident, for example, that Australia led the way regarding the conceptualization of higher education as a services export following regular and systemic cuts to higher education in the 1980s and early 1990s. It is also important to note that these cuts took place in a context (see Elements A & B) of early awareness of student mobility patterns associated with Pacific Asia, a fast-growing source region for Australia at first and then many other Western countries since the 2000s. Austerity and declining real budgets for higher education in Australia then fuelled the emergence of an assertive Australian state that quickly focused on enhancing and diversifying export earnings via the surveillance, courting, and serving of Asian students within Australian territory such that it is the third largest export earner for the Australian economy after coal and iron ore.[4] Australian university budgets as a whole are now the most dependent, in the world, upon the fees generated by foreign (mainly Asian) students.

Element D: Formalizing and Legitimizing the Reconceptualization

A critically important step to formalizing and legitimizing the reconceptualization of higher education as an export industry is the launch of nationally specific study about the phenomenon, which lays the context for 'official' follow-up reports that subsequently emerge on a regular basis.

In 2006, for example, the New Zealand government contracted Infometrics, a leading Auckland-based consultancy, to produce a model to understand the economic impact of 'export education'. The report's lead author was Dr Adolf Stroomberge, Chief Economist, Infometrics. Dr Stroomberge has a PhD in general equilibrium modelling and 25 years of experience in economic consulting, specializing in economic modelling, econometrics, and public policy research in areas such as education, taxation, savings and retirement, energy and environment, trade and transport. He has been a member of the New Zealand Advisory Committee on Economic Statistics since 1996. As Dr Stroomberge put it, in a weblog entry in *GlobalHigherEd*:

> It had been suspected for some time that the contribution of the export education industry to the New Zealand economy has seen impressive, if volatile growth, to reach around $2 billion in 2007/08. Our research in 2008 sought to establish the truth of these suspicions.[5]

Stroomberge's entry outlines his firm's approach to conceptualizing export earnings, factoring in tuition fees, estimated consumption patterns, etc., with

---

[4] Access Economics, *The Australian Education Sector and the Economic Contribution of International Students* (Sydney: Access Economics, 2009).

[5] Adolf Stroomberge, 'Measuring the Economic Impact of "Export Education": Insights from New Zealand', *GlobalHigherEd Blog*, 7 February 2009, <http://globalhighered.wordpress.com/2009/02/07/measuring-the-economic-impact-of-export-education-insights-from-new-zealand/>.

explicit acknowledgement of the limitations of their adopted model. In the end, Stroomberge suggests that our:

[E]stimates show that in 2008 the economic impact of New Zealand's export education industry was $2.1 billion, implying a four-fold increase since 1999. Few industries would be able to claim an average growth rate of 16% pa for almost a decade.

Canada adopted a similar approach, hiring an immigration consultant (Roslyn Kunin & Associates, Inc.) to calculate higher education export earnings for Canada. Her report, which was profiled by Katherine Geddie in *GlobalHigherEd*, calculated that 'In 2008, international students to Canada contributed $6.5 billion (CAD) to the national economy, provided 83,000 jobs, and contributed $291 million (CAD) in government revenue' and that the 'total value of international education is higher than the value of national exports in coniferous lumber ($5.1 billion) and coal ($6.07 billion)'.[6]

I was involved in some informal deliberations with senior Canadian officials about this issue prior to the issuance of the report contract and it was clear that government officials were unclear where widely circulated but unsourced numbers (in Canada's case the idea that each foreign student generated CDN$25,000 per year) came from, hence a key part of the logic for the study. It is also worth noting that the funds for the study came from the federal government (Foreign Affairs and International Trade Canada), though key provincial ministry officials also helped to frame the nature of the charge for the consultant.

Legitimation of the notion of higher education as an export industry also takes in such reports and deliberations via mechanisms such as intersectoral comparisons (see Table 23.2), which are frequently visualized.

Such visualizations enable the state and other advocates of higher education as an export industry to rationalize framing it as an industrial product of sorts, one with significant economic value that can and should contribute to the national economy. Numbers matter, but when they are visualized in such a format, they are more comprehensible, they have the potential to travel widely (as immutable mobiles), and they can be easily harnessed by stakeholders when needed.

In closing, it is important to think about why these numbers are being sought at this point in history. I would argue that these numbers are being constituted, and debated about, in the context of a significant ideological transition—one that increasingly enables views to emerge of higher education as a driver of economic versus cultural-political change. For example, a decade or

---

[6] Kate Geddie, 'Measuring the Economic Value of Canada's International Education "Industry"', *GlobalHigherEd Blog*, 29 October 2009, <http://globalhighered.wordpress.com/2009/10/29/measuring-the-economic-value-of-canada/>.

Table 23.2 Comparison of international education services with other top exports in goods from Canada to the top ten international student source countries, 2008

Export/ranked	China, Peoples' Republic of	Korea, Republic of	United States	France	India	Japan	Saudi Arabia	Taiwan	Hong Kong	Mexico
1	EDUCATION SERVICES $1.301 billion	COAL $1.272 billion	CRUDE OIL $63.7 billion	AIRCRAFT ENGINES $536.9 million	FERTILIZERS $688 million	COAL $2.3 billion	BARLEY 225.100	UNWROUGHT NICKEL $253.3 million	UNWROUGHT NICKEL $241.3 million	RAPE OR COLZA SEEDS $B21.5 million
2	ACYCLIC ALCOHOLS $869.5 million	EDUCATION SERVICES $846.8 million	LIQUIFIED PETROLEUM $36.3 billion	NON-CRUDE PETROLEUM OILS 307.1 million	DRIED LEGUMES $422.8 million	RAPE OR COLZA SEEDS $1.4 billion	EDUCATION SERVICES $114.2 million	CHEMICAL WOODPULP $138.9 million	GOLD $193 million	MOTOR VEHICLE PARTS $479.2 million
3	CHEMICAL WOODPULP $858.5 million	CHEMICAL WOODPULP $239.6 million	MOTOR VEHICLES $33.7 billion	EDUCATION SERVICES $263.9 million	NEWSPRINT $232.3 million	MEAT OR SWINE $801.6 million	CHEMICAL WOODPULP $65.6 million	EDUCATION SERVICES $127.4 million	RAW FURSKINS $148.3 million	ELECTRONIC CIRCUITS $464.4 million
4	RAPE OR COLZA SEEDS $782.5 million	NICKEL PRODUCTS $220.9 million	NON-CRUDE PETROLEUM $14.6 billion	AIRCRAFT PARTS $242.5 million	EDUCATION SERVICES $225.7 million	LUMBER $760.1 million	UNCOATED PAPER $56.4 million	COAL $118.4 million	EDUCATION SERVICES $127.3 million	MOTOR VEHICLES $332.9 million
5	UNWROUGHT NICKEL $703.9 million	SEMI-CHEMICAL WOOD PULP $145.5 million	MOTOR VEHICLE PARTS $9.9 billion	BLOOD $180.9 million	CHEMICAL WOODPULP $76.7 million	COPPER ORES $737.7 million	TANKS AND OTHER ARMOUR $47 2 million	IRON ORES $86.7 million	MOLLUSCS $65.8 million	TELEPHONE SETS $195.3 million
6	SULFUR $686 million	COPPER ORES $143.2 million	UNWROUGHT ALUMINIUM $5.9 billion	IRON ORES $160.9 million	AIRCRAFT $70.7 million	WHEAT $550.9 million	NEWSPRINT $45.2 million	NICKEL PRODUCTS $80.4 million	EDIBLE ANIMAL $62.8 million	WHEAT $179.1 million
7	FERTILIZERS $534.9 million	UNWROUGHT ALUMINIUM $141.2 million	MEDICAMENTS $4.1 billion	URANIUM $98.4 million	TELEPHONE SETS $62.2 million	UNWROUGHT ALUMINIUM $511.1 million	LIFTING MACHINERY $26.3 million	LUMBER $59.3 million	PLANT PARTS $62.3 million	MACHINERY PARTS $173.6 million

8	SEMI-CHEMICAL WOOD PULP $409.8 million	MEAT OR SWINE $118.4 million	AIRCRAFT $5.1 billion	COAL $88.6 million	GOLD $59.9 million	CHEMICAL WOODPULP $421.2 million	COPPER WIRE $21.1 million	POLYMERS OF ETHYLENE $56.7 million	MEAT OR SWINE $58.5 million	COAL $148.8 million
9	IRON ORES $315.6 million	URANIUM $63.8 million	POLYMERS $3.9 billion	TELEPHONE SETS $86.5 million	COPPER ORES $46 million	COBALT $206.6 million	ASH & RESIDUES CONTAINING METAL $20.6 million	RAW HIDES/SKINS $54.7 million	NEWSPR INT $56.5 million	BARS/RODS OF STEEL $133.2 million
10	RAPE, COLZA OR MUSTARD OIL $269 million	WHEAT $61.6 million	ELECTRICAL ENERGY $3.8 billion	NEWSPRINT $85.3 million	ASBESTOS $44 million	EDUCATION SERVICES $204.5 million	NON-DOMESTIC DRYERS $19.1 million	SEMI-CHEMICAL WOOD PULP $43.5 million	SCRAP PLASTICS $49.4 million	UNWROUGHT ALUMINIUM $127.6 million
NOT IN TOP 10			EDUCATION SERVICES $349.2 million							EDUCATION SERVICES $118.9 million

Sources: RKA's calculation of education services; Trade Data Online—Industry Canada. Kate Geddie, 'Measuring the Economic Value of Canada's International Education "Industry"', *GlobalHigherEd Blog*, 29 October 2009, <http://globalhighered.wordpress.com/2009/10/29/measuring-the-economic-value-of-canada/>.

two ago, it would have been impossible to imagine creating tables such as the one profiled in Kate Geddie's entry in *GlobalHigherEd* in which education is measured against 'scrap plastics' or 'chemical woodpulp'. Thus, a powerful new organizing logic, to use Saskia Sassen's phrase, is emerging: one that reframes higher education as an urban/national/global services industry, for good and for bad.

Second, it is worth thinking about the emerging capabilities to generate such analyses. Interestingly, almost all of the analyses have been generated by consultants working on behalf of ministries of foreign affairs and trade (or equivalent). It is noteworthy that there is little capacity within the state to assess such impacts, at least initially, so representatives of the state rely upon consultants with track records of studying an array of economic development dynamics. Desectoralization is thus a key element in this process of bringing such alternative visions of the uses of higher education to life.

24 Filthy Lucre: Urine for Sale*

Barbara Penner

In November 2010, a curious story began making the rounds on the Internet. Entitled 'Urine For Sale? Durban's in the Market', the piece reported on a South African pilot scheme, supported by a grant from the Bill and Melinda Gates Foundation, that proposes to process urine for nutrient recovery.[1] Urine is rich in phosphorus, nitrogen, and potassium, all key nutrients in fertilizer, and unlocking its potential as an alternative source of phosphorus in particular has become something of a Holy Grail for scientists.[2] But what distinguishes the South African project is its focus on the logistical as well as the technical side of urine processing: how might urine be harvested, collected, and transported in the first place?

As it happens, Durban has a ready supply of urine, thanks to the installation of over 90,000 urine-diversion (UD) toilets in its environs since 2003. These are dry and self-contained sanitation units designed to divert urine into a separate hole from faeces, so that the latter can dry out faster and be disposed of more easily (see Figures 24.1 and 24.2) As part of the pilot scheme, jerry cans have been attached to 500 of these units to capture the urine that would normally soak away into the ground. The cans are picked up once a week and the sum of R30 (about $4.30 USD) is paid to each household for the contents, not

* The author would like to thank Will Rupp, Emma Jones, and Ben Campkin for comments and suggestions in developing this article.

[1] Marine Veith, 'Urine for Sale? Durban's in the Market', *Mail & Guardian* online, 7 November 2010, <http://www.mg.co.za/article/2010-11-07-urine-for-sale-durbans-in-the-market>. The main players in the four-year project are the Bill and Melinda Gates Foundation (who have provided a grant of $3 million USD), eThekwini Water and Sanitation, and the Swiss Federal Institute of Aquatic Science and Technology (Eawag). 'Urine as a Commercial Fertilizer?', Eawag, 14 October 2010, <http://www.eawag.ch/medien/bulletin/20101014/index_EN>.

[2] In 1959, in the essay 'Life's Bottleneck', Isaac Asimov highlighted how the modern sewerage system was dumping phosphorus into the ocean as waste and advocated the use of 'sewage disposal units' that would process it as fertilizer instead. Recent discussions tend to dwell more on the geopolitics of phosphorus mining, especially the implications for America as its domestic supply diminishes. Isaac Asimov, 'Life's Bottleneck', in *Asimov on Chemistry* (New York: Doubleday & Company, 1974): 137–46; and David A. Vaccari, 'Phosphorus Famine: The Threat to Our Food Supply', *Scientific American* (June 2009): 54–9.

Figure 24.1 Urine-diversion toilets of the type favoured by the municipal authorities of Durban, South Africa

a trifling amount in a country where unemployment is high and incomes are low. Durban's water and sanitation division, eThekwini Water and Sanitation, confidently describes pay-for-pee as a win-win scenario: residents financially benefit from using their UD toilets properly while the world benefits from the recovery of phosphorus.

Upon publication, the 'pay-for-pee' story was picked up and reprinted in news outlets from France to China. One can see why. The idea of urine markets seems to come straight from the pages of a bizarre sci-fi novel. Though a few readers posted positive remarks about the scheme, the majority seemed incredulous, treating it as bureaucratic thinking gone mad. But, far from being mad, this initiative is the rational outcome of the global community's recent embrace of market mechanisms as an effective means of encouraging 'correct' sanitation behaviour. The conviction that cash incentives are required to stop practices like open defecation or, in this case, to reconcile poor people to a sanitation technology they believe is inferior, is only the latest example of this logic, but it demonstrates how deeply it extends. Too few seem to ask: What are the limits of this approach?

Figure 24.2 Urine-diversion toilets of the type favoured by the municipal authorities of Durban, South Africa

Essential Diversions

eThekwini Water and Sanitation turned to UD toilets after a cholera outbreak in 2002 when sanitation infrastructure needed to be rapidly rolled out to areas beyond Durban's 'waterborne edge', that is, rural and semi-rural areas outside its existing sewage system. UD toilets were deemed superior to other dry sanitation technologies as they would cost the municipality the least long term; this is because they effectively transfer labour, maintenance, and emptying costs to users who bury their waste into holes they dig themselves on-site.[3] Possibly making a virtue of necessity, eThekwini Water has declared that it now has no plans to extend its sewage infrastructure beyond the waterborne edge due to concerns about water scarcity. For residents unable to afford 'upgrade' options such as septic tanks, UD toilets are set to become a permanent feature of their daily lives.

---

[3] The process by which eThekwini Water arrived at UD toilets is described fully in Teddy Gounden, Bill Pfaff, Neil Macleod, and Chris Buckley, 'Provision of Free Sustainable Basic Sanitation: The Durban Experience' (paper presented at the 32nd WEDC International Conference, Colombo, Sri Lanka, 2006).

While this move towards dry systems seems logical and laudable in a water-stressed country such as South Africa, there is one major problem: many recipients are unhappy with UD toilets. Many explanations are given for their rejection, but the most compelling one is the most elemental. People object to having to handle their own waste. This is not a surprising objection given that African culture generally is faecal-phobic. But in South Africa, where widening access to basic services such as sanitation is fundamental to redressing the social injustices created by apartheid, users are also acutely sensitive to perceived inequities in provision.[4] And the recipients of dry systems need only look to the country's still predominantly white privileged class—who benefit from full-pressure water systems and are certainly not expected to dispose of their own shit—for proof that the distribution of sanitation options largely follows the old race and class lines.[5]

eThekwini Water feels that the easiest way to overcome this resistance is to ensure that UD toilets are used correctly. UD toilets are simple pieces of technology, but they require considerably more effort from users than waterborne 'flush and forget' systems do: the facility must be maintained; the recommended number of people must use it, faithfully keeping their urine apart from their faeces; an appropriate bulking agent (sand or ash) must be used; and, once full, the decomposing chamber must be sealed for two years. If users follow all of these steps, a dry 'humus' is produced that is not offensive to handle. If they do not (as very often appears to be the case), the contents of the UD toilets quickly become disgusting, reinforcing users' perception of them as inferior. More seriously, in eThekwini Water's view, non-use or misuse of the facilities can lead to contaminated water sources and spread disease.

Encouraging correct use, then, is essential to the UD toilet programme's success. Beyond safeguarding public health, eThekwini Water has real incentive to transform users' attitudes. As a large-scale roll-out of a dry sanitation technology—Durban's UD toilet programme is one of the largest in the world—it is an important test case, one that can establish the viability of such technology. And improving sanitation is now on the global radar, thanks to the United Nations' Millennium Development Goals (MDGs).[6] While eThekwini

---

[4] A useful overview of the ANC's key policy statements up to 2002 regarding infrastructure is provided by Patrick Bond, *Unsustainable South Africa: Environment, Development and Social Protest* (Scottsville: University of Natal Press, 2002): 185–242. See also Nozibele Mjoli, 'Review of Sanitation Policy and Practice in South Africa from 2001 to 2008; Report to the Water Research Commission (31/03/2010)' (Pretoria: Water Research Commission, 2010). Available to download from: <http://www.wrc.org.za/Pages/DisplayItem.aspx?ItemID=8669&FromURL=/Pages/KH_DocumentsList.aspx?su=c6&ms=2%3b67%3b>.

[5] For a fuller version of this argument, see Barbara Penner, 'Flush with Inequality: Sanitation in South Africa', Places, 18 November 2010, <http://places.designobserver.com/entry.html?entry=21619>.

[6] It is presently estimated that 2.6 million people in the world do not have access to basic sanitation, which results in 5,000 children dying every day of diarrheal diseases. The United Nations' initial target was to halve these numbers by 2015, as part of Millenium Development Goal 7: Ensure Environmental Sustainability (though sanitation impacts on other MDGs as well, notably Goal

Water has several options for making UD toilets more palatable (making them easier for children and the elderly to use would be one way to start), its preference for urine harvesting conforms to the prevailing wisdom about how best to deal with local indifference or resistance to sanitation. Rather than addressing the deep social and cultural roots of the problem, market mechanisms are deployed to bring them round.

Pee Equity

The rise of market logic in sanitation circles can be traced back to the 1980s when many projects failed because users rejected free toilets provided for them by the state or by NGOs.[7] Since then, the consensus has emerged that it is not enough to supply toilets: users must want them and, if they don't, must be persuaded to want them, using a combination of hygiene education and business techniques to stimulate demand. As Melinda Gates recently put it, the toilet must be repositioned 'as a modern, trendy device'.[8] She suggests that Coca-Cola, which has penetrated remote areas through aspirational marketing, can serve as a good model for how local views may be altered.

While the comparison between Coke and toilets may seem far-fetched, the approach Gates promotes has a proven track record: for instance, the non-profit organization IDE Canada has greatly increased sanitation coverage in the regions of Cambodia where it operates, due to its decision to market affordable latrines as 'achievable aspiration'—as status symbols. Since IDE demonstrated that EZ latrines are highly saleable if pitched the right way, Cambodian businesses have apparently been lining up for the chance to sell them. To IDE at least, this is the best possible guarantee that they will proliferate. 'Now that the private sector is organized to do this, [sanitation is] spreading like wildfire,' the organization says, claiming that the involvement of entrepreneurs will avoid the 'toxic cycle of dependency' that dogs so many sanitation projects.[9]

4: Reduce Child Mortality; Goal 5: Improve Maternal Health; and Goal 6: Combat HIV/Aids, Malaria and other Diseases.) At the September 2010 Summit on the MDGS in New York, however, the UN announced that it would not meet its target. ('Goal 7: Ensure Environmental Sustainability', United Nations, <http://www.un.org/millenniumgoals/environ.shtml>.) In fact, of all the MDG targets, improving sanitation seems to be one of the furthest off track, a situation blamed on chronically low levels of funding.

[7] A summary of this change can be found in Maggie and Ben Fawcett, *The Last Taboo: Opening the Door on Global Sanitation* (London: Earthscan, 2008): 133–65.

[8] Rebecca Mead, 'The Real Thing', *The New Yorker*, 4 October 2010, 37. See also 'Melinda French Gates: What nonprofits can learn from Coca-Cola', TEDxChange Lecture (September 2010), <http://www.ted.com/talks/melinda_french_gates_what_nonprofits_can_learn_from_coca_cola.html>.

[9] Patrick White, 'A Cleaner Third World, One Toilet at a Time', *The Globe and Mail*, 19 October 2010, A3.

As the 'toxic cycle of dependency' reference underscores, at the core of the new market-led logic is a rather old-fashioned maxim: It's no good giving people something for nothing. Locals must show their governments and donors that they appreciate the value of toilets, either by paying for them in full or in part or by helping to build them, the 'sweat equity' principle. With urine harvesting, sweat equity becomes 'pee equity'. By diverting their urine for collection, users provide the municipality with proof that they have used their UD toilets correctly and are financially rewarded for so doing.

The whiff of nineteenth-century paternalism that can be detected in this approach makes urine harvesting an easy target for criticism. But invoking the nineteenth century also usefully reminds us of some of the larger issues at stake. For much of that century in major Western cities from Edinburgh to Munich, dry systems of human waste disposal were in play alongside water systems and it was by no means obvious that water would win. Following the theories of chemist Justus von Liebig, government officials, sanitarians, scientists, and entrepreneurs dreamed of finding a way to harness the power of 'liquid manure'. Most were driven by a sincere horror of how water closets polluted rivers and wasted the God-given nutrients in human excreta. Most also believed, however, that sewage harvesting could be lucrative—not an unreasonable belief in an age when there was still a working organic economy.

This belief drove the Victorians to put forward a seemingly endless series of plans and patents for sewage farms, earth closets, and even an early UD toilet, Turner and Robertshaw's Patent Divided Closet. (See Figure 24.3; Turner and Robertshaw's advertising suggested that the urine collected in the Patent Divided Closet be used in manufacturing, but did not specify how.) No less a figure than engineer Joseph Bazalgette was seduced by the profitable potential of urine. In 1849, less than a decade before he began to build London's waterborne sewage system, Bazalgette proposed that the Metropolitan Commission of Sewers erect a series of 60 public urinals throughout the city, the construction and maintenance of which would be financed through the sale of undiluted urine to farmers and market gardeners. Backing up his proposal with detailed calculations and costings, Bazalgette reckoned that if each urinal was occupied four hours each day, it would produce 408 pints of urine, and bring in £48 per annum.[10]

Like most of these proposed schemes, Bazalgette's was never realized. Of those that were put into practice (mostly sewage farms), few generated any profits, due to the high cost of collecting and transporting waste and the availability of cheaper forms of fertilizers such as guano.[11] And there was one last

[10] Joseph Bazalgette, *Letter of Mr. J. W. Bazalgette on Establishment of Public Conveniences Throughout the Metropolis: Printed by Order of Court, 22nd March, 1849* (London: Printed by Reynell and Weight, 16 Little Pulteney street, [1849]): 367.

[11] A good overview of these schemes is provided by Jamie Benidickson, *The Culture of Flushing: A Social and Legal History of Sewage* (Vancouver: UBC Press, 2007): 119–26.

Figure 24.3 Victorian-era advertisement for an early UD toilet, the Turner and Robertshaw Patent Divided Closet

problem: people proved to be quite stubbornly attached to water closets, even if that meant their excreta would be too dilute to be of productive use. These factors together ensured the triumph of water systems by the end of the century, although many regarded it as a Pyrrhic victory at best. Karl Marx was certainly not alone when he lamented: 'In London they can find no better use for the excretion of four and a half million human beings than to contaminate the Thames with it at heavy expense.'[12]

Today, the dream of restoring an organic economy has been given a new life, fuelled by fears of water scarcity and dwindling supplies of non-renewable natural resources. Indeed, if one can get past the fantastical sound of pay-for-pee, the economic and environmental case for it is sound. If the scheme proves feasible, human waste might once again become a commodity. Of course,

---

[12] Quoted in John Bellamy Foster, 'Marx's Ecology in Historical Perspective', *International Socialism Journal* 96 (Autumn 2002).

significant schemes already exist that turn shit into gold: biogas digesters which turn human waste into cooking gas (15 million household plants in China and counting); and, more controversially, the 'biosolids' industry which sells the sludge left over from the waste treatment process as fertilizer for agricultural use.[13] In comparison to the latter option in particular, harvesting nutrient-rich and sterile urine seems to be an attractive prospect.

Yet without wishing to deny the validity or the appeal of these economic, environmental, and public health arguments, it is important to note that they can have a negative impact too, creating an atmosphere of crisis in which expediency trumps all other considerations. In this case, for instance, giving people cash incentives to use their UD toilets clearly is a potential solution to the problem of non-use or incorrect use. It fails, however, to address one of the primary reasons for non-use in the first place: the reality of vastly different standards of provision for rich and poor. That this underlying structural inequity goes unchallenged reveals the limitations of a market-led approach to sanitation reform. While pay-for-pee promises to alter users' toilet habits, it does so within the boundaries of a system over which they have little influence. And while pay-for-pee promises to help achieve South Africa's public health goals, it does little to further its civic ones of building a more equitable post-apartheid society.

---

[13] Both of these developments are brilliantly summarized in Rose George, *The Big Necessity: Adventures in the World of Human Waste* (London: Portobello Books, 2008): 123–44, 167–94. For more on the rebranding efforts of the biosolids lobby, see John Stauber and Sheldon Rampton, *Toxic Sludge is Good for You! Lies, Damn Lies and the Public Relations Industry* (Monroe, USA: Common Courage Press, 1995): 99–122.

25 Moody's, Emotions, and Uncertainty in Finance

Jocelyn Pixley

Uncertainty is the elephant in the shop of Anglo-American finance. There is a studied ignorance or blankness to the unknowable outcomes of money's promises. This may be hope or pretence, because even if the UK–US crisis of 2007 had global effects, and showed the impact of the rise in money markets, these changes did not (entirely) remove old emotion-rules of caution. The rules admit—quite rationally—that financial futures are unknowable. Money production from relationship bank lending is created on opinions, intuition, and emotions of trust and distrust. None of this is 'irrational' since making and accepting promises of payment must look forward. Inevitably, unexpectedly, some futures fall apart; but 'innovative' money production by Wall Street and the City was bound to fall apart (sometime). The deals on global money markets to borrow and create packages of promises—blessed mostly by the credit raters' assessments—had no social possibilities for new wealth creation. Little has changed, despite a crash worse than 1929 and another looming. Signs appeared early into the crash, when Moody's went back to being fickle, for example.

Moody's is an aptly named credit rating agency. It became one of the key handmaidens to the UK–US financial sectors, which place impossible burdens upon credit raters to predict which loan 'product' concocted for sale in markets is creditworthy and which will default. As this chapter shows, raters can be fickle and moody only when deferential to the sector. If not, it attacks. This case is one of many depressing patterns since prudence lessened and trust became fleeting.

Competing financial centres give rise to a variety of collective emotions—anger about other centres, smugness, and superiority. These are worrying emotions to which the biggest centres and global banks easily succumb. Their democratic governments often follow suit, because financial activity can dominate all other economic activity, as in Britain. This essay takes an example in early 2007 of Moody's credit rating agency based in New York City, with global outreach, and its attempted revisions to its bank ratings.

What this example can show is first, that emotions must vary, often rapidly (from unexpected events), and they invariably promote change as much as respond to changes. Second, confidence in mathematical financial models that are, apparently, predictive, rests on a theory of money and social life that these actors depend upon, at least as an excuse. We must worry about emotions in finance because the theories on which predictive models are based find humans and their organizations wanting, not the futility of predictions. 'Incorrect' reactions of clients are dismissed as irrational/emotional residuals; yet the run on the British bank Northern Rock in 2007 was totally rational.

In behaviour, in contrast, these corporations do not act as though money is a neutral commodity for which statistical-probability models could apply and which, in a modernist hope for control over the future, would suppress emotions. Instead, organizations implicitly act on the basis that money is a claim, credit, and promise. In distrust, they use armies of prognosticators—credit raters, accountants, and analysts—to guess the ability of other firms and countries to repay their debts and fulfil promises. Banks used to take the dangers in lending, but increasingly try to transfer dangers of borrowers defaulting. For example, they sold exposure to the performance of bundles of debt securities as though it was a commodity to bet on. The US 'sub-prime' mortgages were one fiasco, ably abetted by London's 'light touch' regulations.

'Buyer beware,' *caveat emptor*, is an emotion-rule of suspicion in the sector, but one that cannot explain why banks try to transfer danger or pay massive insurance costs. Sunk costs in insurance stand as a pure action showing that actors recognize the (unknowable) chances that things can go wrong and that the future cannot be assessed. It also means these dangers are uninsurable. Yet this 'Lender beware' distrust is a mundane organizational phenomenon, with four global accountancy firms that 'count' in assaying any firm's future value, thousands of legal firms, and three global credit rating agencies that cannot be ignored. But what are they saying?

Every actor that hires Moody's, Standard & Poor's (S&P), or Fitch is in a love–hate relationship. If they do not hire one, their competitors and investment firms suspect they have something to hide. When they do, Moody's or S&P is said to have a conflict of interest, in that they are, apparently, bound to sing for their supper, be 'soft', like accountants. But if they were paid by those wanting the ratings, then that is equally liable to manipulation and to demands for the impossible, namely predictions. Neither would that change the way raters fatally 'advise' firms about how to structure financial promises. Even if raters merely published how they would rate which 'bit' of a security as an AAA or junk or D (for default),[1] a bank could comply quite creatively, or hide crucial factors from rating checklists. Raters' excuses for serious 'miscalls', whether justified or not, are that banks lied to, and put 'pressure' on, Moody's, S&P, and Fitch.[2]

---

[1] Jocelyn Pixley, *Emotions in Finance: Distrust and Uncertainty in Global Markets* (Cambridge University Press, 2004: 148–51; <Jocelyn Pixley, *Emotions in Finance: Booms, Busts and Uncertainty>* Second edition, (Cambridge University Press 2012: 248–50; 255–63).

[2] Bank for International Settlements, 'Credit Ratings and Complementary Sources of Credit Quality Information', *Basel Committee on Banking Supervision Working Papers*, No. 3 (August 2000); this was a

Moody's gave a global warning about bank creditworthiness in early 2007. This telling story was later forgotten in the ensuing US–UK bankruptcies, but in 2005 Moody's had announced it would change its rationale for assessing banks by including *a likely bailout* by governments. Why? The unstated problems, apart from criticisms mentioned, were, first, that these agencies were unable to cope with increased responsibility because, in the absence of well-funded regulators, or with 'light touch' regulators, credit raters had, haphazardly, become private quasi-regulators of the entire financial sector. Few pension fund or municipal council managers across the world were permitted to invest in anything without a magical A+. But credit raters have no legitimate state authority to subpoena witnesses, investigate actors under oath, or make accusations of fraud, deception, predatory lending, embezzlement, insider trading, or front running (such as the US Senate investigation: the Levin Report, 2011, or the police).

Second, the new universal or fully integrated banks in Anglo-America such as Citigroup, Macquarie Bank, or Royal Bank of Scotland were 'too big to fail'. They claimed they could trump small competitors because they could afford rising compliance costs; they increasingly engaged in structured finance to sell on debts, and lent (created near money) with light covenants to hedge funds and private-equity firms. Moody's in effect said in 2005 it could not assess banks. The huge array of new 'products', according to a naysayer at the Bank for International Settlements (also in 2005), meant that 'system-wide exposures have become more opaque due to the growing complexity of risk profiles, to the interconnections across different market segments and to the scarcer information about the exposures of some of the new key players'. The positions of banks and their counterparties were unclear. No one could assess the new debt securities (despite requirements that Moody's et al. do so), and no one admitted that collateralized debt obligations (CDOs) for example, some from 'sub-prime' mortgages for people with little to zero income or assets, could not be priced. Banks had outsourced via syndication various bits of the loans—in arms-length relations that they alleged were spreading risk, that is, dangers.

Moreover, senior managements were reticent about lack of knowledge of these mathematical products. Theirs was simple lack of bravery under competition noted in Pixley.[3] Profits initially were excellent for the most risky parcels rated lower by the raters. Everyone purchased this stuff. As long as good performance of people paying mortgage interest brought an income stream to the

---

defence of the increased use of credit raters as quasi-regulators and of their accuracy. Compare this to the horrifying documentation of Moody's as 'deferential' and facing 'pressure' from banks, in the Levin Report, 2011, 307–13: 'Wall Street and the Financial Crisis: Anatomy of a Financial Collapse', Majority and Minority Staff Report, *Permanent Subcommittee on Investigations, United States Senate* (Carl Levin, Chairman; Tom Coburn, Ranking Minority Member), 13 April (pdf download, US Senate).

[3] Jocelyn Pixley, 'Time Orientations and Emotion-Rules in Finance', *Theory and Society* 38, 4 (July 2009): 383–400.

security, valuation could be avoided. In a so-called rising market, claims of a financial product are validated. The repackaging of synthetic securities was so comprehensive that institutional investors—as we now know—were unaware that many contained sub-prime exposures, 'teaser' rates, and defaults for some years. Nor did they know that Goldman Sachs was betting against the same products it aggressively sold.[4]

In March 2007, Moody's published its first, revised ratings taking account of the likelihood of banks being bailed out by governments. Among analysts of major banks, the new ratings created an 'uproar'. Moody's had carefully warned of this new approach to rating banks two years beforehand, but Moody's results shocked the financial field. The press cited, in particular, the fact that Iceland's banks, of all banks, suddenly gained the same AAA ratings as the US Treasury and Exxon Mobil.[5]

It was shocking—during that (brief) moment before spring property sales started in the USA, and the number of institutional doubters was rising. Property prices, on which the mortgage securities depended on to rise, had fallen since 2005 (!). Moody's use of bailouts supposed a dire situation. It suggested the enthusiasm for property debt by Wall Street firms was coming unstuck and that debts could not be sold on indefinitely. Others worried that too many bailouts over 30 years had diluted responsibility for the dangers of uncertainty. When the debt edifice crashes, suddenly lofty bank principles of no state 'interference' reverse. Banks plead for state bailouts; politicians are forced to accede, or risk bank runs and worse. How did Moody's respond to its bank critics?

It was craven. Moody's quickly backed off, saying it would place 'greater emphasis on banks' intrinsic creditworthiness', which was increasingly difficult to uncover. Banks had 'booked' as 'revenue' the *unrealized* mark-to-market 'prices' of debt 'assets' and had extrapolated into the far future their current income streams from issuing stuff like derivatives (as a 1990s CEO of Barclays makes clear about the UK).[6] This was non-existent wealth. At the time, the *Financial Times* calmly explained that 'the saga was sparked by a debate over the degree to which it could be assumed that governments would support banks in a crisis'. S&P said—against its direct competitor—that 'it is impossible to forecast accurately state intervention'.[7]

[4] The Levin Report op. cit. This US Senate report also charges that the CEO of Goldman Sachs misled the inquiry about this 'big short' of 2007.

[5] For a quick summary of Iceland's fallout and the crisis, see *Inside Job*, director Charles Ferguson's 2011 documentary. It also interviews key actors cited here; see also Pixley 2012: 181–5 op. cit.

[6] M. Taylor, 'Innumerate Bankers Were Ripe for a Reckoning', *Financial Times*, 16 December 2007, 11.

[7] J. Glover, 'Moody's Revision Follows Analyst Uproar', *International Herald Tribune*, 12 April 2007; R. Beales, 'Uproar Forces Moody's into U-turn Over Banks' Ratings', *Financial Times*, 2 April 2007, 17; and for following quotes on the issue.

We understood in early 2007 that back in 2005, 'Moody's embarked on a review of bank ratings methodology and concluded that the risk of a large bank default had fallen in recent years because most governments would intervene to prevent this'. What a telling sign! Things had become so precarious to Moody's efforts to rate banks that support—worse, 'total bailout'—was elevated into a rating plus. Here was a warning that a crisis of probabilistic-technical risk models was at hand, but banks poured scorn on Moody's at the time. Critics (e.g. BNP Paribas) suggested that Iceland's banks had liabilities about four times Iceland's GNP, doubting that government's ability to bail out banks. Of course, but why blame Moody's for grasping at straws? Early 2007, no fears were to be permitted. The prospect for Moody's of imminent blame for errors caused *its fear*, and banks greeted the warning as a hated fear. After the run on Northern Rock late 2007, the bankruptcy of the UK–US finance sectors became the horror of 2008. Royal Bank of Scotland's was the largest bailout; the payments system nearly collapsed.

Technical risk management is an emotional bulwark against the idea that money is different from commodities, until promises fail. Claims about future profitable ventures may be upheld in later reckoning, or not. Money looks forward. Banks' purposes are to take the dangers, but the thought of bailouts and interbank lending became 'reassuring' while money market competition pushed banks onto the dangerous grounds they resumed by 2010. Moody's then became fickle in downgrading governments. Yet banks create money by bank loans that are deposited and all used as money; banks loan out deposits (loans) many times over. Loans are bank assets. As well, banks all engage in interbank lending to tide each other over. That lending rate is an expression of trust between banks, which collapsed 2007–8. In 2011 authorities in Europe, Japan, the UK, and the USA investigated whether major banks (Barclays, UBS, Bank of America, etc.) manipulated the interbank rate during those years.[8]

Moody's appeared to suggest in early 2007 that bank practices were frightening since banks confidently assumed they had outsourced dangers (with Moody's approval). Moody's then assumed governments would prevent defaults. It could not assess bank creditworthiness and was frightened.

This example shows some emotions in finance. High finance rarely has national tendencies, and instead competes against firms, states, and key centres. Moody's use of bailouts in assessment was inadmissible just when corporate

---

[8] D. Oakley, 'Crisis Probe Puts LIBOR in Spotlight', *Financial Times*, 16 March 2007, 16; Lex, 'Little White LIBOR', *Financial Times*, 27 March 2011, 18; B. Masters and M. Murphy, 'Barclays at Centre of LIBOR Inquiry', *Financial Times*, 25 March 2011, 1. (LIBOR = London Interbank Offered Rate. In comparison, see Chapter 22 on LIBOR by Donald MacKenzie.) Moody's may have suspected the manipulation subsequently revealed about big global banks. The irony is that 'markets' failed to weed out malfeasance, nor did these private, profit-oriented quasi-regulators, but these trends, blessed by these exact same dubious claims, continue. Global banks are still being saved (including some major European banks), and many populations are paying for mobile capital's irresponsibility.

blame, guilt, double-dealing, and fear were rising over these securitized packages of promises. Although belief that is mostly faith and hope gives a comfort more fleeting than ever, money is an impersonal chain of promises involving emotions of trust and guaranteed by society through our agents, governments. We might worry less about money's emotions if their mundane necessity for caution, not trust in flimsy projections, were admitted. Hope is not a plan.

26 **Credit Rating Agencies**
Timothy J. Sinclair

As he pulled out of his driveway, Bill Rangaroa didn't think too much about the highway he was going to use that morning to commute to his workplace, some 30 miles from his home in Orange County. It was a new highway, but this was America, the land of blacktop. Rangaroa did appreciate the fact that the road was new, smooth, and direct. He didn't like that he had to pay a toll to use the road, though, and it worried him that his neighbour and good friend, Jason McBreslin, who had been laid off from the Northrop factory, visited his family less than he used to because of the new toll. What Rangaroa did not know was that it was no accident the road he was using was now a toll road. The major credit rating agencies, Moody's Investors Service and Standard & Poor's, had helped instigate the toll.

The major American credit rating agencies have been around since the second decade of the twentieth century. Their origins lie in the gathering of statistical information about American railroads and new settlement lands, for investors in New York and Europe, making up for the relatively weak data-gathering capacities of the US federal government at the time. The transition between issuing compendiums of information and actually making judgements about the creditworthiness of debtors occurred between the 1907 financial crisis and the Pujo hearings of 1912. The growth of the bond rating industry subsequently occurred in a number of distinct phases. Up to the 1930s, and the separation of the banking and the securities businesses in the United States with passage of the Glass–Steagall Act of 1933, bond rating was a fledgling activity, carried out as a supplement to the data compendiums. Rating entered a period of rapid growth and consolidation with this legally enforced separation and institutionalization of the securities business. Rating became a standard requirement to sell any issue in the USA after many state governments incorporated rating standards into their prudential rules for investment by pension funds in the early 1930s. A series of defaults by major sovereign borrowers, including Germany, made the bond business largely a US matter from the 1930s to the 1980s, dominated by American blue chip industrial firms and municipalities. The third period of rating development began in the 1980s, as a market in low-rated, high-yield (junk) bonds developed. This market—a feature of the newly released energies of financial globalization—saw many new entrants participate in the capital markets. Today, Moody's and Standard & Poor's issue ratings on approximately $30 trillion worth of debt securities and it can fairly be said that the agencies have become a global form of private market regulation covering municipalities in Russia, corporations in Europe, and national governments around the world.

The rating process is highly confidential. The agencies assemble analytical teams to undertake research, meet with issuers, and prepare a report containing a rating recommendation and rationale. This team presents its view to a rating committee of senior agency officials that makes the final determination in private. Debt ratios are important in the analytical determination. Although raters make comments that support the idea that rating mixes qualitative and quantitative data, producing a fundamentally qualitative result, a judgement, they are very quick to use the cloak of economic and financial analysis and, as it were, hide behind the numbers when it is easier than justifying what may in fact be a difficult judgement to a potentially hostile issuer (see Chapter 25 by Jocelyn Pixley).

Assumptions about how the public world should interact with the private are central to the analytical determinations made in the rating process. Public goods provide an example. Public goods are those for which no market can exist. Any provision of them must be made by government, if they are to be produced at all. However, debates occur about whether any particular good or service is really a public good, or can in some form be provided by the markets or some combination of market and government. These policy debates often revolve not so much around the question of provision as such, but over the price and quantity of supply.

Different resolutions of these conflicts are evident to anyone who has driven on freeways in southern Ontario and western New York. In Ontario, these roads have traditionally been free in the sense that the driver pays no fee for travelling any particular distance. As soon as the same driver crosses the border into the Niagara frontier region of western New York State it is different. Almost immediately the driver is required to pay to use the I-190. When Bill Rangaroa drove his family the several thousand miles of the Trans-Canada Highway from coast to coast during his vacation in the summer of 2010, it was toll free.

Bond rating agencies reinforce a more privatized pattern of supply of social goods in the USA and increasingly elsewhere. Their focus on the financing arrangement reinforces a pattern of provision with heavy emphasis on identifying revenue-producing projects that are not dependent on general revenue sources derived from taxation. From a rater's point of view, this makes sense when taxation sources are perceived to be less reliable than other types of income, because of their vulnerability to political gridlock and recessionary contraction, amongst other things. Dedicating revenue sources has the effect of specifying, reducing, and allocating risk. However, dedicating revenue has implications beyond public finance. Influencing the public/private goods distinction also has consequences for the way in which costs are allocated across the economy and the access that different social groups have to government-provided goods. Financing roads and bridges from tolls rather than taxes rations access by lower-income drivers. This is the direction of policy change affecting Rangaroa and his friends. In December 1998, the 407 ETR (Express Toll Route) opened just north of Toronto.

It would be wrong to suggest that rating agencies always get their way and bring about the sort of policy outcomes they want. Rating agencies have faced major challenges from the rapidity of innovation in financial markets and have been subject to constant review by the US Congress since the Asian financial crisis of 1997–8. This escalated greatly after the Enron scandal of 2001–2 and the global financial crisis that commenced in the summer of 2007. However, as a part of the market infrastructure of globalization, the agencies certainly share important common assumptions about the separation of economic and political life that work well for them. Although it may irk Rangaroa to have to pay a toll, he can't easily blame government for this development. Private regulatory authorities, such as the credit rating agencies, are a powerful feature of globalization.

27 Globalization's Freelancers, Democracy's Decline: Harvard, the Chubais Clan, and US Aid to Russia*

Janine R. Wedel

The reorganizing, post-Cold War world of the late twentieth and early twenty-first centuries opened up opportunities for actors to fulfil functions once reserved for the state.[1] The new circumstances demand that we pay attention to the agency and agendas of the actors who play key roles in issues from foreign to finance policy—roles that can crucially affect outcomes of all kinds. A momentous episode of American foreign policy during the 1990s— US economic aid to Russia via advisers from Harvard University—illustrates the point. In that story, a small group of trans-state actors with their own self-serving agendas significantly shaped relations between nations.

US economic aid to Russia is a case of what I have called 'transactorship', a form of collusion between the representatives of parties on opposite sides. In transactorship, 'transactors'—representatives of the parties (sub-national groups, nations, and/or international organizations) that have been separated, culturally, societally, and perhaps geographically—arise to build bridges among parties. While formally representing different parties, transactors form

---

* For further documentation and analysis, see: Janine R. Wedel, *Collision and Collusion: The Strange Case of Western Aid to Eastern Europe*, 2nd edn (New York: Palgrave, 2001), Chapter 4; and Janine R. Wedel, *Shadow Elite: How the World's New Power Brokers Undermine Democracy, Government, and the Free Market* (New York: Basic Books, 2009), Chapter 5. For articles and court and investigative documents pertaining to the Harvard case, see: <http://janinewedel.info/harvard.html>. For updates, see: Janine R. Wedel, 'For the Shadow Elite Failure Often Guarantees Future Rewards', *The Huffington Post*, 14 January 2010, <http://www.huffingtonpost.com/janine-r-wedel/for-the-shadow-elite-fail_b_422939.html>; and Harry Lewis, 'Larry Summers, Robert Rubin: Will the Harvard Shadow Elite Bankrupt the University and the Country?', *The Huffington Post*, 12 January 2010, <http://www.huffingtonpost.com/harry-r-lewis/larry-summers-robert-rubi_b_419224.html>.

[1] The four transformational developments that led to this sea change are detailed in *Shadow Elite: How the World's New Power Brokers Undermine Democracy, Government, and the Free Market* (New York: Basic Books, 2009).

a small, informal group and work together for mutual gain. Although transactors may genuinely share the stated goals of the parties they represent (and they uphold at least the appearance of that representation in public), they develop additional goals and methods of operating that may, advertently or not, undermine the aims of the parties on whose behalf they ostensibly act.

The US–Russia relationship that developed during the 1990s in the service of US economic policy and economic aid to Russia is an example of how transactors can undermine relationships among nations. Policy prescriptions to rebuild the Russian economy promoted by the United States and the international financial institutions (including radical privatization) are well documented, but the intermediaries and structures through which advice and aid were given are much less familiar. The dynamic and unusual web of transnational relations I encountered in Russia in the early 1990s while researching the politics and social organization of foreign aid to the region piqued my curiosity. I conducted hundreds of interviews over a decade with donor and recipient officials, consultants, investigators, and others who vitally shaped the course of Russian economic reform and US–Russia affairs in the aftermath of the Cold War.

The modus operandi of transactorship has seven distinguishing features. Practised together, they make transactors very effective in achieving their goals and very difficult to counter.

One, an exclusive group. Transactors form an exclusive group made up of a delimited, tiny circle of players from each side who acquire enough authority and influence within each party to push forward the goals of the overall transnational group. In this case, two circles came together: the Harvard team representing the United States and the 'Chubais Clan' representing Russia. The Harvard team consisted of a circle of people affiliated with Harvard University and the Harvard Institute for International Development (hereafter the 'Harvard Institute') and associates.

In the late 1980s, players in what would become Harvard's Russia project had begun to develop contacts with members of what would come to be known as the 'St Petersburg' or 'Chubais' Clan, after Anatoly Chubais from St Petersburg. A 'clan', as Russian social scientists and journalists use the term, is an informal, interlocking elite that places its members strategically in official and private positions to promote their mutual political and economic interests. After the break-up of the Soviet Union and the emergence of Boris Yeltsin as president of Russia, members of the Clan came to occupy key positions in and out of government. Made significant by virtue of his access to hundreds of millions of Western dollars, Chubais became an indispensable aide to Yeltsin.

Across the Atlantic, with high hopes for a favourable relationship with its former Cold War adversary, Congress allocated funds through the US Agency for International Development (USAID) to promote economic reform in Russia. Maintaining that this was so important, and that the 'window of opportunity' to effect change was so narrow, Harvard-connected officials in the Clinton administration saw to it that the Harvard Institute was granted special treatment, including exemption from competition in some USAID awards.

The Chubais–Harvard transactors seized a moment of extraordinary flux to become the designated representatives of their respective parties. The Chubais Clan acquired broad powers, ostensibly to execute complex economic reform, and controlled the ministries responsible for privatization and the economy. The Harvard consultants distinguished themselves from their potential American competitors, including others working in Russia, with their aura of prestige and access to top officials in the Clinton administration (mostly Harvard connected, such as Lawrence Summers at the US Treasury), and thus to considerable foreign aid monies. The Harvard team's social-professional connections aided its members' ability to speak as if they embodied the authority and legitimacy of the United States. The Clan's access to these prominent and powerful networks helped it gain the upper hand vis-à-vis other Russian groups, including reform-minded ones, in the struggle for power.

Working together, the Chubais–Harvard partners presided over hundreds of millions of dollars in loans from the international financial institutions and aid from Western governments. The Chubais Clan sought the fruits of the Western, moneyed world; and the Harvard partners offered access to it. In turn, the Russians offered connections that enabled access to the spoils of an unravelling resource-rich state. The interests of the Harvard team and those of the Chubais Clan became closely aligned, if not indistinguishable.

Two, ideology. Transactors operate in a self-propelling team to pursue their own goals fervently. Their goals are always ideological and political as a group (which may also engage in joint financial or social endeavours). The Harvard and Chubais groups shared a zealous devotion to radical and rapid economic reform, as well as considerable energy, ambition, and youth: most were in their thirties.

Key transactors, including Harvard's two principals—economics professor Andrei Shleifer (project director) and legal adviser Jonathan Hay (on-site director in Moscow)—also pursued joint semi-cloaked financial and business goals. Using inside information and access, they invested in securities, equities, oil and aluminium companies, real estate, and mutual funds.[2] Those investments (which the defendants do not deny)[3] were in many of the same areas in which the

---

[2] For details, see United States District Court, District of Massachusetts, United States of America, Plaintiff, v. The President and Fellows of Harvard College, Andrei Shleifer, Jonathan Hay, Nancy Zimmerman, and Elizabeth Hebert, Defendants, Civil Action No. OOCV11977DPW, 26 September 2000, 30; and for example, Thanassis Cambanis, 'US Seeking $102M from Harvard, Pair', *Boston Globe*, 27 June 2002.

[3] Lawyers for Harvard and the Harvard principals (Andrei Shleifer and Jonathan Hay) argued that the investments made by Shleifer and Hay did not affect most of Harvard's work in Russia (see, for example, Thanassis Cambanis, 'Prosecutors Argue Harvard Owes US at Least $34M in Russia Case', *Boston Globe*, 18 December 2002). Harvard's lawyers argued that Shleifer and Hay did not violate the

Harvard advisers were being paid to provide 'impartial' advice to help develop the Russian economy and a legal and regulatory framework for it. In 2004 a federal judge ruled that Harvard University breached its contract with the US government and that Harvard's two principal players conspired to defraud the government. Lawrence Summers, who served as president of Harvard from 2001 to 2006, helped protect Shleifer.[4] In 2005 the case was settled out of court, with Harvard University and the two principals all paying damages.[5] The same three parties also allegedly defrauded an American mutual funds firm working in Russia. (That case was settled out of court in 2002.[6]) A larger network of related interests also appears to have had a stake in the financial success of the transactors.[7] Of course, transactors' goals, while always in the interest of the group, are not necessarily in the interest of the parties they represent or the public.

Three, mutual gatekeeping. Transactors act as gatekeepers for each other. The Chubais Clan was Harvard's avenue to Russia and to its clout and contacts with the Russian government. In turn, Harvard was the Clan's entrée to the eyes and ears of US policymakers and funds.

---

university's agreements with the US government (see, for example, Thanassis Cambanis, 'US Seeking $102M From Harvard, Pair', *Boston Globe*, 27 June 2002).

[4] See, for instance, this article by a former Harvard dean: Harry Lewis, 'Larry Summers, Robert Rubin: Will the Harvard Shadow Elite Bankrupt the University and the Country?', *The Huffington Post*, 12 January 2010, <http://www.huffingtonpost.com/harry-r-lewis/larry-summers-robert-rubi_b_419224.html>; David McClintick, 'How Harvard Lost Russia', *Institutional Investor Magazine*, 24 January 2006; and court documents and depositions at <http://janinewedel.info/harvardinvestigative.html>.

[5] The settlement provided for the recovery of a total of $30 million, with Harvard agreeing to pay $26.5 million, Shleifer $2 million, and Hay between $1 million and $2 million—the exact amount being contingent upon his earnings over the next decade. With Lawrence Summers president of Harvard, the university was prohibited from paying on behalf of either Shleifer or Hay (Marcella Bombardieri, 'Harvard, teacher, and lawyer to pay US $30 m', *Boston Globe*, 4 August 2005).

[6] Forum Financial Group claimed that Hay and Shleifer used their pull with Russian officials to acquire for the company the rights to the country's first mutual fund. They then compelled its owner to sell his interest in the fund. In 2002, Harvard and its two co-defendants quietly settled with the company, denying any wrongdoing by it or the co-defendants. See, for example, David H. Gellis, 'Harvard in Settlement Talks with Forum', *The Harvard Crimson*, 30 October 2002; and 'Harvard Settles With Mutual Funds Company Over Fraud Allegations', *Associated Press*, 8 November 2002.

[7] For example, the endowment funds of two Ivy League universities, Harvard and Yale, gained access to valuable investments through networks inhabited by the Chubais–Harvard associates. Hedge fund manager Nancy Zimmerman, wife of Harvard's Shleifer, managed a portion of the Yale University endowment ('Yale Connection to Harvard Russian Fraud Case', *Yale Insider*, 10 January 2002). Her investment company traded in short-term Russian government bonds (GKOs) and repatriated the profits to the United States beyond the allowable limits set by Russian law. Zimmerman was ideally placed to time these highly lucrative transactions because her husband advised the Russian official making decisions regarding the government's backing of GKOs ('US Complaint and Jury Trial Demand', 25, 27, in *Yale Insider*). See also Bruce Rubenstein, 'Harvard Accused of Ignoring Russian Aid Scam: Academics Rigged Russian Market', *Corporate Legal Times*, January 2001). Meanwhile, Harvard's endowment, the Harvard Management Company, benefited from some of the most valuable privatization deals to which it gained access through networks occupied by the Chubais–Harvard nexus. The deals were officially closed to foreign investors. (For details and documentation, see Janine R. Wedel, *Collision and Collusion: The Strange Case of Western Aid to Eastern Europe*, 2nd edn (New York: Palgrave, 2001): 160–5.)

Transactors of one party elevate and help to create acceptance of the other party's transactors as the most legitimate representatives of that party. In Russia, the Chubais Clan promoted the Harvard advisers as the best foreign economic experts. In the United States, Harvard touted Chubais as the voice of Russia, and the Chubais team was advertised as the 'Young Reformers'. The Western media built up the Clan's mystique and overlooked other reform-minded groups in Russia. Chubais became the quintessential enlightened Russian in the eyes of many US officials and commentators. By anointing Chubais and his associates as the chosen reformers, Harvard bolstered the Clan's standing as Russia's chief brokers with the West and international financial institutions and as the legitimate representative of that nation. In Russia, however, the Chubais team's primary source of clout was neither ideology nor reform, but its standing with—and ability to attract resources from—the West.

Four, supplanting the state. Transactors set up informal structures in order to circumvent standard government processes, transfigure existing government structures, and operate through their own, alternative authorities. As the Chubais–Harvard transactors secured influence on their respective sides, they created their own informal structures that both used and supplanted the organizations and processes of government.

Both the Russian and US environments, albeit by virtue of different processes and to differing degrees, invited actors to monopolize resources and influence and thereby set the conditions for transactorship to flourish. On the US side, the Harvard Institute, bolstered by its access to key officials in the Clinton administration, managed virtually the entire Russian economic aid portfolio—some $350 million, in addition to the $40 million it received directly. It exerted unusual and 'substantial control of the US assistance program' and also 'served in an oversight role for a substantial portion of the Russian assistance program', according to the US General Accounting Office (GAO, the body that monitors how appropriated monies are spent).[8]

In Russia, amid the political, legal, administrative, economic, institutional, and societal flux that accompanied the collapse of an authoritarian system, clans had wide latitude and were subject to few restraints. The Chubais Clan secured expansive powers. The Chubais–Harvard transactors sidestepped the democratically elected legislature, state agencies, and government auditors. They worked through ambiguous not-quite-state, not-quite-private bodies funded by the Western aid they helped control.

Five, executive power. Transactors are disposed to attain their goals through executive branches of government. They eschew legislative and judicial bodies that might encumber or oppose their activities. The Chubais–Harvard transactors realized many of their goals through top-down decisions in the

---

[8] US General Accounting Office, *Foreign Assistance: Harvard Institute for International Development's Work in Russia and Ukraine* (Washington, DC: GAO, November 1996): 3, 317. The GAO is now called the US Government Accountability Office.

executive branch. In the United States, Harvard largely bypassed the usual public bidding process for foreign aid contracts through waivers to competition endorsed by Harvard associates in the Clinton administration. In Russia, the transactors organized the issuance of many presidential decrees—their chief strategy for legal reform. They also empowered an array of ambiguous, foreign-aid funded, might-be-state, might-be-private entities, or 'flex organizations',[9] that are neither clearly state nor private but claim features of both. These flex organizations supplanted state bodies and made end runs around the democratically elected legislature.

Six, pooling roles as a group. Transactors pool multiple roles and statuses that the group can then use to maximize its opportunities. The Chubais–Harvard transactors strategically placed their members in organizations relevant to achieving their goals, be they government bodies, quasi-state entities (flex organizations), NGOs, companies, or the media. They moved their members around to ensure the group's continued influence and continuity of goals. Individuals who had to resign due to corruption charges or having come under political fire were readily replaced by other members of the group.

Seven, overlapping and shifting roles. Transactors are adept at what I call 'representational juggling'—switching roles and sponsors to achieve their interests. The Chubais–Harvard transactors donned all manner of government, political, business, and university hats to best serve their own objectives, but not necessarily those of the nations they supposedly represented. For example, Jonathan Hay, Harvard's on-site director in Moscow, who ostensibly represented US assistance, also was given signature authority over some privatization decisions of the Russian state by members of the Chubais Clan,[10] many of whom also doubled as officials in the Russian government. In roles that overlapped and at times merged, Hay represented Russia, the United States, his girlfriend's (now wife's) company, and the business interests of himself and his associates.

The flex organizations that the Chubais–Harvard players created, ostensibly to carry out economic reform and largely funded by foreign aid, facilitated the transactors' representational juggling. The flexibility built into flex organizations enables their members to move back and forth between state and private status and to attain advantages in one sphere for use in another. The network of flex organizations that the transactors set up and ran enabled them to bypass otherwise relevant government agencies.

---

[9] See Janine R. Wedel, 'Blurring the State–Private Divide: Flex Organisations and the Decline of Accountability', in *Globalisation, Poverty and Conflict: A Critical Development Reader*, ed. Max Spoor (Dordrecht, Netherlands; Boston: Kluwer Academic Publishers, 2004): 222–31; and Wedel, *Collision and Collusion*, 145–53.

[10] Interview and documents provided to author by Russian Chamber of Accounts auditor Veniamin Sokolov, 31 May 1998.

The overlapping and shifting roles assumed by transactors and the ambiguous entities they empower enables deniability. Hay, for instance, could legitimately argue that he had made decisions 'as a Russian, not an American' because he was occupying multiple roles. Such practices obfuscate conflicts of interest. In conflict of interest, an actor can deny the facts, but not the conflict if the facts are true. But with overlapping and shifting roles, it is not necessarily clear what the conflicts are because roles and organizational boundaries are themselves blurred.

In time, the modus operandi of the Chubais–Harvard transactors, revealed in these seven features, served to undermine the stated aims of US foreign policy and assistance, and when the rouble collapsed so dramatically in 1998 and it became clear that the Chubais–Harvard partnership had failed, there were no viable democratic leaders waiting in the wings to replace it. The era of looking to the West for leadership—and to American advisers—was over. The United States had lost the moral authority with which many Russians had credited it during the Cold War.

28 Of Pits and Screens

Caitlin Zaloom

A financial trader sits at a dealing desk in the City of London surrounded by screens. His eyes are fixed on monitors following numbers that flit across his vision. Some digits indicate prices for financial futures—contracts that banks use to hedge and speculate on changes in interest rates—while others denote the number of competitors from London to Singapore poised to whisk away lucrative deals. But not if the trader can generate newer insights about market patterns or move faster than his rivals. Because the screen is anonymous, the trader will never really know who he is dealing with, just as his own identity is masked. The screen pits the man against the market, simultaneously providing intricate connections and independent action. Without looking away, the trader clicks his mouse: join the bid. Again, a second later: exit the bid; buy the offer. He repeats simple actions like these hundreds of times in a day.

Futures trading has not always looked like this. At the Chicago Board of Trade (CBOT), the first futures exchange in the United States, the trading pit provided an arena for futures dealers for more than 150 years. The architecture of the octagonal pit, precise shouts and hand signals, and pencil-etched trading cards made up the original technologies of derivatives dealing. On the trading floor, dealers skimmed money from a global capital that flowed through voices and bodies. Just as an electronic trader's profits now depend on his skill at reading signals on the screen, floor traders' abilities and successes were entwined with the physical form and social life of the pit.

Examining the everyday work of financial exchange—what traders do when they buy and sell futures contracts—raises questions about the social and technological infrastructure of the global economy. How do traders make themselves into the kind of people who can thrive in the risky and relentless world of global trading? How do the technologies that connect them shape the marketplace and traders' actions in it? In the answers to these questions, global financial markets emerge as construction sites where traders, technology designers, and managers are at work to interweave people, skills, and machines according to market ideals. The contrast between Chicago's trading pits and the electronic trading room of a London firm allows us to see one piece of this assembly. First, to Chicago.[1]

---

[1] The material for this essay draws primarily from my ethnography, *Out of the Pits: Traders and Technology from Chicago to London* (Chicago: University of Chicago Press, 2006).

The CBOT tower looms over La Salle Street, Chicago's main financial artery, a public monument to the power of capital that shelters a very private space: the trading floor, a windowless, grey cavern at the core of the exchange. Once the heart of the global derivatives trade, this chamber now stands almost empty. Yet the visible operations of the once-manic trading pits expose patterns more difficult to see enclosed within a screen.

A busy day in the pits looked something like this. The morning flooded the room with colour. Traders needed to stand out in the crowd, so, before entering the floor, they donned jackets decorated with electric-yellow flies, purple and red confetti, American flags. As they waited for the opening bell, they chatted with neighbours as they took their places inside the tiered steps of the octagonal trading pits, clearing their throats and shaking out their arms like boxers before a fight. Clerks shuttled between desks and the pits, checking headphones, straightening stacks of trading slips. As the clock approached 9.30, a storm-eye hush fell over the floor. Some traders raised their gaze to the clock ticking down the seconds, others meditatively lowered their eyes to breathe in the quiet. A harsh electronic buzz sent the room into a pandemonium of shouting, waving, shoving, and running. In the minutes that followed the opening bell, the clamour and chaos of the pits took over, obscuring a finely tuned physical and social order that guided traders' dealing.

On a closer look, the first thing you learned is that size matters. In a trading pit where hundreds of competitors stood shoulder to shoulder, it helped to be brawny and big. A former football player—tall, wide necked, and muscular—could make a thin man disappear. Men who lacked stature need not quit. They could, instead, bulk up, or even buy prostheses. Chicago traders once employed the building's resident cobbler to add inches of dense black foam to the bottom of their scuffed shoes, creating platforms worthy of a catwalk strut.

Size is more than meets the eye. In the market, a trader could become 'big' by taking on more risks than his peers and increasing the number of contracts he could trade in a single plunge. Small men could become huge forces—true 'market makers', respected and sometimes awed by their competitors—if they traded 'size'.

As traders grew bigger in stature, they also won the right to move up the pit steps. The better the trader, the higher his spot, the closer to the busiest brokers. The better the view (and visibility), the easier it was to nab trades. But getting big wasn't easy. It meant taking lucrative trades away from other, bigger traders, guys whose livelihoods depended on their location, and who were willing to fight for their spot. The social ordering of the trading pit was informal but strictly enforced. Climbing to a high step was daunting, even dangerous. Paul, a big trader, was a small immigrant, and when he started in the pits he lacked the social connections and family ties that led many men into the market. But he had ambition, and he liked to take risks. Big ones. As he became successful, Paul tried to climb to the top step, only to have his neighbours pick him up and throw him off. They kept shoving him down, until one day he literally went over their heads to reach a busy broker, who was impressed with the young trader's bravado. Paul made deals that those above him wouldn't make. And he continued making them, embarrassing his neighbours, until finally he stepped up and they let him stay.

The second thing you learned is that traders, whom economists regard as the ultimate self-interested individuals, succeed by working together. Networks mattered. Families took care of their own. Consider the Cashmans. In the 1950s, one brother of ten siblings made his way from the working-class Irish quarter of Bridgeport to the CBOT. Family savings in hand, George elbowed his way onto the steps of the corn pit, throwing out bids and offers, and raking in cash. But the bounty that George created went far beyond the notes he triumphantly distributed to his siblings. One by one he ushered his brothers downtown until the Cashman family had 13 members working on the CBOT floor—fathers, sons, nephews, and even a few female cousins—dealing in and out of commodity futures just as George did on his first days inside the pit.

Markets are shaped by social life, history, and technology, not by supposedly timeless, universal human instincts such as a profit motive. That's the third thing you learn when you spend time with traders—particularly with trading families like the Cashmans. In the dense social world of the trading pits, the Chicago culture of exchange was palpable. Today, only a thin veneer remains, as traders have left the floor for online connections they access solo from their offices, homes, and garages.

The turn of the twenty-first century marked the end of open outcry trading. Now even the most traditional of dealers have been forced onto trading screens. The CBOT, once the envy of its Chicago neighbour, has been submerged by the Chicago Mercantile Exchange (CME), a competitor that responded more decisively to the possibilities of digital markets to form the CME Group. The CBOT and CME used to draw traders from the neighbourhoods and families of the Windy City; now they thrive upon intricate connections between the Chicago exchange and the traders of world financial centres—London, New York, Tokyo—whose deals flash through the digital ether to the servers of the Midwestern marketplace. Many of these traders sit at desks across the Atlantic in the City of London.

On the corner of Walbrook and Cannon streets stands a bronze sculpture of a trader erected to mark the 15th anniversary of the London financial futures markets. As in Chicago, the London pits were filled with shouting and waving men. But this statue, poised at the site of the erstwhile trading floor, is all that is left of London's financial futures floor traders. Although some London dealers still toil face-to-face trading aluminium, copper, and lead, most dealers do business behind orderly rows of computer screens. At Perkins Silver, they perch high in an office tower with views of London Bridge, the Tate Modern, and the Shard. For these online futures dealers, the digital streams of bids and offers originating in Chicago, Frankfurt, and Singapore are the most critical aspect to their dealing, not their prime London location.

The market in which they operate looks very different from the writhing trading floor. The traders sit in neat rows, each solitary behind a set of monitors, smaller panels bearing newswires and prediction tools hovering around a central screen where the bids and offers for European futures tick up and down.

Many traders who attempted the shift from pit to screen struggled, lending desperation to their trades and curses to the room's atmosphere. The first wave of recruits came directly out of the pits below, equipped with a flair for raw face-to-face competition and an aptitude for skimming cash from the global capital currents that flowed through their hands on paper order slips. The charms of Tony Healy, a leering, overweight former bobby, and Freddy, whose trading style was likened to the slashing of *Nightmare on Elm Street*'s undead villain, didn't provide traction in the online markets.

One source of trouble for the ex-floor dealers is the simplicity and anonymity of the trading screen. The software for online trading erases interpersonal interactions from the screen-based markets. The digital interface that online traders confront is made up of simply printed bold black numbers. Surrounding the typeface figures are blue or red boxes distinguishing bid from offer. This is a far cry from the visual chaos and aggressive intensity of the open outcry floor. The traders, however, could not do without clues to their competitors' strategies and proclivities; they watch the patterns of shifting numbers to finger sneaky and stiff Frankfurt opponents and skilful, audacious Chicago adversaries. Although German and American dealers are most likely hidden behind the digits, the competition discussed among the London traders is imaginary.

It is easy to forget that online work is physical work too, but the hunched shoulders and neck rubbing that are constant features of the digital dealing room are reminders that sitting, staring, and button pressing are activities of the flesh. In particular—as any office staffer knows—computer work takes a toll on the hands. Sometimes such distress even endangers profits. The physical world has its revenge on the disembodied marketplace with the involuntary twitch that the traders call 'fat-fingering'. Digital trading centres on spotting a profit opportunity and swiftly clicking the mouse to enter orders. The trouble comes when the synapses misfire and the tools at the end of the hand—the fingers—don't follow directions. While the left button safely joins the bid, the right button, the danger key only millimetres away, sells directly into the bid or buys the offer, establishing an opposite position. Even the more experienced traders sometimes suffer from lapses in manual control. 'Ahh, I've fat-fingered it,' unlucky traders cry with disgust, desperately trying to get out of their positions before losses mount.

Back across the Atlantic in Chicago, online dealing rooms are now established enough to have their own monikers—prop shops and arcades—and these electronic trading centres have repopulated Chicago's markets. Now that the trading floors have emptied, dealers (still overwhelmingly male) haunt office towers around Chicago, trading with competitors that appear only as numbers that flash across their screens.

As in London, Chicago's former floor traders are not the best equipped to make the transition. The technological change from pit to screen is accompanied by a social one. Trained in economic modelling, equipped with ergonomic chairs to unleash mind from body, and outfitted with controls that reconnect intention and finger action, the newest breed of traders joystick their way through more and more complex transactions. One marketplace observer summarized the scene: 'It's getting really *Revenge of the Nerds* around here,' he lamented.

These mathematical sophisticates develop algorithms to draw profit from market patterns. Taking advantage of the lush informational environment, these programs uncover patterns that no human could compute alone, and with unique speed. When they spot an opportunity, these programs whip buy and sell orders through exchanges' matching systems. Floor traders used to exploit their competitors' risk-taking ticks, profiting from trades that anticipated these habits. Now algorithms seek out signals that belie other traders' intentions, identifying markers of their rivals' systems and buying or selling ahead of a detected order.[2]

Sometimes algorithms can also move markets in extreme ways. On 6 May 2010, market indexes fell nearly 6 per cent in five minutes. And recovered 20 minutes later. The 'flash crash' was triggered by a program executing an extensive sale of stock index futures, instruments tied to actual corporate stocks and their markets. Other algorithms reacted to plummeting values by shutting down, accelerating the drop. Prices began to move back toward their previous levels only when the CME applied an electronic brake, also designed to trip under these particular conditions. Human traders then had five seconds to step in to consider their positions, and decide to buy or sell outside the constraints of their automated avatars. The flash crash raises a set of questions that applies far beyond the realm of money dealing: What is the relationship between humans and their machines in the global electronic world? What are the responsibilities that accrue to these new, hybrid systems? Profit's pursuers will certainly fashion inventions with ever greater speed and acuity, and unleash their unintended consequences.

Globalization's protagonists quest for efficient and fast connection that can never be fully realized. For financial traders, this means constantly honing their aptitudes to the demands of the newest market technologies. The shift from

---

[2] Donald MacKenzie, 'How to Make Money in Microseconds', *London Review of Books* 33, 10 (2011): 16–18.

the trading pit to the dealing screen reconfigured the suite of human abilities and technologies that compose the global financial markets. Today, the nerds and their algorithms have the edge, but they too will soon seem insufficient. The idea that the market can be more connected, faster, and more efficient propels new projects forward. The next arrangements are emerging today.

Part IV

Media, Consumption, and Leisure

29 Cigarette Packages: The Big Red Chevron and the 282 Little Kids

*Franck Cochoy**

'Open the door for me, children, your dear little mother has come home, and has brought every one of you something back from the forest with her.' The little kids cried: 'First show us your paws that we may know if you are our dear little mother.' Then he put his paws in through the window and when the kids saw that they were white, they believed that all he said was true, and opened the door. But who should come in but the wolf!

Jacob and Wilhelm Grimm, *Grimm's Fairy Tales*[1]

A few years ago, the economic anthropologist Alain Tarrius issued a very nice book entitled *Globalization Bottom-up*.[2] Tarrius proposed to move away from the conception of globalization as a 'top-down' process imposed by global finance, state decision, and other worldwide strategies. He rather preferred to focus on another aspect of globalization: that of the down-to-earth materialistic and 'subterranean' moves and exchanges carried on by a transnational web of migrants. He showed that these informal activities heavily contribute to shape the contours of our global economy and society. Despite its precedence, actor-network theory helps to move one step further, in refusing the idea of a 'bottom' and a 'top': for Latour, the dichotomy between micro and macro

* This paper draws on an empirical study conducted with Jacques Crave and is an adapted, shortened, and updated version of an article first published in French as Franck Cochoy, Loïc Le Daniel, and Jacques Crave, 'Le grand chevron rouge et les 282 petits chevreaux, ou l'emballage des cigarettes comme dispositif de captation', *Terrains et travaux* 11 (2006): 179–201. I benefited from the support of the Center for Retailing, Handels Business School and University of Gothenburg while writing this paper.
[1] Project Gutenberg, 'The Poject Gutenberg EBook of Grimm's Fairy Tales, by the Brothers Grimm', <http://www.gutenberg.org/files/2591/2591.txt>.
[2] Alain Tarrius, *La mondialisation par le bas: Les nouveaux nomads de l'économie souterraine* (Paris: Balland, 2002).

levels is both meaningless and misleading; the social world is completely 'flat', he says: it is local everywhere.[3] As a consequence, one does not have to study how the local world influences the global one, or the other way round. Rather, one has to describe the devices and objects that enable people (either in state or corporate accounting centres or in ordinary places) to 'localize' or 'globalize' their activities.[4] In this chapter, I want to focus on the particular case of cigarette packs to show how packaging and other 'market things' work along this pattern. Indeed, packaging is both a globalization tool (by means of it, a company may reiterate the same messages all over the world) and a localization device (by means of it, a consumer may identify the product, handle it, carry it or store it, and invent her own identity, behaviour, or fate). I propose to explore this ambivalent power of packaging through an examination of cigarette packs.

It is very easy to adopt the stance of critique as far as cigarette packs are concerned, and describe them as a 'global evil'. Let's take a Marlboro pack. On it, we find a logo, in the form of this big red chevron on a white background. This logo carries us toward the universe of car races, with their values of virility, speed, heroism. On the same pack, we find also a crown with two reared-up horses above a war motto borrowed from Julius Caesar (*veni, vidi, vici*—Philip Morris attacking Gauloises!). In short, chevrons, horses, and Caesar would converge either to deceive us if we are not cautious enough, or to convince us to unveil packaging as a global 'smokescreen' that tries to present as a positive identity what is rather a poison. But a smokescreen may well hide another. Indeed, in focusing our attention on the symbolic global dimension of packaging,[5] critique prevents us to take the other mentions into account. Now, these latter mentions are even more powerful than the ones critique puts forward. The packaging of the same cigarette pack helps us to see what is invisible; it teaches us to look at the product in legal terms; it places us in front of a 'parliament of qualities'.[6] Moreover, its power may be not that of global symbolic worldwide 'marketing' but that of a very local 'market thing' with which consumers interact on a daily and local basis.

In a sense, packaging helps the global social order to move at the local level. We all know that the law relies, curiously enough, on a completely unrealistic

---

[3] Bruno Latour, *We Have Never Been Modern*, trans. Catherine Porter (Cambridge, MA: Harvard University Press, 1993).

[4] Bruno Latour, 'On Interobjectivity', *Mind, Culture and Activity* 3, 4 (1996): 228–45.

[5] Naomi Klein, *No Logo: Taking Aim at the Brand Bullies* (New York: Picador, 2000).

[6] The next two paragraphs sum up and combine arguments presented earlier in: Franck Cochoy, 'Is the Modern Consumer a Buridan's Donkey? Product Packaging and Consumer Choice', in *Elusive Consumption*, ed. Karin Ekström and Helene Brembeck (Oxford: Berg, 2004): 205–27; Franck Cochoy and Catherine Grandclément-Chaffy, 'Publicizing Goldilocks' Choice at the Supermarket: The Political Work of Product Packs, Carts and Talk', in *Making Things Public: Atmospheres of Democracy*, ed. Bruno Latour and Peter Weibel (Cambridge, MA: MIT Press, 2005): 646–59.

maxim: 'Nobody is taught to ignore the law.' Now, thanks to packaging, this maxim lost part of its unrealistic character in order to progressively come into the realm of reality. When today we are reading on our cigarette pack 'Smoking can seriously damage your health' or 'Smoking causes cancer', we guess that there is little chance for the producer to be the actual author of such messages![7] But the sanitary warnings are the latest and most obvious traces of law on packaging. Indications such as content, weight, product composition, far from being the natural expression of products are, on the contrary, the result of a patient work of codification that was largely enforced by the law. As a consequence and through the continuous display of compulsory information, packaging progressively succeeded first to present the letter of the law on a daily basis, and second to convey new ways to evaluate the products. These ways were more analytic and rational; they were as much oriented towards origin and production matters as focused on the product and its consumption. All things considered, by showing the law directly on the product, packaging succeeded in changing the identity of the consumer herself. Thanks to packaging, the consumer became able to take into account new choice criteria, to question the quality of products, to express her point of view and defend her interest, thus sharing a new global consumer identity, beyond her previous entanglement in a peculiar local market.

The branding of the law on the product's body highlights another transformation of the market relationship that occurred by means of packaging. Indeed, packaging transforms the old bilateral relationship between the vendor and the consumer into a multilateral exchange. The packaging appears as a place of expression, a genuine tribune, a forum where a plurality of entities can simultaneously argue to gain the consumer's attention. Thanks to packaging, indeed, the vendor is no more the only actor talking to the client: the vendor must now share his right to speak with the producer, who praises his product and brand in his own way, but also with the sanitary authorities who propose an alternative vision of the product.

Packaging works as a parliament, where sanitary authorities tend to win over a larger and larger majority. On the front side of a Marlboro pack, we may see a large 'Smoking kills' framed by a large black frame. On the back, another black frame even bigger than the first one indicates: 'Smoking clogs the arteries and causes heart attacks and strokes.' On the left side, a third black frame gives the list of some repulsive information: 'Tar: 10 mg; Nicotine: 0.8 mg, Carbon monoxide: 10 mg'... a list which is completed in very small characters, out of the frame, with the global composition of the product: 'Tobacco: 85.0 per cent, Cig. Paper: 6.0 per cent, texturizing and flavor agents, preservatives: 9

---

[7] Nevertheless, one is better to beware of this kind of suspicion (as one has to be vigilant with vigilance matters! See below.).

per cent'. On the right side, another sanitary message warns the young public: 'For adults only'.

Where do these messages come from? From public authorities, of course! Packaging obviously performs the law; it transfers the legal way to look at things toward the public; it plays on adults' bad consciences and worries; it attempts to prevent young people succumbing to the vices that slowly poison their parents' bodies. But is it that certain? Yes and no. Yes, since packaging obviously conveys the law: it teaches the law to everyone without their having to learn it; it gives a miraculous validity to the legal utopia of 'Nobody is taught to ignore the law' (see above). But no, packaging does not completely perform the law, or rather, the law it performs, in spite of appearances, is not always the true one! If packaging does so well its duty of performing the words that are delegated to it, why would not other actors benefit from this performative power of packaging to blur its discourse? Among all the legal messages displayed at the surface of cigarette packs there is an intruder! Which one? The difficulty of the puzzle shows the cleverness of the trick. The intruder is the last element of the messages we quoted; it is 'For adults only'.

This message presents all the appearances of a sanitary warning; its phrasing and meaning are very close to the 14 other allegations listed in the European legislation on tobacco (see for instance: 'Protect children: don't make them breathe your smoke'; 'Smoking when pregnant harms your baby'; etc.). And yet, this message does not come from any official document, neither European nor American, but from a voluntary undertaking of the manufacturer...that in fact is older than the new European directive! Anne Degroux does not hesitate to argue that the 'For adults only' message is a true forgery of the law.[8] But how can we explain that it is a tobacco manufacturer who decides to promote toward the younger consumers a protective warning curiously ignored by the law, without signalling on the pack the different origin of it? 'For adults only', the manufacturer says. Duly noted. Philip Morris is a company that proclaims its corporate social responsibility in displaying its worry about protecting youth. More precisely, Philip Morris's published marketing code reads:

Philip Morris International is totally committed to marketing of its cigarettes responsibly. In that connection, Philip Morris does not market its cigarettes to minors. It is firmly of the belief that cigarettes should be consumed by adult smokers. Accordingly, all advertising and promotions should be directed towards adult smokers only, and not towards minors.[9]

---

[8] Anne Degroux, 'Un exemple de contrefaçon: la communication de l'industrie du tabac vers les jeunes', *Tabac Actualités* 14 (April 2001): 3.

[9] University of California, San Francisco, 'Philip Morris International, Cigarette Marketing Code', Legacy Tobacco Documents Library, <http://legacy.library.ucsf.edu:8080/k/l/v/klv39e00/Sklv39e00.pdf>.

It is in line with this code that from November 1999 the company took the initiative to write on any cigarette pack it produces and sells inside the European Union one of the following warnings: 'For adults only'; 'Wait until you're 18 before smoking'. But this cigarette maker who talks like a regulator whispering 'Minors must not smoke' puts us in mind of the wolf with the paw covered with flour. Do not the younger ones have the desire to turn their backs on childhood and become adults? Is not transgression the means for such a move? Teenagers, like the little kids in the fairy tale, should be all the more cautious about wishing to grow up and become mature, in line with the example they believe to be that of adults.[10]

In order to assess the impact of this strategy, we submitted the bets made at the surface of packs to the test of a quantitative survey oriented toward a privileged target: the pupils of a secondary school for vocational training in Toulouse, France.[11] The initial intent of the questionnaire was, of course, to check if our young kids were capable of spotting the paw of the big red chevron whitened in the flour of law and corporate social responsibility.

If the little kids know rather well what is a goat and what is a wolf, are they able to surely recognize one and the other species at the tone of their voice or at the sight of their paw? The answer of the survey was striking. When they are faced with the message 'For adults only', our kids predominantly attributed it to the law. Even more surprising, 67.8 per cent of the smokers (among which 62.2 per cent saw this message) are the victims of this confusion, while 52.9 per cent of the non-smokers only (among which 36.4 per cent saw the message) are unable to distinguish the voluntary message from a legal warning. This result is all the more remarkable that the mention 'For adults only' is more attributed to the law than true legal warnings, such as 'Smoking may reduce the blood flow and causes impotence' (67.8 per cent against 46.7 per cent). The lesson is very clear: everything happens as if the discernment of the little kids was inversely proportional to their commitment; the more the offered paw concerns them, the more their own life is at stake, the less capable they are of identifying what is behind the whiteness of the paw.

It is now time to draw the moral of this story. If the 'big red chevron' connotes the 'big bad wolf', it also resonates with the figure of Little *Red* Riding Hood,[12] even though there are strong differences between the two! At the intersection of the two characters, we propose the idea of a 'big red riding hood', which we think suits the present case better. When kindly claiming that minors must not smoke, our big red riding hood obviously behaves as a chaperone (the equivalent of 'hood in French'), that is: like a person who

---

[10] Stanton A. Glantz, 'Editorial: Preventing Tobacco Use—The Youth Access Trap', *American Journal of Public Health* 86, 2 (February 1996): 156–8.

[11] We conducted the survey in January 2004; we had 282 respondents.

[12] The homophony is stronger in French: 'grand chevron rouge/petit chaperon rouge'.

is in charge of keeping an eye on the younger ones in order to prevent them from getting into mischief! But the chaperone, this time in its English sense of hood, is big: it's also a large cap able to shelter a wolf. This wolf, in order to attract/divert (*capter* in French)[13] the little kids, may have dipped his paw in the words of the law; he may also have bet both on the double propensity of youngsters to identify with adults and (for this purpose) to break the bans the same adults want to impose on them. As we see, following market devices such as packaging is a good way to account for localization and globalization practices. Instead of starting from 'global forces' or 'local peculiarities' in order to understand the worldwide economy, one does better to look at those particular mediating 'market things' which shape both.

---

[13] Franck Cochoy, 'A Brief Theory of the "Captation" of the Public: Understanding the Market with Little Red Riding Hood', *Theory, Culture & Society* 24, 7–8 (December 2007): 213–33.

30 Collecting and Consumption in the Era of eBay

Rebecca M. Ellis

Chatted with [Tom]. He's been buying Catalin[1] [radio] sets from the US because the exchange rate is good, using eBay...He brought these in from the US double-boxed, with a declared insurance value of only $100, to cut down on the Customs and Excise surcharges. He has previously been bringing in container loads of radios...but says he is unlikely to do this again...Previously, American sets in the UK were quite unusual, but now people can see and bring them in from eBay, especially the smaller sets. People prefer to bring in the sets themselves, on an individual basis.

> Participant observation diary, 2 May 2004, National Vintage Communications Fair, Birmingham, UK

eBay, the e-commerce auction giant, has often been constructed in terms reminiscent of Cairncross's *The Death of Distance*,[2] where the traditional inefficiencies of person-to-person trading such as geographical fragmentation and imperfect knowledge[3] could be offset through computer-mediated communication. Indeed, eBay has been regarded as a classic leveller of economic playing fields,[4] improving the market liquidity for collectables, which are more problematic to exchange than uniform consumer items.[5] eBay, as a

---

[1] Catalin is a trademark name for a particular form of thermosetting plastic or Bakelite material. It is highly desired by collectors because of its bright colours, potential for marbled patterns, and high-gloss finish.

[2] Frances Cairncross, *The Death of Distance: How the Communications Revolution Will Change Our Lives* (London: Orion Business Books, 1997).

[3] David Bunnell and Richard A. Luecke, *The eBay Phenomenon: Business Secrets Behind the World's Hottest Internet Company* (New York: John Wiley and Sons, 2000).

[4] Adam Cohen, *The Perfect Store: Inside eBay* (London: Judy Piatkus, 2002).

[5] Alina M. Chircu and Robert J. Kauffman, 'Strategies for Internet Middlemen in the Intermediation/ Disintermediation/Reintermediation Cycle', *Electronic Markets* 9, 2 (2001): 109–17.

digital intermediary, has created 'new ways in which products are bought and sold',[6] facilitating the global peer-to-peer exchange of goods. It was estimated in 2003 that one-third of eBay sales were international.[7] However, eBay's globalization of exchange does not alone work through the creation of a more perfect market. The 'virtual' objects on the screen do not just materialize in your home: eBay's 'globalization of things' is fundamentally underpinned by social, economic, and logistical infrastructures. Indeed, considerable work and knowledge are required to optimally negotiate the infrastructural layers and complexities involved in an international eBay purchase.[8] In the diary entry above, it is evident that Tom's globalized radio collecting practices are in part determined by the exchange rate, being able to pay in dollars from the UK, and negotiating customs values. The diary excerpt notes people are bringing in small sets from the USA themselves, revealing a key logistical infrastructure that underpins eBay's globalization. The fact that they are small shows the greater potential for the globalized exchange of objects easy to transport.

So, what are the motivations behind buying internationally on eBay that have allowed globalized consumption to flourish there? What infrastructures are needed to facilitate such globalization? Are there any problems with these infrastructures and any backlash against globalized consumption? Does eBay facilitate consumption at other scales? This entry is based on fieldwork on eBay carried out over a two-year period from 2004 to 2006 in the UK, which included focus groups with UK eBay users and interviews with collectors.[9] It should be noted that the 2004–6 period of the fieldwork was comparatively a 'golden age' of consuming globally on eBay for UK buyers, due to the favourable exchange rate of the pound against the US dollar towards the end of 2006.[10] Since the global financial crisis, the pound has fallen, inevitably choking off consumption from countries where the British pound does not go far, and highlighting the importance of one particular infrastructure—the financial system.

---

[6] Matthew Zook, *The Geography of the Internet Industry: Venture Capital, Dot-coms, and Local Knowledge* (Oxford: Blackwell, 2005): 142.

[7] Joseph T. Sinclair and Ron Ubels, *eBay Global the Smart Way* (New York: AMACOM, 2004).

[8] For more discussion of the work and immaterial labour performed on eBay, see Rebecca M. Ellis and Anna Haywood, 'Virtual radiophile (163*): eBay and the Changing Collecting Practices of the UK Vintage Radio Community', in *Everyday eBay: Culture, Collecting and Desire*, ed. Ken Hillis, Michael Petit, and Nathan Scott Epley (New York, Routledge, 2006): 45–61; and Jon Lillie, 'Immaterial Labor in the eBay Community: The Work of Consumption in the "Network Society"', same volume: 91–105.

[9] This fieldwork was conducted during 2004–6 with funding from the UK Economic and Social Research Council (ESRC), from the large grant award RES-000-23-0433 *Virtually Second-Hand: Internet Auction Sites as Spaces of Knowledge Performance*, which is gratefully acknowledged.

[10] See 'Exchange rate graph for GBP in USD', ChipManx Ltd, <http://www.exchangerategraph.co.uk/>.

The 'eBayeur Internationale': Motivations for Globalized Consumption

Buyers are taking advantage of eBay's peer-to-peer global market. The research reveals their primary motivations are to acquire items not available in their own country such as American vintage radios or rare CDs: using eBay to search out rarity, the 'exotic', and 'difference' from the mainstream. Before the Internet, in the case of vintage radios, it was relatively difficult for collectors to acquire sets from abroad without specialist dealers. The advent of eBay has allowed peer-to-peer exchange; buyers can purchase directly from sellers regardless of national borders. Globalized collecting has increased in tandem with greater individual knowledge about what is available, fostered by studying the specifics of eBay's many listings available to a worldwide audience.

Utilizing global price differentials is also part of both collectables and new goods purchasing on eBay, which increases the global flow of goods. Certain small items in the study, such as memory cards, were imported from the USA due to their being much cheaper than the UK retail price. UK radio collectors also took advantage of eBay's increasingly global reach though bidding strategically on different eBay national sites, exploiting newly opened eBay markets to hunt out bargains:

[I]nitially things on New Zealand eBay were quite a reasonable price, and I bought a couple of nice little radios there at…stupid money. But the prices have gone up as…[the market's] got bigger and bigger.

Gregory, radio collector

Such opportunities lessened as increasing numbers of eBay 'lookers' searched these new territories, pushing up prices. Finally, globalized collecting was fuelled by the repatriation of objects: for example, collectors bought rare British items at lower prices from the rest of the world, because their rarity was not appreciated elsewhere. Buying from abroad is often another way to exploit eBay's 'unknown' or 'unknowing' spaces to get 'the bargain'.

The Infrastructures and 'Real Networks' of eBay

In the diary entry at the beginning of this chapter, Tom must trust that the item exists, the seller will post it on payment and that s/he will double-box the item against breakage. eBay trust is based on the buyer's scrutiny of both the item page and the seller's feedback profile from things s/he has previously sold, based on eBay's proprietary feedback system: one of the best known and earliest on the Internet.[11] eBay thus relies on a particular social infrastructure, as promoted by the design of the eBay system, for the smooth operation of global exchange. Other 'physical' infrastructures are also vitally important, and the logistical infrastructures to support eBay's global exchange of goods have become increasingly sophisticated over time.

A geographical perspective on the e-commerce literature has been important in dispelling notions of a new 'weightless economy' in an information age,[12] reinstating the importance of logistics for grounded, non-ethereal commodities,[13] and the importance of information systems infrastructure in redefining geographies through the exploitation of minute differences between places.[14] The growth of eBay into the world's largest e-commerce site has been built on the back of three 'real networks': de facto by Internet infrastructure, but also by financial and delivery infrastructures. eBay has made problems with existing 'real networks' more highly visible in the context of global exchange. For example, in relation to financial infrastructures, banks are seen by our research participants as expensive and highly administrative for foreign exchange (forex) transactions. So eBay transactions tend not to use banks in favour of online payment site PayPal, which has the armchair convenience that eBayers are used to.[15] eBayers often do not bid where forex payments are needed and PayPal is not an option. PayPal was in part created in 1999 as a response to economic globalization and the growing international interconnections of people.[16]

The materiality of eBay items crucially intersects with delivery infrastructures. Certain items are inherently more subject to globalized exchange than others due to their size and weight: for example, stamps circulate globally much less problematically than vintage radios. Indeed, the eBay market for items tends to segment into the local, national, and global. Local items are too big for the delivery infrastructure, and require 'pick-up only'. This non-globalizing

   [11] Paul Resnick and Richard Zeckhauser, 'Trust Among Strangers in Internet Transactions: Empirical Analysis of eBay's Reputation System' (paper presented at E-Commerce Conference, Bodega Bay, California, 2001), <http://www.si.umich.edu/~presnick/papers/ebayNBER/RZNBERBodegaBay.pdf>.
   [12] Danny Quah, 'The Weightless Economy in Growth', *The Business Economist* 30, 1 (1999): 40–53.
   [13] Andrew J. Murphy, '(Re)solving Space and Time: Fulfilment Issues in Online Grocery Retailing', *Environment and Planning A* 35, 7 (2003): 1173–200; Andrew J. Murphy, 'The Web, the Grocer and the City: On the (In)visibility of Grounded Virtual Retail Capital' (Working Papers in Services, Space, Society; Birmingham, UK: University of Birmingham School of Geography, Earth and Environmental Sciences, 2003).
   [14] Feng Li, Jason Whalley, and Howard Williams, 'Between Physical and Electronic Spaces: The Implications for Organisations in the Networked Economy', *Environment and Planning A* 33, 4 (2001): 699–716.
   [15] See Eric M. Jackson, *The PayPal Wars: Battles with eBay, the Media, the Mafia and the Rest of the Planet Earth* (Los Angeles: World Ahead, 2004). PayPal is especially convenient since it was bought by eBay in 2002 and integrated into the eBay site.
   [16] Ibid.

side to eBay may stimulate previously geographically fragmented local markets with better visibility than using the neighbourhood car boot sale or local paper; however, local pick-up often limits the item's market and price potential, particularly for specialist goods. 'National' items have affordable postage within the UK and tend to stay there, as they are too expensive to send abroad compared to their value. But the most mobile global items have the biggest market and price potential. In terms of the global distribution of goods, there has been the cherry-picking of distribution services by sellers through the perspective of a 'chain of accountability'. eBay sellers increasingly require traceability in the global exchange of goods to prove they sent the item and to guard against credit-card chargebacks for non-delivery. Global exchange involves negotiating the risks of global distribution, often through more costly services imposed by sellers. Some sellers will not ship to particular countries because the receiving country's postal system does not provide a traceable system, or because of perceptions of a high incidence of fraud in those countries. Overall, the global flow of eBay goods generally follows paths of financial convenience, a low ratio of postage cost to value, and minimized risk.

There are many problems with globalized distribution networks; for example, fragile items get broken in transit. The level of customs duty and VAT to pay on items is also highly variable between countries: in Canada the threshold is $20 whilst in the USA it is $200.[17] The combination of irreplaceable collectables being broken in the post and the 'shock' of customs charges has meant that some UK eBayers have retreated to buying within national borders. Some have even restricted themselves to eBay buying within driving distance, because of their sadness over the breakage of rare collectables.

eBay obeys the capitalist imperative of globalizing through expansion to new national markets, but intertwines both the global and local, globalization and glocalization processes. As Ritzer states, grobalization involves the imposition on the local of products or ways of doing things by agents such as corporations. Glocalization is concerned with the interpenetration of global and local, with globalization creating a variety of reactions in different areas of the world.[18] The eBay system, as a website and way of buying and selling with certain rules and protocols, involves grobalization: albeit deployed in local languages and with slight differences between country websites. However, in terms of promoting flows of objects at the global or local level, the eBay system supports all geographic scales, with the ability for worldwide searching, national searching, or even searching at incremental distances from a given postcode. This allows consumers and collectors to bring the local more to the fore. The collectors retreating from the global, mostly those with expensive and difficult-to-post items, used the grobalized eBay system to offset the

[17] Sinclair and Ubels, *eBay Global the Smart Way*.
[18] George Ritzer, *The Globalization of Nothing 2* (Thousand Oaks: Pine Forge, 2007).

geographical fragmentation and related imperfect knowledge of offline consumption: to better access and know local markets. Part of eBay's phenomenal success, then, is to be both grobalizing and glocalizing; giving eBay users the flexibility of consuming locally, globally, or both simultaneously, depending on the nature of the objects being exchanged and their grounded experience within the interweaving infrastructures which facilitate global exchange.

31 The Interaction Order of Auctions of Fine Art and Antiques

Christian Heath

It is increasingly argued that we are witnessing significant change in the market for fine art and antiques. It has long been an international market drawing in buyers from Europe, North America, and the Far East, but over the past decade or so it has undergone a significant transformation. New buyers and new types of buyer have entered the market, from countries that hitherto had little representation at sales. In a recent sale of Impressionist, Modern, and Contemporary Art, Christie's reported buyers from 55 different countries had registered to bid and declared that this was now a truly global and international market. Indeed, press coverage of recent sales of art and antiques have increasingly emphasized the ways in which the leading auction houses are transforming how they market and 'choreograph' sales to encompass the new, international rich, the 'ultra-high net-worth individuals', and facilitate bidding from their growing 'global network of private clients, many of whom have never bid at auction before'. These initiatives are seen as a historic development in the art market, and, notwithstanding the financial crisis of 2008, serve to generate record prices for particular works and substantial revenue for the auction houses. This 'global' market fuelled by the wealth of a new rich from countries that in some cases were hitherto largely unrepresented at sales is having a profound impact on both the value and the types of works of art and antique that are sold at auction.

The auction is the primary vehicle through which the value of works of art and antiques is established and provides the resources for the identification of market trends and investment. Long before the emergence of formally based price indexes such as Art Market Trends, Gerald Reitlinger powerfully demonstrated how sales by auction could be used to identify historical changes in the economics of taste.[1] Record prices encourage goods onto the market and in turn enable private buyers and the trade to revalue their stock and collections. The

[1] Gerald Reitlinger, *The Economics of Taste. The Rise and Fall of Picture Prices 1760–1960* (New York: Hacker Art Books, 1982).

auction provides a mechanism to enable buyers, new and old, private and trade, to compete for particular goods, irrespective of their country of origin or the nation in which they are currently based. The auction houses may indeed market particular sales in particular countries or contact particular buyers, but even then it is recognized that there is little correspondence between the location of buyers and the nations they may be said to represent. Indeed, you are as likely to find the new Russian buyer in North London or Los Angeles as in Moscow or St Petersburg and it is not unusual to find, for example, Chinese or Indian collectors bidding at sales in Paris, New York, or even provincial salerooms in England. The ability of the auction to construct or reconstruct the value of goods, to use Charles Smith's term,[2] to legitimatize price and the transfer of the ownership, derives from the neutrality of the process—that it is, and is seen to be, an organization that constitutes the value of goods irrespective of the characteristics of the buyer, the seller, or the 'agent', namely the auction house. In other words, whilst an array of market developments may have a profound impact on the price that particular goods achieve at auction, the characteristics of buyers, including, for example, their country of origin, who they are or represent, their particular interests and the like, are rendered necessarily irrelevant within the auction itself. The ability of the auction to constitute the price of goods of 'uncertain' value and to create stable prices and market 'trends' and the like derives from the ways in which it provides a neutral mechanism that juxtaposes demand and orders competition without regard to the characteristics of the buyer and without favour towards particular individuals or institutions. The global, irrespective of an array of 'global' characteristics, is woven into an organization that serves to render the participation of individuals equivalent, differentiated only with regard to their interest in particular goods and their ability to pay.

Irrespective of the value of goods, marketing of particular sales, the national or international profile of the saleroom, auctions consist of brief episodes of social interaction in which the sale of goods occurs on the strike of a hammer. An auction may involve the sale of up to 500 lots in one day with each transaction taking little more than 30 seconds or less. These repeated episodes of social interaction serve to underpin the valuation and exchange of goods worth billions of pounds each year and provide the foundation to 'global' participation in the market for fine art and antiques. It is within these brief moments of interaction that trust and legitimacy in price and exchange are established and through these episodes of interaction that market trends, investment patterns, and the changing nature of the global economy for art and antiques are accomplished and identified.[3]

---

[2] Charles W. Smith, *Auctions: The Social Construction of Value* (Berkeley: University of California Press, 1989).

[3] See Christian Heath, *The Dynamics of Auction: Social Interaction and the Sale of Fine Art and Antiques* (Cambridge: Cambridge University Press, 2013).

Figure 31.1 The auctioneer acknowledges a bid in the room

Consider the sale of Lot 45 at an evening sale of Old Master pictures at Christie's in London, a rare picture by Ludovico Carracci, entitled 'Salamacis and Hermaphroditus', that had been 'languishing unnoticed' in the store-rooms of Knowle House, Kent for many years. It generated significant interest with buyers from Britain, North America, mainland Europe, and the Far East participating in the sale of the lot. With a relatively conservative estimate, of £800,000 to £1,200,000, the auctioneer started bidding at £550,000 and follow-ing intense competition the painting finally sold for £6,600,000, a record price for the artist. Such was the interest in the sale that Christie's opened adjoining rooms to enable more than a couple of hundred people to attend the sale and arranged for more than 30 staff to take bids from prospective buyers via the telephone. The pictures in Figure 31.1 show a section of the principal saleroom and one of the two banks of telephones manned by sale assistants.

The auctioneer has to deploy an organization, in concert and collaboration with prospective buyers and saleroom assistants, that enables the value and exchange of goods to be rapidly and legitimately established where he may have little idea who is willing to bid, still less the price they are prepared to pay. Consider the following abbreviated extracts from the sale. Bidders included leading London dealers, private buyers from mainland Europe and the Far

East, and a representative for a major North American gallery. To simplify and anonymize their participation, bidders are indicated in the order in which they join the bidding (for buyers in the room B1, B2, and so forth, and for sale assistants SA1, SA2).

A: Lot 45: the Ludovico Carracci (5.5)
    A: Five hundred and fifty thousand pounds (.) to open it
        (0.8) [B1] Six hundred thousand pounds, I see already
        (0.3) [B2]
    A: Six hundred and fifty thousand
        (.) [B1]
    A: Seven hundred thousand
        (0.4) [B2]
    A: At seven hundred and fifty thousand
        (0.4) [B1]
    A: At eight hundred thousand pounds:
        (0.6) (B2 withdraws) [SA1]
    A: Eight hundred and fifty thousand
        (0.3) [B1]
    A: Nine hundred thousand
        (2.6) [SA1]
    A: Nine hundred and fifty thousand
        (0.3) [B1]
        …
    A: Five million eight hundred thousand
        (2.7) [B4]
    A: Six million pounds
        (0.4) [B5]
    A: Six million two hundred thousand
        (4.4) [B4]
    A: Six million four hundred thousand
        (0.2) [B5]
    A: Six million six hundred thousand
        [B4 withdraws]
    A: Last chance. Six million six hundred thousand pounds
        (0.3)
        {Knock}
    A: Sold

At its most basic we can see that the auction relies upon a turn organization in which the auctioneer selectively allocates opportunities to bid to particular participants. Rather than take successive bids from numerous buyers who may be willing to show their hand, the auctioneer establishes what is known as a 'run': he takes bids from two bidders and no more than two bidders at any one time. When one buyer declines the opportunity to bid, the auctioneer looks for a new bidder, and if successful, establishes a new run—taking first come, first served. When only one willing party remains, then the goods are sold—if they have reached their reserve. Moreover, irrespective of the price that buyers may have in mind, the auctioneer escalates the price of goods through a series of standard increments that remain stable throughout successive phases of the sale of the lot. The incremental structure serves to project a series of prices that not only allow all those present to know what it will take to advance the price of the lot, but enable the auctioneer to invite bids during the course of the run by simply announcing the current price and turning towards the underbidder. In other words, the run coupled with the standard incremental structure enables the price of goods to be rapidly and transparently escalated through the most economic of actions, head nods, gestures, and the like, serving to advance the price, until only one bidder remains. Moreover, the bodily orientation and gestures of the auctioneer that accompany successive invitations to bid within the course of a run serve to display to all those present, for all practical purposes, who has the bid and the current price of the lot.

The social and interactional organization of sales by auction enables auctioneers to transparently and systematically escalate the price of goods and with the fall of the hammer transfer their ownership to the highest bidder. It structures and constrains the selective participation of buyers and potential buyers and allows standardized contributions to be rapidly juxtaposed to enable the price and thereby the value of goods to be determined. Demand is expressed and organized in and through this socio-interactional arrangement. The arrangement restricts and formalizes the participation of buyers and potential buyers and primarily constitutes their identity with regard to the prices that they are prepared to bid. The auctioneer elicits, juxtaposes, and displays the source of bids, without regard to an array of potential characteristics of the buyers or the potential buyers; the interactional arrangement is specifically designed to accomplish and display the 'neutrality' of the process, that bids are actual bids on behalf of participants who are constituted solely with regard to their interest in and ability to purchase particular lots. Preserving the anonymity of the participants, whilst simultaneously rendering their contributions visible, is an integral feature of the accomplished legitimacy and trust in the process; that no personal interest, on behalf of the vendor, buyers, or auctioneer is favoured or seen to be favoured within the constitution of the price and sale of goods. As a social arrangement, therefore, the 'global' and the various associated characteristics of the participants are rendered irrelevant within the organization of the sale of particular lots. The international transformation of the market, 'global' participation in sales of fine art and antiques, and the changing nature of taste, are made at home and constituted in and through a routine interactional organization that has changed little over many centuries.

Over the last decade or so we have witnessed the emergence of the Internet auction (see Chapter 30 by Rebecca M. Ellis) and it is delightful to find that a social organization that has enabled the valuation and exchange of goods since at least Roman times has informed the foundation of one of the most successful developments in e-commerce. There were fears that the introduction of the Internet auction might replace more traditional sales of art and antiques and yet notwithstanding the financial crisis of 2008 the turnover of the leading national and international houses has significantly increased. Indeed, far from undermining the traditional auction, the Internet has enabled new forms of engagement in sales and facilitated the participation of buyers whose access to goods and sales was hitherto limited by geographical and even political constraints. A significant proportion of sales of art and antiques now enable remote buyers to participate in live auctions, not only by listening to and viewing the event, but also by placing bids in real time on particular lots in competition with those in the room and others bidding via the telephone or Internet. Like any other contribution, Internet bids are integrated within the ordinary, interactional structure of the auction, and remote bidders set against others in the emerging competition that arises within runs. As with other contributions, the ways in which auctioneers elicit, acknowledge, and reveal bids serve to rapidly escalate the price of goods and establish the occasioned legitimacy of each and every contribution. We find therefore a social interactional arrangement enabling the contingent participation of buyers wheresoever they may be located, irrespective of nationality, identity, and other personal characteristics and making an advanced technology at home within a social organization that has informed the sale of art and antiques since the fifteenth century if not earlier.

32 Intellectual Property

Adrian Johns

Economic globalization has coincided with an information revolution. Unlike the previous heyday of trade liberalization in the late nineteenth century, the core of today's global marketplace is the enclosure, transfer, and use of intellectual products rather than industrial raw materials, or even manufactures. As a result, intellectual property (IP) has become a central element in many of the debates that globalization has engendered. Antagonists claim that the integrity of countless local cultures is at stake; protagonists that the future of knowledge itself depends on strong intellectual property protections. A recent example of the latter was the reaction of European stem-cell researchers to a judicial ruling against patenting the products of such research: the decision, they declared, would 'wipe out the European biotechnology industry in this area'. Globalization has no more controversial aspect than this.[1]

Protagonists of IP and globalization usually focus in the first instance on legal doctrines and philosophical principles, which they explain in the slightly abstracted terms of cost–benefit analysis. Critics tend to zero in on the tensions between such doctrines and principles, on the one hand, and local or indigenous customs (often evoked as if they existed time out of mind), on the other. The conventions of everyday life in which intellectual property operates as a mundane, relatively uncontentious reality are understood far less well. And we know particularly little about how the points of contact between these two domains of law and custom are actively shaped by participants. They are worth attending to, because their definition can be quite an unpredictable, fraught process, beyond exhaustive prior stipulation by either side. It must be managed, with hard work, knowledge, and skill. What guides the creation, conduct, and resolution of contests over globalized IP? How are the borders drawn between what are inchoately distinct, but may *become* clearly opposed, realms? Answering that question leads us into some of the most well-trodden battlegrounds of modern politics: authority, privacy, and accountability.

---

[1] A. Smith (Chair, Wellcome Trust Centre for Stem Cell Research, Cambridge University), quoted in S. Connor, 'Ruling on Stem-Cell Research May Spell End of Research in Europe', *Independent*, 28 April 2011. The literature on these debates is far too large to cite here, but foundational to it were James Boyle, *Shamans, Software, and Spleens: Law and the Construction of the Information Society* (Cambridge, MA: Harvard University Press, 1996) and Lawrence Lessig, *Free Culture: How Big Media Uses Technology and the Law to Lock Down Culture and Control Creativity* (New York: Free Press, 2004).

Intellectual *What*?

What is intellectual property, anyway? It is a legal concept above all, and a rather recent one. It dates from the mid nineteenth century, in fact, when it came into existence in the context of struggles over patent and copyright law in Europe. Earlier, patents, copyrights, and maker's marks had of course existed, but they had fallen under discrete bodies of law. It was in the eighteenth century that the first arguments for some common underlying principle first appeared. The period 1730–75 saw a prolonged series of 'literary property' debates in Britain that culminated in the establishment of 'copyright' as a limited-term, statutory privilege. In those debates, proponents of such a limited concept began to try to persuade their antagonists by urging that literary invention was comparable to mechanical. In the wake of Newton's achievements, and in the midst of the first Industrial Revolution, the relation between natural knowledge, 'mechanic art' (technology), and literary genius was controversial as never before. Paradoxical as it seems to us, it was the upholders of a genuine property in literary works (that is, of a natural and 'perpetual' right) who had to deny that literary and mechanical invention were in any way the same. This was because nobody seriously entertained the idea that the projector of a mechanical invention gained a natural property in its principles: an invention was protected, if at all, only by the artificial expedient of a patent. Those who maintained that literary works were not properly objects of property, on the other hand, insisted that the two realms did share a common trait. But that trait was political-economic, not natural. A temporary, artificial provision such as a patent was therefore appropriate for both.[2]

Only after this exchange had reached its climax did it become plausible to maintain that there might indeed be some shared character underpinning mechanical and literary invention. What began as a rather negative entity was soon transformed into something more. The rise of Romanticism saw the 'creativity' (a word and concept imported from Germany) of both 'inventors' and poets hailed at new levels. To counter continuing attacks from laissez-faire antagonists who decried it as monopolistic, the concept of 'intellectual property' was at length coined to articulate a positive attribute that these two realms—now defined as kinds of creativity—shared. By the end of the nineteenth century a profession had come into existence of intellectual property lawyers. And in that first age of globalization, extending to the outbreak of the

---

[2] This argument is laid out in full in my *Piracy: The Intellectual Property Wars from Gutenberg to Gates* (Chicago: University of Chicago Press, 2009). For the literary property debates, meanwhile, see Mark Rose, *Authors and Owners: The Invention of Copyright* (Cambridge, MA: Harvard University Press, 1993), and Ronan Deazley, *On the Origin of the Right to Copy: Charting the Movement of Copyright Law in Eighteenth-Century Britain (1695–1775)* (Oxford: Hart, 2004). On patenting, see Christine MacLeod, *Inventing the Industrial Revolution: The English Patent System, 1660–1800* (Cambridge: Cambridge University Press, 1988).

First World War, this 'property' was extended across the world. In the great conventions of Berne and Paris, international standards were set up in copyright and patents respectively.[3]

The Intellectual Property Defence Industry

One very important aspect of this process was that intellectual property came into being at the moment when policing in the major Western powers was being brought under the purview of professional, public forces organized by the state. International IP partook only partially of this change. That has had lasting consequences. It means that points of contact are often encountered under the aegis of a largely unknown enterprise that has become one of the most influential of the globalized economy: an intellectual property defence industry.

Policing IP has always been difficult. Transgressions are hard to detect, and even in the early days transgressors often laid claim to a Robin Hood-like populist appeal that made their pursuit politically tricky. Copyright infringements were civil offences, not criminal ones, so the public police were in any case not charged with detecting them. Moreover, it was hard to pin down exactly when a *proprietor*'s practices became excessive, too. There might well be advantages to the owner of a patent or copyright to pursue deterrence, detection, and reprisal privately and beyond the scope of the strict legal right. Even before 1900 owners were doing this: agricultural seed companies employed private detective companies to seek out farmers who seemed to be growing types of apple, say, that they claimed to be proprietary. In point of fact there was no legal basis for such 'intellectual property', but cease-and-desist letters could be awfully persuasive. In the United Kingdom, the music publishers of the Edwardian period recruited their own private force of 'commandos' to pursue music pirates across the land. Again, the legal basis for their actions was virtually non-existent.[4]

Today's intellectual property defence industry has grown from such foundations by making a business out of protecting whatever could be claimed to

---

[3] See, for example, Lionel Bently and Brad Sherman, *The Making of Modern Intellectual Property Law: The British Experience, 1760–1911* (Cambridge: Cambridge University Press, 1999), and Moureen Coulter, *Property in Ideas: The Patent Question in Mid-Victorian Britain* (Kirksville: Thomas Jefferson University Press, 1991). For the internationalization process, the standard source is Sam Ricketson and Jane C. Ginsburg, *International Copyright and Neighbouring Rights: The Berne Convention and Beyond* (2 vols. Oxford: Oxford University Press, 2006).

[4] Daniel J. Kevles, 'Patents, Protections, and Privileges: Intellectual Property Protection in Animals and Plants', *Isis* 98, 2 (June 2007): 323–31; Adrian Johns, 'Pop Music Pirate Hunters', *Daedalus* 131, 2 (Spring 2002): 67–77.

be an object of such property. It deals in prophylactic measures (anti-pirating technologies, lobbying for new laws, etc) as well as in pursuit and detection. International in scope, it acts across frontiers that impede any merely national police force. Because it measures the extent and impact of 'piracy', what society 'knows' about that phenomenon (its economic and social impact, in particular) is largely a product of this industry. Think, for example, of all those statistics reported in the media from about 1980 onwards of the costs to US industry of software piracy. All came from this industry: a General Accounting Office report recently concluded that *none* of the statistics has a traceable and solid social-scientific foundation.[5]

Like the activities it targets, the IP defence industry is an enterprise notable for mediating between areas of policy, law, culture, and everyday practice. It acts at very local levels (sending agents onto farmsteads to search for 'seed pirates', recruiting Hong Kong boy scouts to monitor the Internet for file sharers, and the like).[6] Its scope extends from the sub-microscopic to the universal. Its means are technological, administrative, epistemic, and political. It shares tactics with the pirates themselves, launching denial of service attacks on pirate venues such as The Pirate Bay—which prompt counter-attacks of exactly the same kind from activist groups such as Anonymous. Arguably, the customs of intellectual property in practice owe as much to this industry as to laws themselves. Indeed, far from its being a mere instrument of laws, laws have come into existence in the wake of its efforts, to respond to the knowledge it creates and the problems it faces. When IP becomes the focus of conflicts, as it often does, it is very often as a result of this industry and its enemies.

Tactics and Technologies

The global IP police have three remarkable aspects, to do with politics, social character, and technology. First, they assume *access* rights that a modern, social-democratic society finds questionable in a public force—and that societies have in fact found objectionable since at least the early modern period.[7]

---

[5] 'Intellectual Property: Observations on Efforts to Quantify the Economic Effects of Counterfeit and Pirated Goods' (GAO 10-423, 12 April 2010); Keith E. Marcus, *Intellectual Property Rights in the Global Economy* (Washington: Institute for International Economics, 2000): 100–2. This point could be extended back in time to the decades (beginning around the First World War) when the US publishing industry lobbied against book piracy in Asian countries.

[6] *New York Times*, 18 July 2006, B3.

[7] A comparison may be made with the antagonism to the general warrants sometimes advanced in early modern England as a strategy against pirated and seditious books. John Locke objected to them as a 'mark of Slavery', and Londoners claimed them to be violations of Magna Carta. See Adrian Johns, *The Nature of the Book: Print and Knowledge in the Making* (Chicago: University of Chicago Press, 1998): 131–2.

Because they are global, no mere nation state can match these. Second, they are *hybrid* institutions, made up of both private firms and public bodies, as well as subunits within major corporations (of which DirecTV's 'Office of Signal Integrity' is a good example). Their personnel are often ex-police or ex-FBI officials, and they frequently bring police officers along on their missions. It becomes very hard to tease public from private. And, third, they embrace an old dream: the dream of a reliable anti-pirate *technology*.[8] Proposals for some foolproof device to make piracy either impossible or, as a second best, trackable have arisen ever since the invention of printing in the fifteenth century (think of watermarks, or authors such as Sterne signing every copy of their novels). But such devices have proliferated with digital networks. Technologies of anti-piracy are all about spatial extension—they are means to enact IP rules at a distance—and today's systems are in that sense merely the latest in a long history of technologies of space. Almost all realms of IP now have their versions of such devices: RFID systems in pharmaceuticals; genetic markers in GMOs; DRM encoding in e-books; and so on.

No anti-pirate technology has ever realized the more extravagant promises of its supporters. In all probability, none could ever do so, without the kind of dispersed enforcement infrastructure that this chapter is suggesting is so important. In practice, its adoption means a commitment to a never-ending code race with an amorphous army of rivals—not just hackers and pirates, but interested amateurs too. Since anti-pirate devices tend to ride roughshod over valued but non-algorithmic freedoms such as fair use, they excite substantial resentment in expert communities, and so their rivals never lack for recruits. Anti-pirate technologies generate conflict, in short, because they do what they are designed to: they extend the constraints of rule-based systems into fuzzier (but morally valued) realms of conduct.

In conclusion, it can be said that the IP defence industry—like the piracy it confronts—has become a globalized, hybrid institution par excellence. Its reach extends across the globe, supervening national and legislative boundaries. Yet it also acts at the most mundane of levels—those of the street seller of pirate DVDs in provincial Chinese towns, the Internet user in rural England, or the farmer in Ohio. Insofar as the principles and doctrines of IP law 'cause' political problems, they do so, very often, by being put into action by this industry. And its three outstanding characteristics mean that it raises once again some of the classic problems of Western political history. Its repeated use of strategies that test the legal limits of privacy and access poses the question of citizenship: how do we negotiate clashing rights in a liberal society? Its autonomy, hybridity, and internationalism invoke the question of accountability: who

---

[8] For this theme in the realm of digital media see Tarleton Gillespie, *Wired Shut: Copyright and the Shape of Digital Culture* (Cambridge, MA: MIT Press, 2007).

guards the guards? And its embrace of technology not only poses the question of freedom, but aspires to answer that question at a distance: when are forms of moral conduct legitimately subsumable to (others') rules? These are some of the real reasons why intellectual property in practice is among the most controversial aspects of globalization today.

33 The Curvature of Global Brand Space

Celia Lury

In what has come to be considered a classic article, Theodore Levitt identified in 1985 the arrival of a 'new commercial reality—the emergence of global markets'. Levitt argued that 'Global competition spells the end of domestic territoriality, no matter how diminutive the territory may be' and proposed that differences in national and regional customer preferences were disappearing:

The global corporation operates with resolute constancy—at low relative cost—as if the entire world (or major regions of it) were a single entity; it sells the same things in the same way everywhere.[1]

He continued, 'The earth is round, but for most purposes it's sensible to treat it as flat. Space is curved, but not much for everyday life here on earth.' Since then brand managers have busily set about developing a huge number of global, global–local, and glocal brand development strategies, resulting in a 'flat', albeit multi-tiered global–local market structure in most countries. What this means in practice is that many brands are global in the sense that 'A youth in India is using a Nokia mobile phone, a Lenovo laptop, pulls out a Coke can from a Whirlpool refrigerator, [is] wearing Levi jeans, hops on to a Honda motor cycle wearing Rayban subglasses', while many products, including those of Nokia, Lenovo, and Coca-Cola are often exclusive to a specific territory.[2] But building global brands by flattening the earth does not exhaust the diversity of ways in which brands are now made to make and mark space.

Take the ways in which brand interfaces make visible some (or none) of the multiple places in which the production of branded products occurs. Consider Swatch. A key component of the logo of this brand is its insistent self-identification in relation to Switzerland. Swatch watches display not only the name Swatch (itself a contraction of Swiss and watch) and the Swiss flag, but also the description 'Swiss' on their faces. In addition, much of the promotional literature accompanying Swatch products makes reference to the

---

[1] T. Levitt, 'The Globalisation of Markets', *Harvard Business Review* (May–June 1983): 39.

[2] Ambi M. G. Parameswaran, 'Revisiting Prof Levitt', *Business Line* (2 October 2008). Also available through <http://www.thehindubusinessline.com/todays-paper/tp-brandline/revisiting-prof-levitt/article1112114.ece>.

Swiss-ness of the Swatch ethos. Such references are widely held to have the effect of strengthening consumer perceptions of trust in the quality of Swatch products in what is perceived to be a risky global commercial environment. Thus Nicolas Hayek, one-time Swatch CEO, has gone so far as to claim that the buyers of Swatch are 'sympathetic' to the Swiss: 'We're nice people from a small country. We have nice mountains and clear water,' he says. Indeed, he attributes the company's success to the fact that:

the most important element of the Swatch message is the hardest for others to copy. Ultimately, we are not just offering watches. We are offering our personal culture.[3]

Here Hayek describes the way in which a place of origin may be deliberately designed into the interface of a brand. This design activity enables Swatch products to sell in many local markets by securing the trust of (some) consumers, providing a guarantee of quality, by tying the brand to an origin (a 'personal culture', 'nice mountains and clear water'). This guarantee is indirectly linked to the use of Swiss labour in the manufacture of Swatch products. This is one way of saying that Swatch may be seen as not only a national but also a territorial brand, but perhaps it might be more accurate to say that Swatch is part of a re-territorialization of global flows in the context of a competitive global economy.

In contrast, the Nike brand is less clearly tied to a territorialized place of origin, or indeed, to an origin at all. To some extent, the physical location of the company itself (in Portland, Oregon), dedicated retail outlets such as Niketowns, and sports events sponsored by the company may serve as such an origin. Certainly this perception of the flagship retail outlets, Niketowns, as origins is encouraged not only by the highly charged design of the stores, but also by the range of stock available, typically including all the most recent models of shoes, clothes, and accessories. Alongside such dedicated sites, however, Nike presents itself as original in relation to the almost endless multiplicity of the sites of its products' uses through the brand's elevation (and ownership) of an ethos of competition, determination, and individuality. Just Do It is the brand injunction, and in this 'doing' multiple origins for the brand are brought into being. Of course, it is possible to argue that a culture of competition, determination, and individuality is the national culture of the USA and in this sense there is a parallel between the interfaces of the Nike and Swatch brands. But what makes the interface of the Nike brand so distinctive is that it appears as if there is no need to locate this ethos within territorial boundaries in order to secure its ownership or claim its effects. The brand is not tied to any specific organization or distribution of the production process in this regard: it is de-territorializing.

---

[3] W. Taylor, 'Message and Muscle: An Interview with Swatch Titan Nicolas Hayek', *Harvard Business Review* (March-April 1993): 103.

In each case, as part of such processes of re- or de-territorializing, the brands of Swatch and Nike are *marks of flow* or *shifters*; that is, they are 'markers of the edge between the aesthetic space of an image or text and the institutional space of a regime of value which frames and organizes aesthetic space'.[4] Simmel, at the beginning of the twentieth century, already described the liquidity of money; 'Money is nothing but the vehicle for a movement in which everything else that is not in motion is completely extinguished.'[5] And since then numerous other commentators have described the movements of not only money, but also people, ideas, and risks in terms of flows.[6] But it is Raymond Williams, the cultural critic, who provides one of the most precise and helpful elaborations of how flow can make both re-territorializing and de-territorializing spaces, and does so on the basis of his experience of watching television.[7]

For Williams, flow is *a serial assembly of units characterized by speed, variability, and the miscellaneous*. In developing this definition, he notes the historical decline of the use of intervals between programmes in broadcasting, or rather, he draws attention to a fundamental re-evaluation of the interval.[8] In the early days of broadcasting on radio, for example, there would be intervals of complete silence between programmes. But now, no longer dividing discrete programmes, no longer an interruption or silence, the interval makes a sequence (or sequential progression, one after another) of programmes (or products) into a series or flow. Think here of the role of 'idents', that is, the logos of broadcasting companies, which not only fill the previous gaps or silences between programmes but also sometimes now persist through programmes in the corner of the screen, making possible multiple associations within and across programmes. The true temporality in broadcasting, Williams argues, is not the published sequence of programme items, but flow, that is, the multiple series of differently associated units, some larger and some smaller than the individual programme that is divided and connected by intervals marked with idents. The argument proposed here is that in marketing practices, the logo is similarly able to secure the recognition of the brand *as a constantly shifting set or series of products, services, or experiences*. It marks an open set of relations between products in which those relations may be given a fixed and prior origin, or an origin that is produced again and again, and in doing so, does not so

---

[4] J. Frow, 'Signature and Brand', in *High-Pop: Making Culture into Popular Entertainment*, ed. J. Collins (Malden and Oxford: Blackwell, 2002): 71.

[5] G. Simmel, *The Philosophy of* Money (London: Routledge, 1990): 511.

[6] A. Appadurai, 'Disjuncture and Difference in the Global Cultural Economy', in *The Phantom Public Sphere*, ed. B. Robbins (Minneapolis: University of Minnesota Press, 1996): 269–97; S. Lash and J. Urry, *Economics of Sign and Space* (London: Sage, 1994); R. Shields, 'Flow', *Space and* Culture 1 (1997): 1–5; K. Knorr Cetina, 'From Pipes to Scopes: The Flow Architecture of Financial Markets', in *The Technological Economy*, ed. A. Barry and D. Slater (London: Routledge, 2003).

[7] R. Williams, *Television: Technology as Cultural Form* (London: Routledge, 1993).

[8] Ibid.

much make products move within flat space as organize a space of movement, introducing curves in space into a flat world.

More than this, the use of the brand logo to divide and connect not only produces a sequence of products as a series but also gives the movement of the products they mark the intensive qualities that are produced in the associative relations of specific kinds of series: the intervals may be organized so to produce branded products as the same (the guarantee of consistent quality), or as different, as authentic, fashionable, collectable, or new. Indeed, in most cases brands do not have a single temporality, but rather coordinate multiple temporalities. So, for example, Swatch is organized through the temporalities of both fashion and collecting, marking the design and release of products in relation to seasons, the participation of artists and limited editions. Nike too facilitates collection, but most obviously positions itself beyond the remorseless, collectively imposed changes required by fashion to produce events. In coordinating the series of products that comprise the brand in these different ways, then, logos are markers of *the multiple temporalities* that contribute to the flows of disjuncture and difference that characterize the global economy.[9]

In these and other cases, the spatio-temporal performativity of the brand is a consequence of its organization as an object of the sciences of the artificial, an artefact in the sense outlined by the economist Herbert Simon.[10] Simon argues that an artefact can be thought of as a meeting point—an interface—'between an "inner" environment, the substance and organization of the artefact itself, and an "outer" environment, the surroundings in which it operates'. For Simon design is understood as the organization of an (artificial) entity in terms of an intended purpose, that is, it is the organization of an interface or surface of communication between inner and outer environments. As he says, the 'description of an artifice in terms of its organization and functioning—its interface between inner and outer environments—is a major objective of invention and design activity'.[11] Alternatively put, it is the operation of the interface which means that branding introduces 'the environment into the battle between the adversaries',[12] that is, the organization of the brand as artefact introduces the space of consumption, of markets and everyday life, into the competitive battle between firms.

In this analysis of the space-making capacities of brands outlined above, the surface of the brand is a meeting point or interface for the exchange and communication of information between 'producers' and 'consumers', the economy, and everyday life. But this interface is not to be found in a single place; rather,

---

[9] Appadurai, 'Disjuncture and Difference'.

[10] H. A. Simon, *The Sciences of the Artificial* (Cambridge, MA: MIT Press, 1981).

[11] Ibid., 13.

[12] P. Sloterdijk, *Terror from the Air*, trans. A. Patton and S. Corcoran (Cambridge, MA: MIT Press, 2009): 13.

it appears as if it is drawn in different dimensions in space: on products them-selves; on the surface of wrappings of packaging and publicity; on screens—televisions, computers, cinemas; and within public and private sites—window displays, advertising hoardings, dedicated retail outlets, theme parks and resorts, public spaces, and so on. Indeed, what such examples suggest—to par-aphrase Etienne Balibar[13]—is that the border between economy and society organized by the brand is not at the edge of the economy but in the middle. And in this regard, it seems as if countries and cities may already be organizing to face the challenges of a globalizing world in ways that are remarkably similar to the brand. Sandro Mezzadra and Brett Neilson have revealingly described the operation of the border as a method in precisely this way.[14] Using the examples of body-shop agencies, detention centres, and points-based migra-tion systems, they describe some of the highly technocratic means by which the legal statuses of subjects inhabiting the same political space are multiplied and stratified. In these examples, they are able to show that the operation of the border as a method both closes a labour market and allows a selective openness, a filtering and selection of labour in ways that facilitate processes of production and labour exploitation in terms of what Mezzadra and Neilson call *differential inclusion*.[15] Just as they describe this topological space in terms of the multiplication of labour and differential inclusion, so too might the 'col-laboration' or co-creation of brand users in branding activities be described.[16] The multiple spaces of the brand that are brought into being by the operation of an interface is not a flattened earth but a curved space, produced by the operation of borders in *n* dimensions. Boundaries are drawn in many places in ways that multiply relations with the environment of everyday life while still preserving the internal organization of the brand so that it may be identified and owned. In these and other ways, brands transform and make dynamic the space of value creation, making it possible to build abstract curves of calcula-tion, flows of fashion, collection, and event, newness, and sameness, disjunc-ture and difference, right here on earth.

---

[13] Etienne Balibar, in *We, the People of Europe? Reflections on Transnational Citizenship* (Princeton, NJ; Princeton University Press, 2004), proposes that borders do not exist only 'at the edge of the territory, marking the point where it ends' but 'have been transported into the middle of political space' (109).

[14] S. Mezzadra and B. Neilson, 'Border as Method, or, the Multiplication of Labor', *Transversal* 03 (2008), <http://eipcp.net/transversal/0608/mezzadraneilson/en>.

[15] In a reversed formulation, they also note the argument made by Saskia Sassen that a full under-standing of the tensions and conflicts that mark contemporary citizenship can emerge only from an analysis that works from the edges of the space of citizenship and not from one that operates from the legal plenitude of its centre. That political subject who is 'unauthorized yet recognized' (294) or, in other words, the illegal migrant, is not only subject to exclusion but also becomes a key actor in reshap-ing, contesting, and redefining the borders of citizenship. See ibid.

[16] As Sloterdijk would have it, the brand is a case of 'the new rule according to which the extension of the work to the work's environment is itself to be received as a form of work' (*Terror from the Air*, 76).

34 Bollywood

Vijay Mishra

When a descriptor becomes more than that which it immediately signifies—the concept that it refers to directly—we begin to feel that there is something special, something rather unusual about it. Such a descriptor is 'Bollywood', which now has an entry in even the hallowed *Oxford English Dictionary* (2005): 'a name of the Indian popular film industry, based in Bombay. Origin 1970s. Blend of Bombay and Hollywood'. That the word refers to a film industry situated in Mumbai/Bombay (the slash here is important because without the city's colonial name, 'Bollywood' cannot be generated), a city located in a dangerously chauvinistic Marathi-speaking state, is a pre-given. But how do we address its current circulation as 'Bollywood industry', 'Bollywood bonanza', 'Bollywood fix', 'Bollywood shakedown', 'Bollywood romp', 'Bollywood breaks', 'Bollywood dancing', 'Bollywood calendar', 'Bollywood experience', 'Bollywood culture', 'Bollyweb', and so on? Bollywood is clearly more than a national cinema in that it encapsulates the everyday lives of both the Indian bourgeoisie as well as the Indian lumpenproletariat. In the popular imagination it signifies Indian modernity, and the state itself seems to have accepted this equation as it too reads Bollywood as the nation's pre-eminent transnational and transcultural popular art form. The coexistence of a quotidian reading of Bollywood alongside the state-institutional was readily evident in the closing ceremony of the Commonwealth Games in Melbourne in 2006 and in the near-calamitous 2010 Delhi Commonwealth Games opening ceremony, both of which had a strong Bollywood presence. It was only because Shilpa Shetty was a Bollywood star that the racial slur against her on the British television show *Celebrity Big Brother* (2007) by her 'housemates', model Danielle Lloyd, singer Jo O'Meara and most importantly Jade Goody, the highly-strung English reality show personality, herself of mixed-origin, but upon her death of cervical cancer in 2009 among the most mourned celebrity in the UK, became a big global affair.

Although in terms of number of films produced, Bollywood is only a fifth of the Indian film industry (the total number of films produced by Bollywood since the coming of sound in 1931 is fewer than 11,000, whereas the overall Indian figure is well over 50,000), for most people it is now a catch-all term for Indian cinema as a whole.

Like any postcolonial form, Bollywood cinema for many years dealt with big issues—the idea of the nation state, communal harmony, justice—all rendered through a melodramatic genre which grew out of a combination of the sentimental European novel, the Indian epic traditions, Persian narratives, a fair bit of Shakespeare, and the influential Parsi theatre, the last of these a form which effectively created the theatrical genre that was to become Bollywood cinema. The highest-grossing hits of Bollywood from 1943 to 1994—*Kismet* (1943), *Barsaat* (1949), *Awara* (1951), *Aan* (1952), *Shree 420* (1955), *Mother India* (1957), *Mughal-e-Azam* (1960), *Sholay* (1975), *Hum Aapke Hain Koun* (1994)—show the persistence of these themes and the durability of the melodramatic genre. With the exception of *Hum Aapke Hain Koun*, which introduced a new wave of young film stars such as Salman Khan and Madhuri Dixit, these classics and others of the period were not unlike Hollywood as they reworked the base genre and created subtexts around its great actors (K. L. Saigal, Ashok Kumar, Dilip Kumar, Devanand, Raj Kapoor, Nargis, Madhubala, Meena Kumari), its auteurs (Mehboob Khan, Raj Kapoor, and Guru Dutt), and its film studios. Fanzines fed on all these and it could be said that with a few significant shifts—the arrival of the angry young man character of Amitabh Bachchan being one such rare shift—the form remained more or less intact. Indeed, from *Devdas* (1935) to *Maine Pyar Kiya* (1989), Bollywood cinema was a single interconnected syntagm.[1]

Then came a sudden redefinition, not because of any significant change to the genre itself (which continued to be melodrama) but because of a move away from the hero as a man of feeling (marked by the shift from Rajesh Khanna to the Amitabh Bachchan persona of the angry young man), and, with it, a shift in the mode of production, consumption, and circulation of Bollywood films. In the late 1980s a combination of disco dance and Michael Jackson was superimposed upon the old staple of Bombay popular film, the sentimental song, in films such as *Ashiqui* (1990) and *Dil* (1990). The year, 1990, is important in as much as these two films rethink the erstwhile themes of sentimentality and ethical responsibility, and the earlier movie-making techniques (especially montage, what Salman Rushdie called the magic of the 'indirect kiss') with reference to both the home audience, the new Indian, and diasporic Indian spectator. For India's foremost film theorist and critic, Ashish Rajadhyaksha, 1990 also marks the end of the 'time of celluloid' whose hallmark was an engagement with issues central to the formation of the nation state.[2] Youth, in the form of Shah Rukh Khan, Salman Khan, Amir Khan, Abhishek Bachchan (to name a few), returns to Bollywood with a different kind of excitement that had brought Dilip Kumar, Raj Kapoor, and Devanand to cinema in the late forties and early fifties. But there had also been a major shift in the nature of capital—from the old manufacturing-based wealth to a new kind of wealth which moved swiftly via cyberspace. This wealth was also a virtual wealth made and unmade as well on the Internet. In a postmodern Bollywood the old depth of language and dialogue (hallmarks of classic Bollywood cinema

[1] Vijay Mishra, *Bollywood Cinema: Temples of Desire* (New York; London: Routledge, 2002).
[2] Ashish Rajadhyaksha, *Indian Cinema in the Time of Celluloid: From Bollywood to Emergency* (Bloomington and Indianapolis: Indiana University Press, 2009).

as seen, for example, in the 1953 *Parineeta*) is replaced by a technorealism (seen in the remake of *Parineeta* (2006)) at the level of production, and the global at the level of the mise en scène. This (post)modernity negotiated a new definition of the spectator and a new definition of the subject of cinema. Great box-office hits since 1994—*Gadar: Ek Prem Katha* (2001), *Dhoom 2* (2006), *Ghajini* (2008), and *3 Idiots* (2009), the last of these the highest-grossing Bollywood film ever—reflect the changes in theme, movie-making techniques, and implied spectator.

The figures for Bollywood now are quite staggering, especially for an industry which was given 'industry status' only on 10 May 1998: a $3.5 billion dollar per year industry which employs some 2.5 million people, ticket sales close to $4 billion every year, and a growing international market for the films in the 'new' Indian diaspora of late capital.[3] In the first decade of the twenty-first century, films such as *My Name is Khan* (2010), *3 Idiots* (2009), *Om Shanti Om* (2007), and *Kabhi Khushi Kabhi Gham* (2001) had box-office collections of between $3.1 million and $6.5 million per film in the USA and Canada and between £1.5 million and £3 million in the UK. Not surprisingly, the overseas market has begun to provide between a quarter to almost a half of worldwide (that is, including Indian) revenue. Films such as *3 Idiots* (2009), *Dabangg* (2010), *Ek Tha Tiger* (2012), *Dabangg 2* (2012), *Yeh Jawaani Hai Deewani* (2013) have had combined local and international collections of between $36 million (for *Dabangg*) and $65 million (for *3 Idiots*). The short time span of these figures indicates the exponential demand for Bollywood in the UK and USA/Canada Indian diaspora at the turn of the twenty-first century even if 'India's share in the global film industry, valued in 2004 at $200 billion, was less than 0.2 per cent'.[4] One would have expected better returns from the UK but even there the Bollywood market 'accounted for just 1.1 per cent of gross box office in 2004'.[5]

At the level of spectator, the implied viewer was no longer made up primarily of Hindi-Urdu-speaking Indian denizens and those in the Middle East or the old Indian plantation diasporas (Fiji, Trinidad, Guyana, Surinam, Mauritius, and the like) but included, in growing numbers, South East Asians and the people of the new Indian diaspora of late capital. The latter—the well-to-do Indian diasporas of the UK, the USA, Canada, Australia, rich but also uneasy in supposedly multicultural nation states and often unable to connect directly with the nation state's own popular cultural forms—began to emerge as the target audience, while in India too the growth of a new middle class with disposable incomes created lifestyles seemingly similar to those of Indian youths

[3] Vijay Mishra, *The Literature of the Indian Diaspora: Theorizing the Diasporic Imaginary* (London; New York: Routledge, 2007).

[4] Daya Kishan Thussu, 'The Globalization of "Bollywood": The hype and hope', in *Global Bollywood*, Anandan P. Kavoori and Aswin Punathambekar, eds (New York: New York University Press, 2008).

[5] Ibid.

in the diaspora. Bollywood captures this new consumer class across national boundaries. Again with a difference. Bollywood has a remarkable mediating function, in as much as it relocates, re-presents and repackages contemporary culture for re-consumption by the diaspora. The shift from Bollywood as a postcolonial form (aimed at defining the nation, its values, and so on) to Bollywood as a transnational form responding to a new consumer community whether within India or in the diaspora is now its fundamental characteristic. The hype around Bollywood, if not its global box-office success, however limited, captures this trend. At the forefront has been Yash Raj Films, a film company which quite self-consciously feeds the diaspora with values which it, the production company, feels will alleviate the diaspora's unrelenting unhappiness for being untimely ripped from their homeland.[6] Additionally, the impact of cable and satellite television was also enormous. B4U (a British Bollywood movie channel launched in London in 1999) is now 'available on eight satellites in more than 100 countries'.[7] With fanzines such as *Cine Blitz, Filmfare, Movie*, and *Stardust* available globally online and in hard copy immediately after production, the Bollywood experience is growing into a worldwide phenomenon.

Implicit in the collaborative and cosmopolitan Andrew Lloyd Webber–A. R. Rahman musical *Bombay Dreams* (2002) is a whole new definition of the subject of the Bollywood film. The basic themes of love, desire, and separation, of the lure of the city and its material benefits, of the stability of the family are all there, but these are being slowly transformed at the levels of discourse, representation, and theme. At the level of discourse languages proliferate—Punjabi and English (as in *Kal Ho Na Ho* and *Dhoom 2* (2006)), regional dialects (as in *Omkara* (2006)), Bombay slang (as in *Lage Raho Munnabhai* (2006))—the English word 'love' replaces its Urdu-Hindi equivalents; at the level of representation the old 'Bombay realism' is replaced by a distinctly Bollywood technorealism and this distinctiveness is readily obvious in films such as *Don* (2006; a remake of the original Amitabh Bachchan *Don* of 1978) and *Dhoom 2*, where Bangalore software seems to replace carefully designed stage backdrops and production studios. At the thematic level, another feature surfaces which may be noted with reference to two recent adaptations of Shakespeare and a classic sentimental film: *Maqbool* (2006 based on *Macbeth*), *Omkara* (2006 based on *Othello*), and *Dev D* (2009). In the first two Shakespeare is modernized in very Indian ways: in *Omkara* with the use of Indian dialects; in *Maqbool* with its subtext of the Bollywood film industry itself. In *Dev D* (2009) the great intertext of Bollywood sentimentality—*Devdas* (1935, 1955, 2003)—is recast with the character of Chandramukhi transformed into an assertive

---

[6] See Sangita Gopal, 'Sentimental Symptoms: The Films of Karan Johar and Bombay Cinema', in *Bollywood and Globalization*, eds Rini Bhattacharya Mehta and Rajeshwari V. Pandharipande (London: Anthem Press, 2010), pp. 15–34.

[7] Thussu, 'The Globalization of "Bollywood"'.

courtesan/prostitute whose cinema life captures a notorious Delhi school sex scandal involving a young student, a pimp, and her paramour.

With all the claims of globalization and transnationality, Bollywood has not been able to capture the worldwide success of the Bollywood-inspired *Slumdog Millionnaire* (2008), which collected an astronomical $378 million at the box office, a figure when placed in context, and if Thussu is to be believed, that is not much less than Bollywood's share of the total global market. Bollywood remains different, and largely inaccessible, in its totality, to people not immersed in its form. For, in the end, it tries to be modern without throwing away its thematic grounding in rather ancient ways of doing things (seen as late as 2006 in the film *Babul*) and these ways will always insinuate a different, an Indian, splitting of reason. Borrowings from Hollywood (storyline, music, mise en scène) notwithstanding, the argument about Bollywood as a 'hype' and in its late modern form as a new technoreality comes together graphically in Sanjay Leela Bhansali's 2003 version of the P. C. Barua– Bimal Roy classic *Devdas* (1935/1955), based on Saratchandra Chattopadhyay's 1917 sentimental novel in Bengali of that name. In Bhansali's high-tech version of the film the homage is neither to the writer of the novel nor to P. C. Barua and Bimal Roy (as the credits in the film declare) but to 'Bollywood', which now takes over *Devdas* and models it in its new image; the cinematic fidelity is not to an earlier form but to the film's own postmodern, simulacral modes of representation. The shift from Bollywood as a postcolonial form (aimed at defining the nation, its values, and so on) to Bollywood as a transnational form responding to a new consumer community whether within India or in the diaspora is now its fundamental characteristic.

35 Global News (Service) Networks

Gerard Toal

A plane plunges from the sky and crash-lands deep in Amazonia. Within an hour, readers on yahoo.com have a concise summary of the known particulars of the event. Mobile phone subscribers have a 'breaking news' alert on their handhelds. A few hours later there is video footage accompanying television reports in France and French-speaking Africa. Spanish-language newspapers have an updated summary of the event in the next-day editions accompanied by lurid photographs. So also do English-language newspapers across Asia and Australia. The world recoils, for a moment, at the 'horror in the jungle'.

The everyday work of global news service networks is the translation of plane crashes, wars, assassinations, sports, entertainment, and the latest breakthroughs in health, science, and technology into a global informational product: world news events as a 650-word story, a 90-second video, and a portfolio of photographs. On the top floor of a building recalling an earlier age of time–space compression, the Southern Railway Building at 1500 K Street in Washington DC, is the hemispheric headquarters of one of the three major Western newswire services still operating, Agence France-Presse (AFP), the others being Reuters and Associated Press (AP). If newsworthy events happen in the Americas, they flow through this office that is staffed around the clock by personnel operating its three language newswires (English, French, and Spanish), photographic banks, and modest video-feed facility. AFP boasts that it produces from 400,000 to 600,000 words in text, between 2,000 and 3,000 photos as well, about 80 news graphics, and 30 video clips every day.

AFP is the oldest news service in the world, founded in Paris in 1835 by Charles-Louis Havas as Agence Havas. A pioneer in the gathering, packaging, and disseminating of news as a commodity for sale to newspapers and other sources, Agence Havas became an incubator for the news service industry. Employees Julius Reuter and Bernhard Wolff later left to set up rival news agencies in London and Berlin. The three companies eventually carved up the European world into exclusive news zones. This arrangement came undone in the early twentieth century as states went to war, governments clamoured to control information, and radio accelerated news cycles. Yet international newswire service companies adapted and adjusted. Agence Havas was reborn as Agence France-Presse at the end of the Second World War and became an informational news service arm of the French state. This changed in 1957 when the French parliament established AFP as a public corporation but run as a commercial business. Granted full editorial independence, it nevertheless relies on indirect subsidies from the French state and has three of its 15-member board appointed by the French government.

AFP's mandate is the gathering and dissemination of news that is scrupulously accurate and neutral. In effect it is a worldwide mediation and translation network. Its own description captures part of the ambition: 'With a team of 4,000 people spread across 165 countries, AFP covers the world 24 hours a day in eight languages, delivering the news in video, photos, text and graphics.' What is opaque is how this occurs. Two aspects of this are worth elucidating. The first is the process of 'covering the world'. Central to this is the company's own worldwide web: a central headquarters in Paris, five regional centres, and reporters and stringers spread across all those countries. But just as important is the AFP style, the process by which events get distilled into text, and, to a lesser extent, as images, graphics, and video. All AFP staff and stringers are trained in the voiceless writing required by the organization. The style book sets out what is required: accuracy, clarity, neutrality. The AFP style should be 'placeless' while the news content as close to the event site as possible.

The second is the process of 'delivering the news' and for this we need to trace how a story makes it onto the AFP newswire. In the case of an Amazonian plane crash, as soon as the AFP office in São Paulo learns about the event, a reporter writes a story with the initial details from the primary source. This might be local television footage (AFP offices subscribe to a service that allows them to tap into the broadcast feed of television stations across a country). An in-house reporter will be dispatched to the scene or a freelance journalist, known as a 'stringer,' hired in the vicinity. AFP has followed the lead of other news organizations and now requires their reporters to carry laptops to send in their stories, as well as digital cameras to provide images and video feed.

Stories, from the field or from a colleague a few metres away, are fed into the AFP intranet and arrive in the computer terminal inbox of the 'slot editor' for a particular language newswire. The slot editor has the 'hot seat', usually centrally located, in any newsroom floor. Her job is to manage the flow of incoming stories and edit them, serving as a guarantor of the AFP style and a gatekeeper on the organization and tagging of particular stories. The position is demanding, with the occupant rarely able to leave the seat for an extended period—for lunch or dinner—during the eight-hour shift. Workers describe their job as having to get into the flow of the news feed. Most report themselves mentally drained after their shift.

Once a story is 'subbed' (i.e. edited and tagged) by the slot editor, it is released into the AFP wire and channelled into a particular stream—politics, business and economics, sports, lifestyle, etc. Supervising the process is a desk chief, a deputy, and then the bureau chief, the latter two positions located in glass offices removed from the open newsroom floor but with a view of it. Making the collective connectivity possible is a dark windowless office stacked with computer servers, terminals, wires, and cables, a space with its own separate air-conditioning system to prevent this box room overheating.

The proliferation of the Internet and advent of specialized digital media websites have significantly undermined traditional newspaper publishing. While most newspapers have adjusted and invested in company websites, they have also had to make deep staff cuts. Global news service networks are needed more than ever by newspapers but they are also adjusting to the turbulent media environment. On the one hand, they now provide their newswires and other content to clients such as web portals—yahoo.com displays AFP stories—but, on the other hand, doing so dilutes their proprietary content and undermines their traditional business of selling to newspapers and other traditional media. Most news service wires have adapted by selling specialized bundles of services, with particular rules of attribution and distribution, to different segments of the new digital media landscape, but some are experimenting with moving away from their traditional style towards more 'voice'- and 'personality'-based reporting. AFP is experimenting with reporter blogs but is fortunate in being insulated, more than Reuters or AP, from financial pressures by its special relationship to the French state. To the multinational staff in the Washington newsroom these changes are part of their everyday life of globalization. Dark humour accompanies everyday life on the news floor, with jokes about being galley slaves, mere stenographers, or part of the AFP Borg expressing their condition. 'The world at your fingertips' is AFP News's slogan for its new mobile phone-alert service packages. Getting it there is the job of those who have assimilated to the AFP assemblage and work its cybernetic systems 24/7.

36 How Rounders Goes around the World

Sumei Wang and Elizabeth Shove

By most accounts the English game of rounders travelled to the USA where it was transformed into baseball and played so widely during the American Civil War that it became what was, by the 1870s, referred to as America's national game. Baseball, which is now extremely popular in Canada, Central and South America, and in many Asian countries, is currently cited as *the* 'national' game not only in the USA,[1] but also in Dominica,[2] Japan,[3] and Taiwan (see Figure 36.1).[4] We use this intriguing case of simultaneous internationalization and national appropriation to compare ways of conceptualizing the global diffusion of practice.

One dominant interpretation is that baseball, and other forms of organized sport, such as cricket, have been simply carried from one country to another often by colonizing powers—and it is true, trajectories frequently follow this pattern. Having crossed the Atlantic and become established as a distinct entity, baseball was exported to Japan in the 1850s by American soldiers and teachers, and especially by those based in coastal ports where extraterritorial authority was granted.[5] Within a few decades, and partly in keeping with the Westernizing ambitions of the Meiji restoration, baseball was established across the Japanese state school system. When Japan colonized Taiwan in 1895, the Japanese took baseball with them, again introducing it into schools but this time as part of a deliberate project of assimilation, and as a means of 'civilizing' the native 'barbarians'.[6] Baseball has not been unscathed by these movements from the UK to the USA, from the USA to Japan, or from Japan to Taiwan.

[1] Frederick Ivor-Campbell, 'Many Fathers of Baseball: Anglo-Americans and the Early Game', in *The American Game: Baseball and Ethnicities*, ed. Lawrence Baldassaro and Richard A. Johnson (Carbondale: Southern IllinoisUniversity Press, 2002).

[2] A. Klein, 'Yo Soy Dominicano: Hegemony and Resistance through Baseball', *Sport in Society* 10, 6 (2007): 916–46.

[3] Donald Roden, 'Baseball and the Quest for National Identity in Meiji Japan', *American Historical Review* 85, 3 (June 1980): 511–34.

[4] S.-Y. Hsieh and C.-F. Hsieh, *Taiwanese Baseball Since 1906* (Taipei: Fruition Publishing, 2003); Junwei Yu and Dan Gordon, 'Nationalism and National Identity in Taiwanese Baseball', *NINE* 14, 2 (Spring 2006): 27–39.

[5] Roden, 'Baseball and the Quest for National Identity in Meiji Japan'.

[6] Yu and Gordon, 'Nationalism and National Identity in Taiwanese Baseball'.

Figure 36.1 Baseball may be officially the 'national pastime' of the United States, but its popularity has transcended continental boundaries, especially in Asia

Carrying is never that simple and the meaning of the game is evidently dynamic. To begin with, playing baseball in Japan symbolized some kind of privileged, Western, and specifically American identity but later, and as a Japanese export to Taiwan at the end of the nineteenth century, it expressed and reproduced the new '*bushido*' or '*samurai*', core values of the Japanese warrior and a traditional spirit of 'blood and guts'.[7] Yet this is also not a simple narrative of appropriation. Unlike Trobriand Island 'cricket', elements of baseball have remained sufficiently intact to allow 'the game', as an internationally recognized entity, to develop and extend into new territory.

Alongside accounts of diffusion and appropriation we explore the parallel possibility that always-localized reproductions of practices such as baseball commonly sustain standardized 'elements' (including rules, competences, and material infrastructures) that constitute the necessary conditions and ingredients of their expansion and global circulation.

---

[7] Roden, 'Baseball and the Quest for National Identity in Meiji Japan'; W. W. Kelly, 'Blood and Guts in Japanese Professional Baseball', in *The Culture of Japan as Seen Through its Leisure*, ed. Sepp Linhard and Sabine Früstück (Albany: State University of New York Press, 1998).

This works in different ways. We have already noticed contested interpretations of the sport as it is positioned in relation to an existing complex of meanings.[8] Although people in Taiwan were initially suspicious of Japanese colonizers' attempts to impose baseball, many enjoyed the experience of playing and those who were very good particularly enjoyed beating the Japanese at their 'own' game.[9] Along with many other experiences associated with Japanese colonization, baseball gave Taiwanese islanders, who had not until then thought of themselves as a unified group, a common point of reference. In this context, the meaning of baseball was in effect captured, reconfigured, and reproduced (but, crucially, still with the same rules, forms of competence, and material equipment) as an integral part of generating an emergent 'national' identity.

The role of baseball became still more complex when the Republic of China took over Taiwan in 1945, when the island was governed by Nationalist troops (also known as the Kuo-Min-Tung, the KMT), and when immigrants from mainland China became the island's new elite. Partly because baseball was so strongly associated with the former Japanese rulers, it was actively discouraged by the KMT. If anything, this strengthened its importance as part of a shared memory for those Taiwanese islanders who had experienced Japanese rule. In the first decades of the KMT's rule,[10] watching baseball was one of the few occasions when native Taiwanese could be themselves, dressing in shorts and slippers, chewing betel nuts, and eating from Japanese-style lunch boxes, reproducing a way of life they took to be comfortable and normal, but that was denigrated as vulgar by the new middle-class elite from mainland China. From this we highlight the further point that baseball is also not only a site of symbolic expression: it is also actively implicated in making national and ethnic identities.

Despite discouragement by the state, and despite Taiwan losing its status as a member of the United Nations (in 1971) and international recognition in subsequent years, Taiwan's baseball teams kept winning titles in *international* tournaments. Middle-aged people in Taiwan, whether of native origin or immigrants from mainland China, consequently share the collective experience and excitement of staying up late to watch baseball games held in the USA, and of welcoming teams as 'national' heroes when they returned home with trophies. Baseball once again seems to have done some 'capturing' work of its own, crossing ethnic and cultural divides by becoming popular among Chinese mainlanders in Taiwan. From this perspective, it seems that recruitment to baseball—whether as player or supporter—is relevant in redefining

---

[8] Douglas B. Holt, 'How Consumers Consume: A Typology of Consumption Practices', *Journal of Consumer Research* 22, 1 (June 1995): 1–16.

[9] Hsieh and Hsieh, *Taiwanese Baseball Since 1906*.

[10] Hill Gates, 'Ethnicity and Social Class', in *The Anthropology of Taiwanese Society*, ed. Emily Martin Ahern and Hill Gates (Stanford: Stanford University Press, 1981).

differences not only between Japan and Taiwan but also within Taiwanese society. In the constant redefinition of ethnic boundaries and imagined communities, baseball has been an embedded and also constitutive element. This is so for spectators as for players.

Taiwanese baseball has shaped and is shaped by a confluence of multiple national and ethnic histories and by processes of local adaptation. Ironically, baseball has been capable of carrying and reproducing these diverse cultural forms precisely because key elements, such as the rules, the equipment, and the competences involved, have remained relatively stable. Yet this 'stability' is obviously not total. Under Japanese colonial rule, baseball was typically played by members of an educated elite who had access to proper facilities and equipment. In becoming a sport for all in post-war Taiwan, material compromises were required.[11] Prior to the 1970s, poorly funded community teams used rubber balls and improvised with handmade gloves of folded paper, both innovations being important in turning baseball into a game that could be played almost anywhere and by almost anyone—not only by male athletes but also by women, children, and older people too.

What does this brief account of baseball's career, especially in Taiwan, reveal about the globalization of practice? Baseball is played in many countries and when they come together in international competition, players compete on formally equal terms. It seems that the standardizing infrastructure of rules defining the field, the method of play, and the (ideal) bat and ball have enabled its circulation. Most obviously, rules permit competitions, which when played at the international level, arouse and provide a focus for nationalistic passion and association. Less obviously, it is because the game is defined by certain minimum requirements that core elements of playing can travel: likewise, it is because baseball exists as a provisional but still recognizable entity in its own right that it can be given and that it can carry meaning.

Does this mean that globalization of baseball is made possible as the result of creeping or sometimes enforced diffusion? Shove and Pantzar argue that the reproduction of practice is an unavoidably situated process, consisting as it does of the active integration of new and existing elements of image, meaning, material, and competence.[12] Accordingly, traces of colonialism, ethnicity, class, and nationalism are inextricably embedded in Taiwanese baseball and are so in ways that are reproduced through and as the game is played today. To an extent, we go along with this argument and agree; the playing fields are definitely not identical.

---

[11] Hsieh and Hsieh, *Taiwanese Baseball Since 1906*.

[12] Elizabeth Shove and Mika Pantzar, 'Consumers, Producers and Practices: Understanding the Invention and Reinvention of Nordic Walking', *Journal of Consumer Culture* 5, 1 (March 2005): 43–64. See also Elizabeth Shove, Mika Pantzar, and Matt Watson, *The Dynamics of Social Practice: Everyday Life and How it Changes* (London: Sage, 2012).

This leads to the somewhat puzzling conclusion that when teams compete in international leagues, they are not, in fact, playing exactly the same game. In making sense of this seemingly paradoxical situation, we have suggested that it is the relative stabilization of certain elements of the game (field, bat, ball, rules) that allows it to move in some recognizable way, and that allows it to intervene in, and to acquire multiple characteristics as, a multiply localized practice. This analysis leads us to reject one-way accounts of diffusion and colonization that position baseball players as victims of some sort of global invasion. It also challenges the view that seemingly global trends are outcomes of entirely local reproduction. Instead, we have pointed to mediating tensions and dynamics including those that simultaneously sustain the possibility of international competition, the concept of a 'national' game; and the more complex ways in which participation in baseball—whether as player or fan—is directly and actively part of reproducing and also transforming shared memories, excitement, talent, and cultural and ethnic identities.

We therefore argue for an approach that deals equally with two related processes: one being the circulation of constitutive elements—including rules and equipment however approximately defined—the other being their situated and very active integration along with other ingredients such as those of cultural significance and accumulated competence. Our conclusion, then, is that seemingly global practices are formed of multiple and successive integrations of the old and the new, the native and the foreign, the customized and the standardized—and that it is by these means that rounders goes around.

Part V
Health and Nature

37 Biodiversity and Globalization

Geoffrey C. Bowker

It's amazing the language that gets used around so-called invasive species. New Jersey refers to the 'alien invaders' amongst us where California talks about 'zebra mussel outlaws'. In the days since 9/11 a fair amount of the protecting-the-homeland talk has been taken up by environmentalists. We don't want these foreign agents coming into our country and wreaking untold havoc, now, do we? It's a long way from the heady days of the nineteenth century when there were societies to turn parts of the United States into bucolic England—one such had the goal of importing and nurturing every plant mentioned in Shakespeare.

It's an odd term, 'invasive species'. It reminds me of the (circum)locutions folks indulge in when they talk about the 'homosexual community'—it sounds like a reasonable term till you try to imagine its other—the non-invasive species, or the 'heterosexual community'. The unmarked categories (native species, heterosexuals) are not, so the rhetoric goes, a single unit—they are doing just what they should be doing until the outsider comes along to threaten them. Let's stay with the species, since I don't want to strain the analogy. It's sort of in the nature of species to be invasive. I've never met a good species that wasn't. Certainly not our own—we are invaders par excellence—living in a wider set of environments than most other entities on earth. We bring our invaders with us (cats, for example, are a major source of biodiversity loss in Australia—since the marsupials there did not have natural predators in the available trophic slot). We have invaded many landscapes with our wheat, corn, and soy. We have ourselves internally been invaded countless times, and are the better for it—infants who don't get a good dose of their mother's bacterial colonies in the birth process are at a significant health disadvantage. Bring a species to a new place, and of course it will try to survive.

And then there's the problem of what the natural environment is. Take the Midwest of the USA—that part of it that I know well (the 'I' states— Iowa, Illinois, Indiana) live in the rainshadow of the recently created Rocky Mountains. The prairie landscapes which have developed there are still basically in their early stages—there are few or no 'native' species—everything is an invader. Further, when restorationists try to preserve the ancient prairie, they tend to preserve a period when the Native Americans—who were practising fire management of the landscape—were already changing it significantly. So in principle preserving the prairies becomes a somewhat tortuous question of preserving what might have been had there not been two waves of human invasion. I'm a little unclear on why precisely this is worth doing.

I live in the redwood forests. Second growth—billions of metric feet got shipped out, built with, used to fire kilns, and so forth till the slaughter stopped. In the troubled area I live in, the invasive madrones have come into the environmentally disturbed area and have clawed out a foothold. They tend to get pretty good press. The poor old French broom doesn't (isn't it nice when you can associate nationalities to epidemics—just like the Spanish flu?)—many of my friends pull these out of the ground whenever they see them with nary a qualm at the destruction they are causing.

So we arrive at the point where I am generally asked if I'm being just deliberately ornery or whether I have something to say. Surely no one wants lantana or cane toads in Australia, French broom in California, and zebra mussels coursing through our waters? Well, I guess not—it does sadden me to see any species die, and if one species is doing a lot of killing in new territory (excepting ourselves, I guess) then there are arguments for eradication. However, if we are truly living in one world right now, and are truly travelling as much as we seem to want to (as a species), then I don't think that people jumping up to see if there're any insects in the undercarriages of jets in Hawai'i is really going to do much for the very long term. It's like the British obsession with stopping the 'spread' of rabies—millions of dollars spent keeping a pretty harmless disease (when is the last human victim you can think of?—and it's endemic in Europe) out of the United Kingdom—united against invasion.

We need to recast the debate—and as with so many issues in our technoscientific world, we can use a similar argument for humans and for non-humans. Creating Maginot Lines, massive walls against Mexican immigrants or between the Palestinians and the Israelis is bound to be a failed endeavour, as well as being wrong-headed. Maintaining purity is a massive amount of work and all historical examples show is that it always fails. ('Beware of purity, it is the vitriol of the soul,' as Tournier's Robinson Crusoe says.) There's a wonderful book by Arthur Waldrup called *The Great Wall of China: From History to Myth*, where he shows that the Wall stood at a site of great exchange—often the nomadic hordes invaded through it, became Sinicized, and then sat around (became sedentary) for several generations till the next invasion through the Wall. Similarly with nature. If we insist on deploying the communications technology we do (and I'm personally looking forward to a day with fewer planes, but more airships, since I do love to travel) then we should accept other species as our fellow travellers. If we don't get so het up about invasion, we may get some really unfortunate things happen along the way (the loss of some great species) but we will be acting much more naturally.

The biodiversity debate that isn't happening in this country needs to be careful not to get caught up in cheap and easy rhetoric borrowed from myths of racial purity and crazed aliens. We need to be, socially and naturally, cosmopolitan. The dialectic of differentiation (let's keep people and plants on reservations, as different linguistically and phylogenetically as possible) and uniformitarianism (let's all speak English and eat corn) is key to the social and natural dynamics of globalization. And in both cases there is a political urgency to eschewing the canonization of difference.

38 Mobility and the Medical Image

Catelijne Coopmans

It's 7 June 2011, and Katsumasa Itakura arrives at the Retinal Vascular Imaging Centre (RetVIC) in Melbourne, Australia. The young ophthalmologist from Hiroshima University, Japan, has come for a one-year stint as a visiting PhD student. Katsu, as he prefers to be called, will be working with a very special collection of images: retinal photographs of atomic bomb survivors from Hiroshima and Nagasaki. Katsu is the second person from Hiroshima University to come to RetVIC and learn how to analyse these images for retinal vascular signs. Copies of the retinal photographs of about 2,500 adults are already waiting for him, having travelled to Melbourne on DVDs some two years ago in the suitcase of his predecessor.

Those who work at RetVIC are used to the arrival of people, and even more so images, from all over the world. The storage cabinet shown in Figure 38.1 houses eye images from South Korea, Japan, India, Singapore, Taiwan, the United States, Canada, Norway, Finland, and a number of Australian cities. At the point of origin, these images may have been used for the screening or diagnosis of eye disease, but here they are processed for research purposes. RetVIC is a hub for the analysis of retinal vascular signs, which are the features, patterns, and changes of the small vessels at the back of the eye made visible by retinal photography (Figure 38.2).[1] These signs are increasingly valued for their potential use in predicting and monitoring small-vessel-related afflictions of the eye, and also of the brain and the heart. Together with the reputation of RetVIC's staff—and in particular that of its director, Professor Wong Tien Yin—this has generated demand for the centre's services among researchers who possess collections of retinal photographs.

RetVIC's operations, and indeed its very existence, demonstrate the global mobility of medical images. Here, as elsewhere, the flow of images from many places into one hub requires two forms of 'delocalization'. First, images have to be physically displaced, and this has been greatly facilitated by the change from film-based to digital imaging that has gradually occurred over the past

---

[1] For an overview of the uses and potential uses of retinal vascular imaging, see G. Liew, J. J. Wang, P. Mitchell, and T. Y. Wong (2008), 'Retinal vascular imaging', *Circulation: Cardiovascular Imaging* 1(2): 156–61.

Figure 38.1 The storage cabinet at RetVIC, Melbourne contains a world of images. Photograph by author

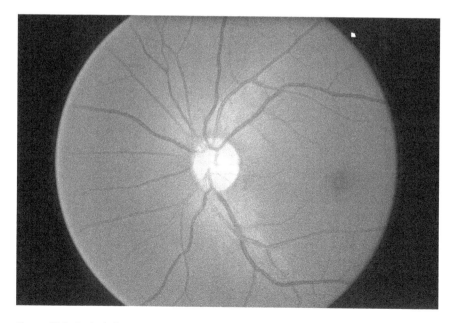

Figure 38.2 Retinal photography shows the condition of the vessels at the back of the eye. Image courtesy of the Retinal Vascular Imaging Centre (RetVIC), Centre for Eye Research Australia

two decades. Medical images no longer need to be analysed in close prox-imity to the bodies from which they are generated. Technically, they can be treated exactly like any other type of electronic information; indeed, these images have become part of the digital data streams that feature so promi-nently in our imagination of the global. Clinical teleradiology services, in par-ticular, are the manifestation of a utopian vision of digital circulation whereby images are transferred at the click of a button to places in a different time zone, with lower labour costs, or where the promise of an attractive lifestyle has drawn highly qualified professionals.[2] A centre like RetVIC does not offer quick-turnaround clinical services, but it nevertheless partakes in the vision of a technology-enabled, global differentiation of expertise that attracts images from anywhere in the world to a single locale for specialized analysis.

The second form of delocalization involves the removal or neutralization of features that tie an image to its place of origin.[3] These could be personal identi-fying details or technical peculiarities due to local variations in image produc-tion. When images are analysed for research purposes, the way such features might unduly affect findings is a cause for concern. At RetVIC, incoming col-lections of retinal photographs first undergo preparation to turn them into the kind of neutral and comparable data that analysts—or 'graders' as they are called—can work with. This job usually falls to Lauren Hodgson, the grading coordinator. She will copy them from DVD onto RetVIC's server, and gather all photographs centred on the optic disc into a specific vessel measurement subfolder. Images of right and left eyes are separated. To prevent technical variations from confounding the grading, Lauren also sorts images accord-ing to the camera angle and magnification settings used in their production. Finally, she will remove personal identifying details if the sending party has not already done so. Lauren explains:

---

[2] The website of the Telemedicine Clinic, for example, highlights that its consultants serve cli-ents in the United Kingdom and Scandinavia out of offices based in Barcelona (overlooking the Mediterranean) and Sydney (overlooking the Opera House). Teleradiology is, however, less pervasive than the utopian vision of digital circulation might lead one to expect, because the outsourcing of diag-nostic interpretation within and beyond national health systems is significantly curtailed by concerns and regulatory stipulations regarding credentials, liability, information privacy, and confidentiality. See R. D. Smith, R. Chandra, and V. Tangcharoensathien (2009), 'Trade in health-related services', *The Lancet* 373: 593–601.

[3] Stripping away 'locality' and 'particularity' is integral to the process of producing knowledge claims with universal aspirations. For a vivid account of the dialectic of gain and loss that characterizes scientific knowledge production, see B. Latour, 'Circulating reference: sampling the soil in the Amazon forest', in *Pandora's Hope: Essays on the Reality of Science Studies* (Cambridge, MA: Harvard University Press, 1999): 24–79. This form of delocalization also resonates with Berg and Goorman's 'law of medi-cal information', which proposes that 'the further information has to be able to circulate (i.e., the more different contexts it has to be usable in), the more work is required to disentangle the information from the context of its production' (M. Berg and E. Goorman (1999), 'The contextual nature of medical information', *International Journal of Medical Informatics* 56: 51–60 (quote at p. 52)).

You don't want to introduce any subconscious bias into thinking 'Oh, these are old people, so it should be a certain way,' or 'These are diabetics, so I expect to see…whatever.' It's best to know as little as you can about the images, particularly if you're just doing the software grading. You really need to know nothing about the images; just open them and grade them, whatever you get.

By the time a grader sits down behind a set of computer screens to analyse a series of images, there are few clues as to where or whom the images have come from. This, of course, is precisely the point: it helps to configure the grading as a form of perception that is 'objective' in the sense of being unburdened by expectation. Presented in standardized sets, images are organized to become interchangeable. And so, in fact, are the graders, whose interpretative judgement is standardized through training, reliability testing, and the use of tools such as grading protocols and computer-supported detection for retinal vessel measurements. These arrangements help make retinal vascular signs calculable and they qualify RetVIC as a 'centre of calculation'.[4]

This, then, is the setting in which Katsu finds himself, the setting in which he will soon begin to analyse the retinal photographs of atomic bomb survivors from Hiroshima and Nagasaki. The images in question were taken between 2006 and 2008 as part of a longitudinal study of the effects of radiation on the health of survivors and their children.[5] At RetVIC, the images will be graded to determine the impact of radiation on 'vessel narrowing' in the eye and the way that this correlates with eye diseases such as glaucoma and age-related macular degeneration. The project owes its genesis to RetVIC's grading manager, Dr Ryo Kawasaki, who, through the contacts he maintains in his homeland of Japan, helped arrange for the images to come to Melbourne for analysis. Collaborations of this kind are common at RetVIC, and yet there is something crucially different about this case: the images will be analysed at RetVIC, but not by RetVIC's own graders. As Ryo explains: 'We don't access the images here, although we keep the images on the grading stations. But myself, Lauren, no one touches the images.' The images are off limits to anyone

⁴ A 'centre of calculation' is a place designed for the accumulation, combination, and synthesis of information. Centres of calculation harbour the means to act upon the world based on abstractions and generalizations. B. Latour, *Science In Action: How to Follow Scientists and Engineers Through Society* (Milton Keynes: Open University Press, 1987).

⁵ The earliest Japanese and American investigations into the health effects of radiation were started within days and weeks of the bombing in 1945. The first significant finding came from an ophthalmic survey initiated in 1949 related to radiation cataracts. The retinal photographs discussed here were collected as part of the Adult Health Study, a clinical research programme on the long-term health effects of exposure to atomic radiation. The programme is based on biennial health examinations that include a general physical exam and various imaging and biochemical tests. About 20,000 subjects have been followed since 1958; these were selected from a much larger lifespan study on atomic bomb survivors and control subjects instigated in 1950. See <http://www.rerf.jp> (accessed 24 November 2013). For a relatively recent discussion of health research on Japanese atomic bomb survivors, see H. Brown (2005), 'Hiroshima: How much have we learned?' *The Lancet* 366 (6 August): 442–4.

but Katsu, who was sent by his superiors at Hiroshima University to learn how to grade and work with the collection. In this way, the images from Hiroshima and Nagasaki remain firmly attached to the context where they came from.

There is a folder on RetVIC's server for the retinal images from Hiroshima and Nagasaki, and no access restrictions prevent other graders from opening it. Yet the special status of these images is understood by all. Ryo, Lauren, and Katsu talk about this in practical terms: if the project is assigned to Katsu, then why should anyone else care about accessing these images? Others are busy enough as it is with their own work! But the exemption of these images from RetVIC's usual procedures also has a moral connotation. Ryo hints at the reasons why the overseas processing of data from Japanese atomic bomb survivors is considered a sensitive issue—reasons that are amply discussed in historical accounts of radiation-effects research after the Second World War.[6] In the years after 1945, US-led research on the health of the *hibakusha*, the atomic bomb survivors, became mired by mistrust and accusations of exploitation. The Atomic Bomb Casualty Commission in charge of coordinating this research became increasingly unpopular among the *hibakusha* and their supporters as it transpired that data and specimens had been sent out of Japan to the United States for analysis, that early findings were reported in US journals in English only, and, in particular, that the research took a detached, scientific approach that did not extend to the provision of medical care for the survivors. Although the *hibakusha* were hailed as 'the most important people living',[7] the benefits of their participation in the research appeared to accrue predominantly to US scientists and the US military. Several reforms and reorganizations since the early days, and in particular the establishment of the Radiation Effects Research Foundation that has been jointly run and funded by Japan and the United States since 1975, have placed control over what happens to survivors' data more firmly, although not exclusively, in Japanese hands.[8]

This history is folded into the project on which Katsu is going to embark, and its continuing resonance is evident from the fact that besides Hiroshima University and RetVIC, the Radiation Effects Research Foundation also participates in the present collaboration. The greatest care is taken to maintain trust in the analysis of survivors' retinal photographs, lest it be seen to echo earlier

[6] See, for example, H. Brown (2005), 'Hiroshima: How much have we learned?' and M. S. Lindee, *Suffering Made Real: American Science and the Survivors at Hiroshima* (Chicago, IL; London: University of Chicago Press, 1994).

[7] This is a quote from Robert Holmes, the director of the Atomic Bomb Casualty Commission from 1954 to 1957, highlighting how survivors of the bombing have been seen as a 'scarce and precious intellectual resource'. In M. S. Lindee (1994), *Suffering Made Real*, p. 4–5.

[8] Whereas its predecessor, the Atomic Bomb Casualty Commission, was established in 1947 by the US National Academy of Sciences with funding from the US Atomic Energy Commission, the Radiation Effects Research Foundation was set up as a non-profit foundation under Japanese civil law on the premise that 'research continue in full partnership between Japan and the US'. See <http://www.rerf.jp> (accessed 24 November 2013).

highly problematic outflows of data from Japan.[9] On account of RetVIC's reputation as a global centre of expertise, the Japanese images are dispatched to Melbourne, and yet their analysis is organized as a decidedly Japanese, even a Hiroshima-specific, affair. On account of their digital nature (and their status as research materials), these medical images are as 'mobile' as other images flowing into RetVIC, but at the same time they are entangled in historical, political, and cultural circumstances that circumscribe this movement.

Katsu's very special assignment shows how the passages through which medical images travel not only contribute to an interconnected world, but also highlight national boundaries and the stakes involved in crossing them.[10] Katsu's physical displacement from Hiroshima to Melbourne warrants the passage of the *hibakusha*'s retinal photographs out of Japan. This passage is temporary, for the images will stay at RetVIC only for as long as this researcher from Hiroshima University is also there. Katsu's presence in Melbourne thus satisfies conditions that could not be satisfied either in Hiroshima (or elsewhere in Japan), where retinal grading expertise is scarce, or by RetVIC's own graders, who have the expertise but lack the personal, embodied connection to the sites where the bombs were dropped. When asked about his own view on this unique position, Katsu says: 'It's a bit of a responsibility, I guess. I'm honoured to be in this project. And also, I was born in Hiroshima and grew up [there]. I am not one of the survivors but I feel some connection to [them], so ... it means something to me.'

The retinal photographs from Hiroshima and Nagasaki are like other images in that they will be analysed at RetVIC according to well established, universally recognized protocols for the grading of retinal vascular signs—protocols in which the graders at RetVIC are expert. Katsu is like other graders in that he will be trained in the use of these protocols until he can claim confidence in his results upon achieving good intra- and inter-grader reproducibility scores. Yet at the same time, the images from Hiroshima and Nagasaki will *not* become interchangeable with others, and by the same token Katsu's

---

[9] Assurances of high-quality science are not by themselves sufficient to maintain this trust. The handling of *hibakusha* data requires both thoroughness and sensitivity—*care* in more than one sense of the word. This is in marked contrast with a past in which 'to many Japanese, particularly the residents of Hiroshima, devotion to "pure science" [on the part of medical researchers] represented an inappropriate, dehumanizing attitude toward the suffering of the survivors.' M. S. Lindee (1994), *Suffering Made Real*, p.147.

[10] In focusing on the transnational movement of medical images, this chapter extends my earlier work on efforts to build a digital infrastructure for mammography within the UK. See C. Coopmans (2006), 'Making mammograms mobile: suggestions for a sociology of data mobility', *Information, Communication & Society* 9(1): 1–19. In that article, I examine the painstaking negotiations and arrangements that help constitute certain kinds of digital flow and exchange as 'valuable' and 'ethical'. In this chapter, the value and the ethics of sending medical images abroad are worked out through an arrangement that brings images in contact with international expertise while retaining, and even strengthening, the connection to their context of origin.

job will *not* become interchangeable with that performed by any other competent grader. The images' special status—the history they embody—is continually kept in view by the presence of the ophthalmologist from Hiroshima University. By the same token, Katsu's ties to the city where he grew up are continually enacted by his work with these images.[11] At a time when the global circulation of medical images is strongly associated with visions and technologies of delocalization, sometimes the opposite prevails, and the mobility of images *renders present* the context of origin, as opposed to leaving it behind.[12]

[11] A parallel can be drawn with the 'local' ties that enable—and are arguably strengthened by—the transnational mobility of medical images in teleradiology services. For example, most offshore radiology services supplying the United States employ radiologists who were trained in the United States. The average radiologist working for NightHawk Radiology Services (which is based in Idaho, USA, but has offices in Sydney, Australia, and Zurich, Switzerland) is said to hold 38 state licences and be on the staff of more than 400 hospitals. R. Steinbrook (2007), 'The age of teleradiology', *New England Journal of Medicine*, 357(1): 5–7.

[12] The research for this chapter was conducted as part of the project 'Asian Biopoleis: Biotechnology and Biomedicine as Emergent Forms of Life and Practice' funded by the Ministry of Education, Singapore, and the Humanities and Social Sciences Division in the Office of the Deputy President (Research and Technology) at the National University of Singapore, Grant Number MOE2009-T2-2-013. Denisa Kera, Ryan Bishop, Gregory Clancey, and Antonio Alvarez provided helpful feedback on an earlier draft. Special thanks are due to RetVIC staff, particularly to Katsumasa Itakura, Lauren Hodgson, and Ryo Kawasaki for telling me about their work, and to Wong Tien Yin for facilitating, in June 2011, the visit to RetVIC during which the materials for this chapter were gathered. Since the chapter was written there have been some changes at the Centre for Eye Research Australia, and as of April 2013 many of the people and the work formerly belonging to RetVIC have been incorporated under a new Clinical Trials Research Unit. They still do analysis for retinal vascular signs and are still receiving eye images from around the world.

39 e-Solutions to Sharing Information in Child Protection: The Rise and Fall of ContactPoint

Christopher Hall, Sue Peckover, and Sue White

Recent history of child protection policy in England has been characterized by strong reaction to tragedies where children known to agencies are killed by their parents/carers. High-profile media coverage has been followed by government inquiry (in private or public) and new legislation to address the identified deficiencies. A frequent criticism has been that different professionals failed to 'share information' about the child and family circumstances and to bring disparate threads together. Had all the information been adequately scrutinized, the argument goes, the risks to the child would have been clear. The report of the Victoria Climbié inquiry in 2003 concluded that there were 12 occasions where professional intervention could have taken place, but critical signs were missed.

There have been a number of developments to address poor communication between child welfare professionals, perhaps the most controversial being ContactPoint. The subject of pilot projects since 2003 and enshrined in the Children Act 2004, ContactPoint was a database which would include information on all 11 million children in England—their name, age, gender, address, school, GP, parent's/carer's details, and the services involved with the family. Professionals were to be able to look up a child's details, check which agencies were working with them, and indicate their own involvement. In this way, it was argued, concerns could be shared more effectively and joint plans developed. ContactPoint could also indicate if a standardized assessment of the child's needs, known as a Common Assessment Framework (CAF), had been completed. Pilot databases were developed in 12 'trailblazer' areas between 2003 and 2007, and nationally ContactPoint started to be used by selected local authorities during 2009. However, the project was opposed by the new coalition government and ContactPoint was switched off in August 2010. The standardized assessment, the CAF, has been maintained.

ContactPoint was typical of a number of information and communication technologies (ICTs) developed by the Labour government, accompanied by a good deal of magical thinking about their potential to eliminate human error.[1] ICTs can input, transfer, and store large amounts of data from multiple sources. In the Climbié case, a database could have easily identified that she was not at school nor registered with a doctor. A wide range of other concerns about children were to be prevented by early identification, tracking (a word used in the original name of ContactPoint), and strong preventive action.

There was widespread opposition to ContactPoint, perhaps because it epitomized the intrusive character of the 'surveillance society'. Along with the development of electronic identity cards and associated National Register, and the Vetting and Barring scheme (which held data on anyone working with children in a voluntary or paid capacity), the government was storing large amounts of data on citizens and allowing checks to be made by diverse agencies. Christine Bellamy summarizes the concerns—the sheer amount of information being stored, the security and integrity of the information, and widespread sharing of the data, sometimes for purposes other than those for which they were collected (known as function creep).[2] ContactPoint would have allowed some 300,000 child welfare professionals to access the personal details of children, despite only a small proportion receiving intervention by such services.

Our ethnographic research project, funded by the Economic and Social Research Council e-Society programme (2004–7), examined the early implementation of the project. It was less concerned with privacy and security issues than with how ContactPoint was used by professionals in their everyday practice. In our view ICTs are not necessarily threatening if the panoptic ambitions of the promoters are not realized in practice.

First, did the professionals embrace new technology? Professionals have different work patterns. Some, like social workers, are office based, and completing electronic forms and consulting databases are routine. Others, however, spend little time at the workstation. Teachers, for example, are in the classroom, only logging on in 'non-contact time'. There is often a computer in the classroom but little opportunity to work undisturbed or confidentially. Health visitors (community-based nurses) traditionally have few IT resources and IT skills, with notes routinely handwritten and access to a computer limited (although this has changed in recent years). Midwives move between hospital, clinic, and home visit, and struggle to log on in any setting. Youth workers are

---

[1] Dave Wastell and Sue White, 'Technology as Magic: Fetish and Folly in the IT-enabled Reform of Children's Services', in *Children's Services at the Crossroads*, ed. P. Ayre and M. Preston-Shoot (Lyme Regis: Russell House, 2010): 107–14.

[2] Christine Bellamy, 'Alive and Well? The "Surveillance Society" and the Coalition', *Public Policy and Administration* 26, 1 (January 2011): 149–55.

often 'street based' or 'detached'. Even if professionals have access to a computer, they tend to see themselves as 'people workers': their real work is with children. Their working day is not organized around e-office routines; they can easily be defeated by being timed out, frozen screens, and similar hazards. Their knowledge of children is crucial but communicating it may not be facilitated by ICTs.

Second, how is the information inputted? The basic details of the child's ContactPoint record were created from existing databases (often inaccurately); however, records of other professional activity relied on each professional indicating their involvement. Even accepting the 'technophobe' issues mentioned above, deciding to make an entry was not straightforward. At what point does a play worker consider that they are 'working' with the child in a 'concerned' way in contrast to the other children at the centre? In the pilots, we found widespread reluctance by professionals to use the technologies, creating a problem. If a professional looks on the database and sees no services on the child's record, they will have to decide whether this accurately depicts the child's lack of involvement or the reluctance by other professionals to make an entry. If ContactPoint is inaccurate it will not be used; if it is not used it will be inaccurate. One of the pilot databases was closed down, partly because of the lack of a 'critical mass' of use.

Third, what and when is 'information' to be 'shared'? Indicating a professional's involvement on ContactPoint requires making a judgement about whether worries are sufficient to share and how best this is achieved. It may entail taking on responsibilities to coordinate others' actions, colleagues may need to be persuaded, and relations with children and parents may be compromised. Each audience needs to be convinced that present services are inadequate and other interventions are required. This entails more than merely 'sharing information', but strategic action and careful negotiation. Facts need to be set within contexts, hoping that others will draw similar conclusions. It is hard to imagine how decontextualized systems such as databases will manage the nuances of such delicate information exchanges.

Our conclusion, then, was that there were serious problems with the everyday operation of ContactPoint in terms of access, accuracy, reliability, and consequently its use. Using ContactPoint involves a range of moral choices about how the worker constructs 'concern' about children, much more complex than the technical process of logging on.

ContactPoint was switched off in August 2010. The Conservative Party had indicated its opposition before the election in a paper called 'Reversing the Rise of the Surveillance State' (2009). ContactPoint was particularly associated with the National Identity Register, which was physically destroyed. The minister, Damien Green, said: 'Laying ID cards to rest demonstrates the government's commitment to scale back the power of the state and restore civil liberties.'

So are we now in a less intrusive state and is this better for vulnerable children? The government is certainly moving towards a smaller state (partly but not entirely because of cuts in public services). There is a view that there should be fewer national mandates, with local areas encouraged to develop their own solutions. A recent review of child protection has suggested reducing regulations that are seen as getting in the way of skilled professional practice.[3] Even so, the government has considered a replacement for ContactPoint. The National Signposting Service would be restricted to the surveillance of those already heavily involved in the system, but note how the minister uses similar justifications to those for ContactPoint: 'quick and reliable'; 'Experience and research have shown the potential value of a quick and reliable means of discovering whether a child or young person has been or is the subject of a child protection plan and/or whether they are or have been a looked-after child or young person.'[4] The Munro report has not supported this project, which has been accepted by the government, for now. Similarly, the National eCAF was to be a database indicating all children where a CAF has been completed electronically, potentially containing details on many more children than the National Signposting Service. This project was also abandoned in May 2012.

Even if new national databases are not established, there are databases of children at a local level. At least one of the original 'trailblazers' has maintained a local version of ContactPoint, considering it has become embedded in practice. This system relies on voluntary involvement, but with the associated inaccuracies. Several local authorities have databases to coordinate the management of the CAFs. Furthermore, systems of multi-agency working enable professionals to have access across education and social care, although health databases are often unable to link up. Recent observation of a social-care referral team demonstrated the wealth of information already recorded in local databases, as well as the continuing struggles to maintain their accuracy. The strong encouragement for coordinating responses to early intervention in several government-sponsored reports suggests continuing impetus for mechanisms for sharing information of early concerns, probably on a database.

At a time where child protection is being promoted in terms of improving skilled interventions by workers and services are facing severe cutbacks, the presence of the database remains, with its panoptic potential but also its inaccuracy and unreliability. The impact of techno-magical thinking on everyday practice remains seriously underexplored, ignored not just by social scientists, but also by scholars in information systems. It remains a pressing empirical problem.[5]

---

[3] Eileen Munro, *The Munro Review of Child Protection: A Child-Centred System* (London: HMSO, 2011).

[4] *Hansard*, 17 January 2011.

[5] Dave Wastell and Sue White, 'Myths, Facts and Thought Styles…and a Rallying Cry for Civic Engagement', *Journal of Strategic Information Systems* 19, 4 (December 2010): 307–18.

40 Globalizing of Bananas: Of Rhizomes, Fungi, and Mobility

Mimi Sheller

The banana is not simply one of the world's most popular fruits by coincidence. It exists in its current form through a surprisingly wide range of global systems that have been assembled (and contested) to produce it: agriculture, agronomy, transport, labour, migration, tourism, diplomacy, and global governance. It is also implicated in other kinds of cultural discourses such that it travels freighted with racial, gendered, and sexual implications. When the banana surfaces as icon and problem—whether in Hollywood musical numbers or tense diplomatic stand-offs—it connects far-flung parts of the world and condenses complex meanings in an excessive way.[1] Bananas are prime agents for reconnecting distant social networks and the more-than-human worlds to which they are vitally indebted. Above all, bananas are mobile, along with the diseases that stalk them, tracing the uneven topologies of global circulation.

How is a soft yellow fruit produced via complex interconnecting systems of global transportation, migration, communication, politics and regulation, culture and media? These global systems do not simply move the banana, but instigate it as a material intertwining of commodity markets, living plants, and fungal diseases;[2] as a fruitful yet fragile relation between infrastructures, landscapes, and migrants;[3] and as a compelling object of popular cultures, performing arts, and comedic routines.[4] In particular, 'entwined biological, economic,

---

[1] This article is based in part on Mimi Sheller, 'Skinning the Banana Trade: Racial Erotics and Ethical Consumption', in *Geographies of Race and Food: Fields, Bodies, Markets*, ed. Rachel Slocum and Arun Saldanha (Farnham: Ashgate, 2013), 291–312.

[2] Dan Koeppel, *Banana: The Fate of the Fruit that Changed the World* (New York: Hudson Street Press, 2007); Mike Peed, 'We Have No Bananas', *The New Yorker*, 10 January 2011.

[3] Phillipe Bourgeois, *Ethnicity at Work: Divided Labor on a Central American Banana Plantation* (Baltimore: Johns Hopkins University Press, 1989); Mark Moberg, *Myths of Ethnicity and Nation: Immigration, Work and Identity in the Belize Banana Industry* (Knoxville: University of Tennessee Press, 1997).

[4] Cynthia Enloe, *Bananas, Beaches and Bases: Making Feminist Sense of International Politics* (London: Pandora, 1989); Maria Warner, *No Go the Bogeyman: Scaring, Lulling and Making Mock* (New York: Farrar, Straus, and Giroux, 1998).

and cultural processes shaped efforts to create and recreate the export banana.[5] What we call the banana is materially heterogeneous, and therefore unstable and potentially unsustainable:[6] talk, bodies, texts, trucks, architectures, pesticides, markets, boxes, and jokes—all of these and many more are implicated in and perform the banana.

In terms of global importance and gross value of production, bananas (and their cousins, plantains) are the fourth most important global food crop after rice, wheat, and corn, being a dietary staple for hundreds of millions of people in developing countries.[7] Although most of the bananas grown in the world are not exported, it is arguably the transnational banana industry from the late nineteenth century onward that launched the economic system of globalization in its modern form. The United Fruit Company (UFC), founded in 1899, epitomized the modern multinational corporation through its horizontal and vertical integration and stranglehold over Central American 'banana republics' (controlled by banana corporations and their interests). Beyond their economic reach, powerful banana companies have long been involved in nefarious political activities—ranging from UFC's involvement in the 1911 military coup in Honduras and overthrow of Guatemala's first democratically elected government in the 1950s,[8] to Chiquita's $25 million fine in 2007 after admitting to supporting Colombian terrorist groups in the 1990s. The rise and fall of the banana industry have had major impacts on entire countries, not only in Central America but also in the Windward Islands in the Caribbean, where 'banana politics' drives elections, labour migration, subsistence-level family survival, and the shifting economies of the illegal drugs trade.[9]

The banana plant is not a tree, but a giant herb and a rhizome. Cultivated bananas are seedless and parthenocarpic, meaning that they form fruit without fertilization by forming side shoots and suckers. Contrary to its potent phallic associations, the plant is sterile; this means that the gene pool of bananas never really changes over the generations. It also means that banana plantation techniques depleted biological diversity and simplified the topography in a way that aided the diffusion of disease and increased its hosts.[10] By the

---

[5] John Soluri, 'Banana Cultures: Linking the Production and Consumption of Export Bananas, 1800–1980', in *Banana Wars: Power, Production and History in the Americas*, ed. Steve Striffler and Mark Moberg (Durham: Duke University Press, 2003): 69.

[6] John Law, *Organizing Modernity* (Oxford: Basil Blackwell, 1994).

[7] Craig Canine, 'Building a Better Banana', *Smithsonian Magazine*, October 2005, <http://www.smithsonianmag.com/people-places/banana.html>.

[8] Peter Chapman, *Bananas: How the United Fruit Company Shaped the World* (Edinburgh: Canongate, 2008).

[9] Michel-Rolph Trouillot, *Peasants and Capital: Dominica in the World Economy* (Baltimore: Johns Hopkins University Press, 1988); Mark Moberg, *Slipping Away: Banana Politics and Fair Trade in the Eastern Caribbean* (New York: Berghahn Books, 2011).

[10] Stuart McCook, *States of Nature: Science, Agriculture, and Environment in the Spanish Caribbean, 1760–1940* (Austin: University of Texas Press, 2002).

1920s, intensive monoculture on huge plantations in Central America assisted in the spread of a fungal disease, *fusarium oxysporum*, commonly known as Panama disease, though it originated in Asia.[11] Monocultures of the Gros Michel variety—the best banana for long-distance travel—'came at the cost of ecological vulnerability', triggering an assault of plant pathogens that 'assumed plague-like proportions in Latin America and the Caribbean'.[12] Devastation of hundreds of thousands of acres of banana plantation across the Americas led to conversion to the less desirable Giant Cavendish variety by the 1960s.

Mobility systems are a crucial part of the globalization of bananas: both the systems moving bananas (and their pathogens) from crop to shop, and the systems moving workers from one plantation zone to another. Operating at the intersection of peasants and global capital,[13] the ecological vulnerability of banana plantations produced a 'persistent impermanence' and 'enforced mobility' as uprooted workers were enticed to new banana zones, producing ethnic/racial rivalries and tensions.[14] With the reduction of transatlantic journey times by the use of steam-powered ships, the invention of refrigeration, and the development of new forms of ethnically marked branding (such as Senorita Chiquita Banana; see Figure 40.1), bananas were the first tropical fruit to be popularized as a long-distance mass-market commodity. In 1959, the Standard Fruit Co deemed boxed bananas 'the greatest innovation in the history of the banana industry'.[15] Banana fleets were not only the first vessels to have built-in refrigeration systems, but since the 1980s banana growers have developed controlled-temperature warehousing and uniform ripening through the use of ethylene gas. At the same time, the boxing and branding of bananas had major impacts on small farmers who were obligated to invest in (and internalize the costs of) the increasingly specific packing techniques to make their crop globally mobile.[16]

Despite these technological advances, however, disease continues to threaten the banana. Plantations of the Cavendish variety remained susceptible to another Asian fungal disease, Black Sigatoka (*Cercospora musae*), and plagues of nematodes; aerial spraying of pesticides and fungicides contributed to the poisoning of water systems, destruction of avian populations, and the sterility of thousands of Central American banana workers.[17] This prompted

---

[11] Claude W. Wardlaw, *Green Havoc in the Lands of the Caribbean* (Edinburgh: William Blackwood and Sons, 1935).

[12] Allen Wells, 'Conclusions: Dialectical Bananas' in *Banana Wars: Power, Production and History in the Americas*, ed. Steve Stiffler and Mark Moberg (Durham: Duke University Press, 2003): 321.

[13] Trouillot, *Peasants and Capital*; Larry Grossman, *The Political Ecology of Bananas: Contract Farming, Peasants and Agrarian Change in the Eastern Caribbean* (Chapel Hill: University of North Carolina Press, 1998).

[14] Moberg, *Myths of Ethnicity and Nation*; Wells, 'Conclusions: Dialectical Bananas'.

[15] Soluri, 'Banana Cultures', 72.

[16] Moberg, *Slipping Away*.

[17] Wells, 'Conclusions: Dialectical Bananas', 323, 325.

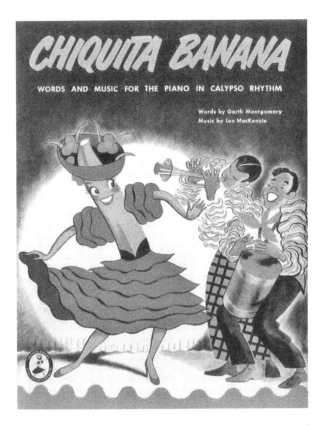

Figure 40.1 Bananas have occupied many more spaces than just the breakfast table. This 1940s-era sheet music, for example, demonstrated a mix of various forms of consumption, aspiration, and spatial assumptions in the American consumer market

the creation of the International Network for the Improvement of Banana and Plantain (INIBAP) in 1985. Part of the International Institute of Plant Genetic Resources (IPGRI), INIBAP founded a transit centre to house the genetic diversity of worldwide bananas, hosted by the Catholic University of Leuven, in Belgium. The transit centre currently contains 1,175 different kinds of banana plantlets growing in test tubes and forms part of a worldwide network, now known as Bioversity, holding diverse food plants 'in trust' for humanity, a kind of global Noah's Ark. A research institute in France is sequencing the banana genome, while scientists in Australia are trying to genetically engineer Cavendish bananas resistant to fungal attack.[18] Meanwhile, though, global market forces and trade regimes are busily shaping bananas to other logics and mobility systems.

---

[18] Peed, 'We Have No Bananas', 34.

Following the formation of the Single European Market in 1992, the European Union became the world's largest market for bananas (35–40 per cent) and the dismantling of various countries' preferential regimes for bananas became one of the most contentious trade issues. By the 1990s five billion bananas a year were being consumed in the United Kingdom alone.[19] The 1990s 'banana wars' between the European Union, the United States, and several South American and Caribbean producers broke out over preferences and barriers for bananas grown by small Caribbean farmers versus those grown by American corporations in huge Central American plantations. The entire incident reflects the complex flows of trade, diplomacy, governance, and historical relationships across the Atlantic world, and above all pitted the discourse of neoliberal globalization against a discourse of global justice and fair trade.[20]

In 1999 the World Trade Organization ruled that the EU banana regime violated global trade rules, and that the USA was allowed to impose $191.4 million in sanctions. The EU eventually agreed to phase out its tariff system by 2006, threatening the livelihood of tens of thousands of small Caribbean growers in the Windward Islands.[21] This made Fair Trade certification the most viable route left to European markets, and transformed how bananas are sourced and marketed, especially in UK supermarkets. Global trade policies today remain inseparable from ethical questions: What should we eat, from where, produced by whom, under what conditions? The 'ethical banana' is a product and a figuration of these processes, as new kinds of ethical consumption disrupt the spatial distances and temporal gaps between agricultural producers and consumers, and refold the relation between the North and the South through alternative trade networks.[22]

The question of the ethical banana is seldom linked to questions of global racism and transnational migration; yet these too are crucial to the mobilities of the banana. A relational ethics must come full circle and recognize the interconnected systems of mobility that link commodity markets to human migrations, and world-trade regimes to racially based immigration policies. As a tropical export crop, bananas depend on a racialized labour force that is marked as 'black' or 'brown', and controlled by restrictive visa regimes. Bananas thus help to construct the racialized spaces of global inequality. There

---

[19] Warner, *No Go the Bogeyman*, 360. For comparison, the current figure in the USA is approximately 7.6 billion bananas eaten in 2008.

[20] Karla Slocum, 'Discourses and Counterdiscources on Globalization and the St. Lucian Banana Industry', in *Banana Wars: Power, Production and History in the Americas*, ed. Steve Stiffler and Mark Moberg (Durham: Duke University Press, 2003).

[21] Myers, *Banana Wars*.

[22] Moberg, *Slipping Away*; Sarah Whatmore and Lorraine Thorne, 'Nourishing Networks: Alternative Geographies of Food', in *Globalising Food: Agrarian Questions and Global Restructuring*, ed. David Goodman and Michael Watts (London: Routledge, 1997); Laura T. Raynolds, 'Re-Embedding Global Agriculture: The International Organic and Fair Trade Movements', *Journal of Agriculture and Human Values* 17, 3 (September 2000): 297–309.

is a connection, then, between the macro level that we call 'the global' (with its debates over trade regimes and free trade) and the micro level of a personalized corporeal ethics that recognizes the global interdependence of who eats and who goes hungry, who produces and who consumes. Small gestures such as the marketing of ethical bananas may have some real impact on global trade systems by promoting worker participation in economic democratization.[23] Fair trade bananas intervene in the market in a way that potentially makes legible the systems of (im)mobility, market regulation, and racialization that perform inter-corporeal connections across global scales.[24]

Nevertheless, in the final analysis disease may do far more than the ethical banana ever will to illustrate the limits of human control of such complex systems. In late 2002, Dr Emile Frison, who heads INIBAP, published an article in the *New Scientist* warning that 'edible bananas may disappear within a decade if urgent action is not taken to develop new varieties resistant to blight'. Frison announced plans to map the genetic blueprint of the banana within five years, in order to try to save varieties that are staple foods in many parts of Africa and Asia, where half a billion people depend on the banana and plantain as staple foods. A new, more virulent strain of Panama disease has started to spread. The new strain, known as Tropical Race 4, has proved lethal to a broader range of banana hosts, including the Cavendish. It first appeared in Taiwan in the 1980s, where it wiped out 70 per cent of Cavendish plantations; then spread to Malaysia and Indonesia, has devastated plantations in China and the Phillipines, and has most recently spread to northern Australia and South Africa—and will almost inevitably reach central Africa and Latin America some time soon. No known pesticide is effective against it for long. As one banana grower in Darwin, Australia, put it: 'Shit's gonna *move*. Americans are snookered. They'd better wake up and realize it, or they're not going to have any bananas to eat.'[25]

The Cavendish banana as a global commodity may soon disappear, leaving in its wake only the many local varieties that can resist this disease but are unsuitable for export; or perhaps a new high-tech genetically engineered alternative. Thus the banana of the future pivots on two possibilities, or a combination thereof: either re-localization of more fragile varieties of the plant, with reduced mobility (and impact on staple food crops), or hyper-globalization of a super-banana in the form of a patented genetically modified organism whose mobility will be in the hands of private corporations. In either case the contestation of banana politics around social justice, agrarian survival, and the ethics of global markets will only intensify.

---

[23] Mimi Sheller, 'Bleeding Humanity and Gendered Embodiments: From Antislavery Sugar Boycotts to Ethical Consumers', *Humanity* 2, 2 (Fall 2011): 171–92.

[24] Sarah Whatmore, *Hybrid Geographies: Natures, Cultures, Spaces* (London: Sage, 2002); Moberg, *Slipping Away*.

[25] Peed, 'We Have No Bananas', 20.

Part VI

Order and Control

41 **Forms that Form**

Nicholas Gill

Asylum seekers and 'illegal' migrants usually hit the headlines when some sort of event occurs: the 'escape' of detainees, the involvement of asylum seekers in criminal acts, the passing of a numeric milestone that supposedly illustrates the 'flood' of asylum seekers entering developed countries. Less media attention is given to the everyday technologies that structure asylum seekers' experiences, often hiding unequal power relationships beneath a facade of routine and repetition. Take, for example, the paper forms that confront an asylum seeker from the moment of their entry into countries such as the UK. Almost everything an asylum seeker experiences in a country such as the UK is governed, monitored, or recorded in some way through these forms: their claim for asylum, the support they receive at the various stages of the determination process, and the legal procedures that accompany them. They are a currency of legitimacy that asylum seekers have no choice but to trade in.

The British government provides subsistence support to asylum seekers who would otherwise be destitute in the UK, but to apply for this support the asylum seeker must navigate a 35-page form-based interrogation about the number of dependents they have, the value of their assets (including jewellery), the inadequacy of their current accommodation, the location and status of their original, and any subsequent, claims for asylum or support, and their health and disability status. Figure 41.1 provides an extract from the application form.

After various questions and sections such as those exhibited in Figure 41.1 that quiz the applicant on income, savings, dependants, and a range of other personal information, the form provides two full pages for 'additional information'. Here the applicant is invited to construct a narrative that will be appealing to the sensibilities of those making the decision. An acceptable, pitiable version of oneself is to be produced, emphasizing the helplessness of the applicant, the worthiness of their cause, and, underneath all this supplication, the authority and legitimacy of state actors to judge on these very criteria.

Refused asylum seekers in the UK have the right to support if they are facing destitution while they are continuing to make 'reasonable steps' towards leaving the country. The support amounts to £35 per week that is loaded on to an 'Azure' card that they can use in certain supermarkets (this system means that they receive no cash). But they are often reluctant to claim this support, because they must agree to be deported at a later date if they claim it. As a result,

	Can you liquidate this asset? Yes ☐ No ☐
- Land in the UK? *	Yes ☐ No ☐
	If yes, what is the value of the land in the UK?
	Currency:
	Can you liquidate this asset? Yes ☐ No ☐
- Land outside the UK? *	Yes ☐ No ☐
	If yes, what is the value of the land outside the UK?
	Currency:
	Can you liquidate this asset? Yes ☐ No ☐
- valuable jewellery *	Yes ☐ No ☐
	If yes, what is the value of the jewellery?
	Currency:
- TV, DVD, electrical goods *	Yes ☐ No ☐
	If yes, what is the value of the goods?
	Currency:
-car, vehicle *	Yes ☐ No ☐
	If yes, what is the value of the car/vehicle?
	Currency:
52. Do you wish to add another material asset? *	Yes ☐ complete annex C
	No ☐ go to question 53
53. Do you have any of the following monetary assets? *	You must select any or all of the monetary assets you have
- Cash held in the UK? *	Yes ☐ No ☐
	Value:
	Currency of assets:

Figure 41.1 Extract from 35-page form for application for government support while claiming asylum, issued by the UK Border Agency and called an Asylum Support Application Form (ASF1), <http://www.ukba.homeoffice.gov.uk/sitecontent/applicationforms/asylum/asylumsupportform.pdf> (accessed 22 November 2013)

fewer than one in ten of the refused asylum seekers thought to be in the UK are in receipt of co-called 'Section 4' support; the rest choose destitution. For those that do take the support available, the Section 4 application form lays bare the soul of the applicant: everything—from credit history to pregnancy, illness, marital status, degree of destitution (with evidence), and the unconditional compliance of the applicant with future Home Office demands—is required.

Forms such as the applications for support have a number of immediate effects. First, they *condition* the asylum seeker's voice. For the vast majority, the forms will not be in their mother tongue, so they may have to find help to fill in the forms. Positioning the applicants as objects of charity from the outset, workers in 'One Stop Services' around the country, or lawyers that are increasingly rare, work to translate the experiences of asylum seekers into terms that are legally legible and appropriate. These actions, while often well meaning, can have the side effect of forming accounts in ways that cannot avoid impoverishing them.

Second, they *obscure* the complexity of asylum cases from the very people who have to make decisions on the basis of the forms. Decision makers in 'Regional Asylum Teams' are often located in suburban sites well away from asylum-seeker populations, as a consequence of recent moves to devolve aspects of the asylum system. These back-office workers are asked to make a judgement about asylum seekers that they have never met and will never meet. The forms mobilize a detached, partial presentation of the asylum seekers they describe, distilling 'facts' from emotions, abbreviating long histories of often arduous travel, and curtailing accounts of suffering and loss to small boxes on a page. This disembodiment of the asylum seeker's story deprives decision makers of the human contact they could benefit from in order to make an informed decision.

Third, the forms demand that the asylum seeker is able to mobilize a specific constellation of artefacts, proofs, documents, copies, memories, and photographs to corroborate their stories. In this way such forms *are themselves formative*. They insist that the asylum seeker collects about them a set of materials without which they are not recognized as complete. These include asylum registration cards, passports, birth certificates, medical declarations, certified letters from medical professionals, marriage certificates, identity cards, driving licences, medical evidence, flight tickets, copies of other applications, and legal permissions. Without at least some of these, the issue is not whether or not they are genuine, but whether they can collect the relevant bits of paper to allow them access to a forum in which a judgement about their genuineness can be made. One can only be an asylum seeker with these accompaniments, demonstrating the profound interconnections between material and political status. Therefore it is with these that a proper asylum seeker is defined. The entire process insists that the applicants take up the language, rituals, and rites of the state, even if they are to be told they are to be deported or refused.

Fourth, these forms also express something to the asylum seekers who are obliged to fill them in. In this sense they are *performative*—they perform the dominance of the state by making compulsory a series of movements in time and space without which the asylum seeker becomes subject to the consequences of administrative or legal proceedings. Asylum seekers are required by the Nationality, Immigration and Asylum Act (2002) to make their asylum claim as soon as reasonably practicable once they have arrived in the UK, which can be taken to mean as little as within three days. For all sorts of reasons, this puts stress upon asylum-seeker populations, not least because they can only apply for asylum at ports or in London (a second within-country asylum-screening centre for initial applications was closed in Liverpool in 2009). A range of other spatio-temporal requirements accompany the asylum determination process: applicants often have to visit local reporting stations every few days, they can be asked to move to anywhere in the country at short notice, they must attend interviews at specific dates and times, sometimes with their families, and they must complete and return all forms issued to them within the prescribed time limits. All these processes make clear to the applicant that it is the state that dictates the uses to which they can legitimately put their time, as well as the places that they can legitimately occupy.

Forms are part and parcel of the business of managing asylum seekers. On the one hand they are seen as necessary—any government will attempt to keep track of its population. But they are also intrinsically political, affronting mobility and stamping the authority of the state on populations that are on the move. Asylum seekers simply don't have the means to organize and resist the unrealistic demands put upon them to fill in forms that require extensive knowledge, documentary substantiation, and rapid reading and writing skills. Nor, very often, do charities and aid agencies working on their behalf. A report published by Positive Action for Refugees and Asylum Seekers (PAFRAS), a charity, found that, of 56 refused asylum seekers surveyed, the majority subsisted on less than £5 per day and over two-thirds of them had been tortured in their home countries. They received help from family and friends (45 per cent), charities (28 per cent), and churches (19 per cent). Faced with the poverty and ill health of these populations, 'the burden of support is falling on refugee communities, faith groups, religious institutions, and voluntary organizations, who sometimes literally save people's lives, ensuring that they do not starve'.[1] Notions such as the 'Big Society' in the UK, which has contributed to a contraction of funds available to these organizations, ratify and perpetuate this precarity.

---

[1] Diane Taylor, *Underground Lives* (Leeds: PAFRAS, 2009; <http://www.irr.org.uk/pdf2/Underground_Lives.pdf>): 11.

As a result of the desperate need to respond to the immediacy of the plight of many claimants, asylum aid agencies are forced to speak the language of the state, working with asylum seekers to fulfil the demands of the forms that structure their work. For these agencies and the asylum seekers they help, the age of globalization is a world away. The endless tasks they are required to perform, such as the forms they must complete, constitute the grit and dirt that choke the cogs of global liberalization.

42 Accounting for the Calculating Self

Peter Miller

[W]ith the aid of the morality of mores and the social straitjacket, man was actually *made* calculable.[1]

Sociologists once saw a link between accounting and capitalism.[2] That link was then forgotten, or at least overlooked, for half a century or more. Recently, sociologists have been busy rediscovering the economy.[3] This rediscovery needs to be extended, however, to include the multiple and differentiated calculative infrastructures that make and shape the economy and economic relations.[4] It needs to be extended also to include the links between these calculative infrastructures and the ways of governing individuals, actions, and entities.[5] There is little point in studying practices of governing separate from the objects that

[1] Friedrich Nietzsche, *On the Genealogy of Morals*, W. Kaufmann and R. J. Hollingdale, trans. (New York: Vintage Books, 1969 [1887]): 59.

[2] Peter Miller, 'Calculating Economic Life', *Journal of Cultural Economy* 1, 1 (2008): 51–64; Peter Miller and Michael Power, 'Accounting, Organizing, and Economizing: Connecting Accounting Research and Organization Theory', *The Academy of Management Annals*, 7, 1 (2013): 557–605.

[3] Ash Amin and Nigel Thrift, *The Blackwell Cultural Economy Reader* (Oxford: Blackwell, 2004); Koray Çalışkan and Michel Callon, 'Economization, part 1: Shifting Attention from the Economy Towards Processes of Economization', *Economy and Society*, 38, 3 (2009): 369–98; Koray Çalışkan and Michel Callon, 'Economization, part 2: A Research Programme for the Study of Markets', *Economy and Society*, 39, 1: 1–32; Michel Callon, ed., *The Laws of the Markets* (Oxford: Blackwell, 1998); Paul DiMaggio, ed., *The Twenty-First-Century Firm: Changing Economic Organization in International Perspective* (Princeton: Princeton University Press, 2001); Neil Fligstein, *The Transformation of Corporate Control* (Cambridge, MA: Harvard University Press, 1990) and *The Architecture of Markets: An Economic Sociology of Twenty-First-Century Capitalist Societies* (Princeton: Princeton University Press, 2001); Karin Knorr Cetina and Alex Preda, eds, *The Sociology of Financial Markets* (Oxford: Oxford University Press, 2004); Donald MacKenzie, *An Engine, Not a Camera: How Financial Models Shape Markets* (Cambridge, MA: MIT Press, 2006); Donald MacKenzie and Yuval Millo, 'Constructing a Market, Performing Theory: The Historical Sociology of a Financial Derivatives Exchange', *American Journal of Sociology* 109, 1 (July 2003): 107–45; Neil J. Smelser and Richard Swedberg, eds, *The Handbook of Economic Sociology* (2nd edn, Princeton: Princeton University Press, 2005).

[4] Liisa Kurunmäki and Peter Miller, 'Calculating Failure: The making of a calculative infrastructure for forgiving and forecasting failure', *Business History*, 55, 7 (2013): 1100–18.

[5] Anthony G. Hopwood and Peter Miller, eds, *Accounting as Social and Institutional Practice* (Cambridge: Cambridge University Press, 1994); Andrea Mennicken and Peter Miller, 'Accounting,

are to be governed, and the ideas that animate such practices. Put differently, if objects, ideas, and practices for governing economic relations fit each other, this is because they have been made to fit, and we need to pay attention to the ways in which they have come to be aligned.

The focus of this chapter is on one particular part of this calculative infrastructure—accounting—and how the instruments and ideas of accounting make the constituent parts of the economy visible as an economy, and amenable to intervention. More specifically, it is about accounting for the calculating self—how ways of calculating go hand in hand with forms of personhood. For making people responsible is as much about conceptions of the person as it is about the performativity of a particular set of calculative practices. Over 30 years ago, it was said that we go in search of our selves through the genitals.[6] Today, we find who we are through the incessant calculations that we perform on ourselves and others. The following five propositions set out schematically and very briefly what 'accounting for the calculating self' means.

First, it means attending to the distinctive capacity of accounting to act on the actions of others. This derives in large part from the ability of accounting to make comparable the incomparable, by distilling things into a single financial figure.[7] This is more than quantification, calculation, or commensuration, and it is more than 'trust in numbers'.[8] Many other bodies of expertise quantify, but in doing so they only facilitate comparisons of things that are already comparable. Accounting takes things much further, by financializing them, by distilling substantively different kinds or classes of things into a single financial figure (the return on investment of a division, the net present value of an investment opportunity, the financial ratios of a company). Accounting abstracts from the qualities of things, and places them on an equal footing, one far removed from the messy reality of manufacturing automobiles, extracting oil, or delivering health care. This allows connections to be formed with a whole set of other calculations, whether those of actuaries, engineers, health economists, regulators, statisticians, and many others. And this chain of calculations allows those within and beyond firms and other organizations to both act on their own actions and seek to influence the actions of others.

Territorialization and Power', *Foucault Studies*, 13, 4 (2012): 4–24; Andrea Mennicken and Peter Miller, 'Michel Foucault and the Administering of Lives', in Paul Adler, Paul du Gay, Glenn Morgan, and Michael Reed, eds, *The Oxford Handbook of Sociology, Social Theory and Organization Studies: Contemporary Currents* (Oxford: Oxford University Press, 2014); Peter Miller and Nikolas Rose, 'Political Power Beyond the State: Problematics of Government', *British Journal of Sociology* 43, 2 (June 1992): 173–205.

  [6] Richard Sennett, *The Fall of Public Man* (Cambridge: Cambridge University Press, 1974): 74.

  [7] Peter Miller, 'Accounting and Objectivity: The Invention of Calculating Selves and Calculable Spaces', in *Rethinking Objectivity*, Allan Megill, ed. (Durham, NC: Duke University Press, 1994).

  [8] Wendy N. Espeland and Michael Sauder, 'Rankings and Reactivity: How Public Measures Recreate Social Worlds', *American Journal of Sociology* (2007), 113, 1: 1–40; Theodore M. Porter, *Trust in Numbers: The Pursuit of Objectivity in Science and Public Life* (Princeton: Princeton University Press, 1995).

Second, accounting for the calculating self means paying attention to the ideas of personhood that are brought into play in all these attempts to act on the actions of others. It concerns what Nietzsche called the possibility of breeding an animal with the right to make promises.[9] For the individual capable of anticipating and assessing what is to be done, and how, requires the capacity to calculate and compute. It is such an entity that accounting has long sought to fabricate. A whole set of ideas of personhood come into play here. The 'decision maker' is one such idea, which has characterized managerial discourses since the 1930s, and remains at the heart of much of the pedagogy of accounting. 'Responsibility' accounting is another such idea. Both ideas operate by imposing a sort of moral constraint or template on actions carried out under their aegis, defining and constraining the possibilities for action. In Hacking's terminology, such categories 'make up people', that is to say they change the space of possibilities for personhood and action, and they do so in a reciprocal relationship with the instruments that make actions calculable.[10] And they are linked, in turn, to the articulation and valorization of such categories in political and moral discourse.[11]

Third, accounting for the calculating self means examining the assemblages within which accounting operates, rather than focusing largely or exclusively on the instruments themselves, as if they alone were sufficient to explain their effects. For the calculative instruments of accounting are simultaneously social and technical. They always operate within historically specific assemblages, whose only unity is that of the co-functioning of their components. A particular tool or device remains marginal, or little used, until there exists a social machine or collective assemblage that is capable of animating it.[12] Deleuze cites the example of the stirrup, which gave the knight lateral stability, allowing the lance to be tucked under one arm, and benefit derived from the horse's speed.[13] This made possible, he argues, a new military unity. For this 'technical' development was, in turn, linked to the complex assemblage of feudalism, which imposed an obligation to serve on horseback in return for the grant of land. Likewise, with the accountant's toolkit. This arms the manager, the board member, or the regulator with a set of instruments for assessing and comparing the performance of others. This, in turn, is linked to obligations derived from an assemblage of social relations based on an ideal image of

---

[9] Nietzsche, *On the Genealogy of Morals*, 57.

[10] Ian Hacking, 'Making Up People', in *Reconstructing Individualism: Autonomy, Individuality, and the Self in Western Thought*, Thomas C. Heller, Morton Sosna, and David E. Wellbery, eds (Stanford: Stanford University Press, 1986).

[11] Miller and Rose, 'Political Power Beyond the State'.

[12] Stuart Burchell, Colin Clubb, Anthony Hopwood, John Hughes, and Janine Nahapiet, 'The Roles of Accounting in Organizations and Society', *Accounting, Organizations and Society* 5, 1 (1980): 5–27; Miller, 'Margins of Accounting'.

[13] Gilles Deleuze and Claire Parnet, *Dialogues* (Paris: Flammarion, 1977).

the market, and the concomitant aspirations of making people's behaviour fit such an image. The instruments of accounting are always already part of such assemblages, multiplicities made up of many heterogeneous terms, alliances, liaisons, and contagions.

Fourth, accounting for the calculating self is also about creating calculable spaces. Put differently, territorialization is intrinsic to the forming of assemblages, for there is no assemblage without territory. The calculative instruments of accountancy not only transform the possibilities for personhood. They also construct the calculable spaces that individuals inhabit within firms and other organizations, by making visible the hierarchical arrangement of persons and things. Whether it is an actual physical space such as a factory floor, or an abstract space such as a 'division', a 'cost centre', or a 'profit centre', the calculative instruments of accountancy—in association with those of the architect, the engineer, the industrial psychologist, and many others—make up and link up such spaces into an operating ensemble whose performance can be known and compared with others that are both proximate and distant.[14] The territorialization achieved enables the entity to be represented as a series of financial flows, evaluated according to a financial rationale, and acted upon from both within and beyond in order to enhance such flows.

Viewed in these terms, accounting for the calculating self is about much more than exploring how individuals and organizations manipulate or distort numbers, how they 'cook the books'. It is about a distinctively modern form of power, one that can operate with ease 'at a distance', and in a manner wholly in tune with contemporary notions of responsibility, choice, and performance, whether in the corporate world or in the world of public services. The calculative practices of accounting can, that is to say, be viewed as 'mediating instruments'.[15] This refers to the ability of an instrument to carry within it at least a dual set of ideas, whether they pertain to science and the economy, medicine and finance, or engineering and industry. Mediating instruments operate as means of representation and means of intervention, linking up discrete domains and activities, yet remaining distinct from the object of intervention. This allows aspirations, actors, and arenas to be connected, but via a particular instrument rather than directly. In this way, medical, scientific, and engineering categories can be interdefined with political and economic categories. Local ways of thinking can, likewise, link the larger political culture with the everyday doings of a multiplicity of actors. And

---

[14] Peter Miller and Ted O'Leary, 'The Factory as Laboratory', *Science in Context* 7, 3 (1994): 469–96.

[15] Peter Miller and Ted O'Leary, 'Mediating Instruments and Making Markets: Capital Budgeting, Science and the Economy', *Accounting, Organizations and Society* 32 (2007): 701–34; Mary S. Morgan and Margaret Morrison, eds, *Models as Mediators: Perspectives on Natural and Social Science* (Cambridge: Cambridge University Press, 1999); M. Norton Wise, 'Mediating Machines', *Science in Context* 2, 1 (1988): 77–113.

domains as diverse as health care and banking can be made to look remarkably similar, as the instruments used to assess and act on them come to be shared.

The term hybridizing captures well this process of mixing up and linking up very different types of things. For we are confronted daily with imbroglios that jumble up apparently discrete things such as science, politics, economy, law, and so on.[16] Despite constant attempts to demarcate, impurity is the rule and hybrids are the norm. Hybridizing can, of course, assume various forms, and not all practices, processes, and expertises hybridize with equal ease. Once formed, a hybrid may revert, as in the botanical world. Or the newly formed hybrid may stabilize for a while. And once hybridization has occurred, it can commence anew, as the recently formed hybrid comes into contact with others. The calculative practices of accounting are particularly interesting in this respect, as they are inherently hybrids, formed and reformed as they have been at the 'margins' of more than one discipline.[17]

Accounting practices are constantly engaged in a dual hybridization process, seeking to make visible and calculable the hybrids they encounter, while at the same time hybridizing themselves through their encounters with other bodies of expertise. One can see this at work in the context of the ongoing attempts to reform and marketize health care in the UK and many other countries.[18] And one can see it equally in the very different domain of microprocessors, in the oddly named 'Moore's law', which embeds within itself a cost function and a technological trajectory.[19] Accounting is not unique in its ability to hybridize, to act as a mediating instrument. But it is distinctive in its ability to link together widely differing actors and aspirations into an operating assemblage with the aim of making markets. The aspirations of those devising new microprocessors and new processes for fabricating them have no necessary affinity with those seeking annual cost reductions. The aspirations of those inventing new techniques for hip surgery have no necessary affinity with those seeking to give health-care consumers more 'choice'. More generally, those seeking to enact responsibility and devolve decisions have no necessary affinity with

[16] Liisa Kurunmäki, 'A Hybrid Profession—the Acquisition of Management Accounting Expertise by Medical Professionals', *Accounting, Organizations and Society* 29, 3–4 (April–May 2004): 327–47; Liisa Kurunmäki and Peter Miller, 'Modernising Government: The Calculating Self, Hybridisation and Performance Measurement', *Financial Accountability and Management* 22, 1 (February 2006): 87–106; Bruno Latour, *Science in Action: How to Follow Scientists and Engineers Through Society* (Milton Keynes: Open University Press, 1987); Peter Miller, Liisa Kurunmäki, and Ted O'Leary, 'Accounting, Hybrids and the Management of Risk', *Accounting, Organizations and Society* 33, 7–8 (October–November 2008): 942–67 and 'Calculating Hybrids', in *Calculating the Social: Standards and the Reconfiguration of Governing*, Vaughan Higgins and Wendy Larner, eds (Basingstoke: Palgrave Macmillan, 2010).

[17] Miller, 'The Margins of Accounting'.

[18] Kurunmäki and Miller, 'Modernising Government', and 'Regulatory Hybrids: Partnerships, Budgeting and Modernising Government', *Management Accounting Research* (forthcoming).

[19] Miller and O'Leary, 'The Factory as Laboratory'.

those seeking to enhance and calculate the economic returns of such newly created responsibility centres. But this affinity can be forged and enacted (or at least attempted) through the increasingly prevalent calculative practices that go under the name of accounting.

This alerts us to a fifth and final characteristic of the panoply of instruments that makes up what is today called accounting—their ability to travel. We have, of course, long been aware of the important role played by those forms of knowledge that are stable, mobile, and combinable.[20] And we have also been alerted to the important role that technologies of inscription and calculation play in historically specific modalities of governing.[21] But we need to know much more about how, and under what circumstances, some instruments travel and others do not. Put differently, some ideas and practices travel 'light', while others may be too heavy to travel easily. Standard costing, for instance, seems able to travel light, and was equally at home in the very different assemblages of the Soviet Union and the United States in the early decades of the twentieth century. Ratio analysis, developed initially for purposes of credit reporting in the United States across the second half of the nineteenth century, and now an integral part of accounting, also seems able to travel readily across both national boundaries and the boundaries that used to demarcate the corporate world and public services. Audit, likewise, seems to travel almost effortlessly across a vast range of territories.[22] Accruals accounting, in contrast, seems to travel less easily, as does programme budgeting. This suggests that we still have much to find out about the ways in which accounting creates calculating selves, and how this takes place within specific assemblages that are constantly forming and reforming.

[20] Latour, *Science in Action*.
[21] Miller and Rose, 'Political Power Beyond the State'.
[22] Michael Power, *The Audit Society: Rituals of Verification* (Oxford: Oxford University Press, 1997). See also Andrea Mennicken, 'Connecting Worlds: The Translation of International Auditing Standards into Post-Soviet Audit Practice', *Accounting, Organizations and Society* 33, 4–5 (2008): 384–414.

43 Replaying Society to the World through CCTV

Daniel Neyland

Closed-circuit television (CCTV) cameras are a frequent feature of urban life across cities of the developed world. In this chapter I suggest that CCTV systems are involved in the production of versions of society (who and what was where at what time; who and what was out of place and why). I will argue that the ubiquity of CCTV now leads to calls for society to be replayed at particular moments of crisis. Such replays can be mobilized to many locations through TV, newspapers, and the Internet, making CCTV narratives of society broadly available. However, these replays involve a great deal of practical work, first to build narrative, and second to ensure that narratives remain consistent under conditions of mobility.

Introduction

In the UK there is little certainty regarding the number of CCTV cameras in operation.[1] CCTV systems do not simply and straightforwardly produce images of activity in the areas where they operate. Instead such systems involve complex interactions between multiple people (e.g. CCTV staff, police officers, CCTV managers, shoppers, suspects, loiterers, kids) and things (e.g. cameras, monitors, fibre-optic connections, pens, paper, street lighting). On occasions these interactions operate to make sense of urban activity in real time, as the activity happens. More frequently, CCTV archives are used to retrospectively reconstruct previously overlooked footage as potentially relevant for making sense of events that have been subsequently reported. In both scenarios attempts are made to articulate 'what is going on' in the images. Images are thus never left to talk for themselves but are instead always delivered (to media, to courts of law, during press conferences, in CCTV sales pitches) with a narrative that tells a story of the people and things apparently in the image. Attempts are made to gain corroboration that the narrative is an indisputable

---

[1] Daniel Neyland, *Privacy, Surveillance and Public Trust* (London: Palgrave Macmillan, 2006).

property of the images. To look at how CCTV narratives of society are produced, demanded, and made available, I will analyse the operation of CCTV around the London bombings of July 2005.

Producing Society

The work done to produce a replay of society for 7 July 2005 involved five (sometimes overlapping) aspects. First, police officers accumulated CCTV footage. There are so many CCTV systems in major UK cities that part of the standard package of measures for preparing for possible terrorist attacks involves mapping all the CCTV systems for a city and establishing who owns and runs those systems. In the immediate aftermath of the bombings, police officers were sent to multiple locations to collect CCTV footage, mostly on tape but also in computer hard drives. This produced around 200,000 hours of CCTV footage.[2] Second, this footage had to be categorized and indexed. There remains no automated system for drawing together multiple types of CCTV imagery, nor is there an automated system for searching through footage to establish which people moved from place to place, from camera system to camera system. Police officers had to watch tapes and then note on a database a standard set of descriptors for each individual who entered a frame of footage. Third, given that the police had 200,000 hours (or around 22 years) of footage, selections had to be made on where to start searching and what to follow. Underground and train stations were selected as a start point. CCTV staff experienced in picking out the suspicious (such as pickpockets) were drafted in to help make selections. Fourth, selections were made in line with developing investigations of the wrecked trains and bus. This led to the development of scenarios: the bombers were not suicide bombers and so bags or packages separated from owners became the appropriate category of suspicion; they were suicide bombers, so identifying those on buses and trains became paramount; they were known terrorists, so should be checked against terrorist intelligence; they were 'clean skins' and so would be unknown. Fifth, choices to follow the movements of particular people had to be worked back to the database: each time a potential suspect was selected for scrutiny the database was searched for the times and places where someone of that description appeared on a tape.

This method eventually led to the development of a CCTV-based narrative of three suspects travelling from Leeds and meeting another in Luton, train

---

[2] James Carless, 'Too much information', government video, <http://www.governmentvideo.com/article/27514>.

travel from Luton to London, the would-be bombers going their separate ways at Kings Cross and images of the would-be bombers on their respective modes of transport. A selection of people (the four suspects, potential accomplices, victims) and things (backpacks, a car, explosives) were singled out from the mass of ordinary life and clearly circled in preparation for their use in the narration of terror. Making the 'suspects' stand out required this work. Using the same method, this narrative was subsequently widened out backwards to incorporate a previous meeting between three of the suspects at Luton nine days before the bombings and forward through the release of images of suspects involved in the 'failed' bombings of 21 July that year.

Demanding Society

Simultaneous with this work to produce a convincing replay of society for the events leading up to the bombings, demands were being made for such a replay to be made available. These demands came from a variety of directions. First, police forces issued a call for further information. This included a request for further images to contribute to the narrative: 'Were you there? Did you see anything suspicious? Did you take any pictures?'[3] Second, a variety of media sources began to talk of the promise of CCTV evidence prior to any actually being released.[4] Third, this demand for society to be replayed for the period around the bombings was voiced most strongly by the 7 July 'Truth Campaign', which argued that CCTV footage was being held back by the police, encouraging a variety of conspiracy theories.[5]

Making Society Available

In the aftermath of the 7 July bombings, the Metropolitan Police ran a series of press conferences and issued press packs providing a detailed CCTV-based replay of society. The press conferences and packs acted as devices to hold the images and narratives together and situate the narratives as properties of the

---

[3] 'Can You Help?' poster, South Wales Police (2005), <http://www.south-wales.police.uk>.

[4] 'London Bombs Killed "At Least 50"', BBC News, 8 July 2005, <http://news.bbc.co.uk/1/hi/uk/4663931.stm>; Patrick Hennessy, David Harrison, Daniel Foggo, '"Foreign Terrorist Cell" Was Behind London Bombings', Telegraph, 10 July 2005, <http://www.telegraph.co.uk/news/uknews/1493717/Foreign-terrorist-cell-was-behind-London-bombings.html>.

[5] Mark Honigsbaum, 'Seeing Isn't Believing', Guardian, 27 June 2006, <http://www.guardian.co.uk/uk/2006/jun/27/july7.uksecurity>.

images. The replay of society featured a narrative of people and things out of place, neatly circled and delineated from the masses of ordinary people and things, made indisputably suspicious by the CCTV evidence—which showed images of young men entering a train station and standing by ticket barriers. Through the narrative we came to know that the men were not ordinary men but terrorists, the backpacks were not ordinary bags but bombs, their entry into the train station was not an ordinary journey but the prelude to a terrorist act, and standing by ticket barriers was not ordinary hanging around but the final confirmatory conversation of terrorists dedicated to carrying out their acts. Take away the narrative and it may appear as no surprise that the police had to put in so much work to make the suspects suspicious. However, the images were never delivered without the narrative. The images and the narrative of the images featured in reports on TV news, newspapers, and websites around the world.[6] The police-issued narrative and CCTV footage oriented *The Times* description of the image of one suspect 'mounting the stairs at Luton station', as 'chilling'.[7] The image was equally 'chilling' across the UK—for example in the *Daily Mail*,[8] *Scotsman*,[9] and *Sun*,[10] in the USA for MSNBC[11] and CNN,[12] and in India for the *Tribune*.[13] The work done to separate out the images, build a narrative through those images, and make that image-based narrative available, globalizing these replays of society, slipped away as 'chilling' terror became a property of the image rather than a result of the work done to select images and build the narrative used to tell a story through the image.

[6] Associated Press, 'CCTV Captures London Clues', FoxNews, 27 July 2005, <http://www.foxnews.com/story/0,2933,163776,00.html>.

[7] Daniel McGrory, Dominic Kennedy, Michael Evans, and Philippe Naughton 'CCTV Pictures Show London Bus Bomber', *The Times*, 14 July 2005.

[8] Martin Smith, 'Chilling First Picture of the Four Bombers Together', *Daily Mail*, 17 July 2005, <http://www.dailymail.co.uk/news/article-356052/Chilling-picture-bombers-together.html>.

[9] 'London Bombs Home-Made from Pharmacy Ingredients', *Scotsman*, 15 July 2005, <http://news.scotsman.com/uk.cfm?id=1610072005>.

[10] Oliver Harvey, 'Story of a Day of Terror', *Sun*, 7 July 2006, <http://www.thesun.co.uk/sol/homepage/news/special_events/7_7/article54836.ece>.

[11] 'CCTV Gives Chilling Glimpse into UK Attacks', MSNBC, 27 July 2005, <http://www.msnbc.msn.com/id/8719858/ns/world_news-attacks_on_london>.

[12] 'Rail Blasts "Almost Simultaneous"', CNN, 9 July 2005, <http://edition.cnn.com/2005/WORLD/europe/07/09/london.attacks/index.html>.

[13] Reuters, 'Minutes Before 7/7 Blasts', *Tribune* (Chandigarh), 17 July 2005, <http://www.tribuneindia.com/2005/20050718/world.htm#3>.

44 The AK-47 as a Material Global Artefact

Tom Osborne

Globalization is not a seamless process. Indeed, in some respects it is not a process at all, but the name we give to a negative phenomenon—to a certain kind of fallout effect. This can be illustrated with reference to the extraordinary proliferation of one global material artefact, the AK-47 Kalashnikov rifle. First produced in 1947, today the AK-47 is certainly a global phenomenon, not restricted to the states of the former Communist bloc and China but a highly mobile artefact with uneven yet global powers of reach. Closely tied to this globalist effect is a localist one; that the spread of the AK-47 owes as much to its take-up in regionalized, ragged theatres of operations as to more structured arenas of conflict.

There are probably between 50 and 70 million AK-47s or derivatives spread across the continents of the world, not just in the hands of state militaries but amongst private citizens and rebel groups.[1] Part of its popularity is no doubt due to its intrinsic characteristics, the genius of Mikhail Khalashnikov in producing a rifle that could be, so to speak, syndicated by the Soviet Union (and, in its sphere of operations, communist China) for easy production across its client states (the Soviet sphere of influence was, in this sense, a model of free trade—even, to stretch an analogy somewhat, a sort of proto space of restricted globalization). It is true that the AK-47 benefits, in all its different models, from a degree of relative simplicity: it has few and easily workable parts and is comparatively light for an automatic weapon, as testified by the fact that it is—often forcibly—used by children in many parts of the world, particularly in African states such as the Democratic Republic of Congo. But as a material artefact the reasons for its global reach are not

---

[1] Briefing Note, 'The AK-47, The World's Favourite Killing Machine', Control Arms, <http://www.controlarms.org/find_out_more/reports/AK_47.pdf>. On the AK-47 and its offshoots see: Charlie Cutshaw and Valery Shilin, *Legends and Reality of the AK: A Behind-the-Scenes Look at the History, Design, and Impact of the Kalashnikov Family of Weapons* (Boulder: Paladin Press, 2000); Edward Clinton Ezell, *The AK-47 Story: Evolution of the Kalashnikov Weapons* (Mechanicsburg: Stackpole Books, 1986); Edward Clinton Ezell and R. Blake Stevens, *Kalashnikov: The Arms and the Man* (Cobourg: Collector Grade Publications, 2001); Larry Kahaner, *AK-47: The Weapon that Changed the Face of War* (Hoboken: Wiley, 2006); and Mikhail Kalashnikov, *The Gun that Changed the World* (Cambridge: Polity Press, 2006). The linkage between the AK-47 and processes of globalization is, I believe, attributable to Michael Mann.

simply to do with its innate characteristics as a certain item of technology, nor even with any systematically planned attempt to disseminate it. The AK-47 proliferated because it was there already. Its proliferation is a legacy of the end of the Cold War, indeed is a fallout from that event; and just as globalization is as much the name we might give to a multidimensional fallout of forms of power from the end of the Cold War as it is the name we give to a particular kind of socio-economic and political process, then so is the spread of the AK-47 a material, portable aspect of that multidimensional fallout.

Of course, globalization has had particular effects on the balance of the arms trade in general. The end of the Cold War saw a sharp initial decline in military expenditure in countries outside their own borders by Russia and the USA, with a concomitant relative increase in expenditure within such countries themselves, especially in the less developed world. As a result, the AK-47 has taken on cultural-iconic status. Its image is included in the flag of Mozambique and its coat of arms, on the flag of Hezbollah, and on the logo of the Iranian Islamic Revolutionary Guards Corps. 'Kalash', a shortened form of Kalashnikov, is used as a name for boys in some African countries.[2]

The AK-47 proliferated because there were a host of small and ragged conflicts breaking out across the globe; so there was a demand and it was widely produced and widely available. The obvious case for illustration is Afghanistan. With the collapse of Soviet power, Afghanistan was left with a glut of AK-47s that subsequently found themselves in states and conflicts across the globe—in Africa, Pakistan, the Balkans. Today, variants of the AK-47 are produced in Albania, Bulgaria, China, Egypt, Germany, India, Iraq, North Korea, Poland, Romania, Russia, Serbia, and Venezuela. Arms contractors of various descriptions—whether illegal, private, or governmental—act as brokers and middlemen in the dissemination of arms, especially from the countries of the former Eastern bloc. But the trade is not restricted to less well-regulated or advanced states: for instance, the USA has imported a large number of AK-47s for use by the Iraqi security services, and there are reported to have been 20,000 AK-47s imported into the UK in 2006, their eventual intended destination unknown.

There has been an international campaign—with Oxfam, Amnesty International, and the organization Control Arms at the forefront—for restricting small arms just as previously there was a campaign for restricting the use of landmines. It is an evidently worthwhile cause; with the UN in 2001 agreeing to establish firmer regulations governing small-arms control, especially focused on the AK-47. The debate focuses on supply-versus-demand issues. Against those who would emphasize the control of the supply for weapons are those who

---

[2] These and further items of information on the AK-47 have been taken from the very useful Wikepedia article on this subject, <http://en.wikipedia.org/wiki/AK-47>.

have argued that the context of the demand needs to be understood as well.[3] Of course, supply and demand here necessarily overlap, and this is less a debate over principles as over priorities. If there is little supply there will be less demand. Obviously if you can cut demand you can cut supply. Intervention anywhere along the chain of supply and demand will doubtless have some effect. And yet for all that, one suspects that if there is the will, slaughter will be carried out in any case. And no doubt one could say that if it were not the AK-47 then other weapons would have taken on more or less equivalent roles. Killing, in the final instance, is a social and political phenomenon, not a technological one, although the scale and timing of killing obviously owe a lot to technological availability.

Such issues aside, the example of the AK-47 shows two things. First it illustrates the extent to which globalization, just as with any other phenomenon, is carried by ideational and material artefacts of various kinds, be these types of belief, commodities, or, as in this case, types of weaponry. At the end of the day that is all globalization is: not an abstract process but the name we give to concrete shifts and trends in the distribution of artefacts and forms of power. Indeed, forms of power are carried by artefacts—be these ideational, repressive, or economic. But nor is globalization, understood in these terms, always a breathless question of speed, complexities, and flows, as much of the fashionable literature has suggested. Such artefacts, for instance, are not always those of high and fast technology—computer chips or nano inventions—but can be rather beat-up, second-rate material forms devised for other purposes in other contexts: in other words, exactly as in the case of the AK-47. What matters in globalization is not novelty but availability, reproducibility, possibilities for spread and exportability.

Second, the AK-47 example indicates one way at least in which the landscapes of globalization and of the previous Cold War period are in fact overlapping phenomena. Globalization did not appear in stark and absolute opposition to the Cold War world, and is not a complete break from it. The ghosts of dead generations hang like nightmares on the souls of the living. But these are more like active, undead ghosts—in this case sowing death and disorder in an environment somewhat different and displaced from their origins. The zombie swarms of AK-47s are indeed like legions of the Cold War undead spreading blindly—ideologically un-choosing and un-discriminating—across the globe, artefacts of deathly agency. Globalization was built on the necessary foundations and legacies of the Cold War in that once the ideological context of that bipolar world had been abandoned, what remained was not least its material detritus: its waste, weapons, lost souls, and sundry artefacts. Globalization is as much about the rearticulation of the remains of what was there before as it is about the construction of a newer world—brave, bad, or otherwise.

[3] David Atwood, Anne-Kathrin Glatz, Robert Muggah, 'Demanding Attention: Addressing the Dynamics of Small Arms Demand' (Geneva: Graduate Institute of International Studies, Small Arms Survey, occasional paper 18, January 2006).

45 Human Rights

Sharyn Roach Anleu

Human rights is a term that has wide currency. The discourse of human rights shows up regularly in daily newspapers and on evening broadcasts. Searches on the World Wide Web can generate an enormous and changing literature on human rights posted by organizations and individuals. Particularly in Western countries, human rights are a lens through which instances of suffering, violence, and deprivation experienced by individuals and populations can be viewed or framed. Usually the absence or derogation of rights is the focus of attention, especially in the international arena or global society: news reports describe human rights violations, abuses of human rights, or breaches of human rights. However, we can ask: Why are some instances of pain and suffering regarded as human rights abuses but not others?

The most obvious and accessible place to look for a statement on human rights is the Universal Declaration of Human Rights adopted by members of the United Nations in 1948. Article 1 states: 'All human beings are born free and equal in dignity and rights.' This idea of human rights, then, attaches to all humans, as a birthright—rights are not the product of particular political regimes, legal systems, or cultural values—they are universal. At an abstract, philosophical, or global level, human rights belong to all humans, and do not depend on citizenship status. Nonetheless, the notions of rights, freedom, and equality, which inscribe the Declaration and related covenants, have their roots in Western political values that date back to the eighteenth century, and perhaps as far back as the Magna Carta of 1215. In practice, however, the recognition and content of human rights are far more contingent, contested, and variable than the assertion of their universal existence implies. The actual meaning and constitution of human rights are context driven and inevitably political. In practice individuals are often accorded rights depending on their citizenship status (which is granted by nation states). For example, some residents in a state may have access to employment, education, and health care but lack political rights to vote in elections. This is the case for many migrant workers and overseas students, and there are instances whereby their treatment can be characterized as human rights violations and their recourse to any legal remedies restricted. Another example of how human rights are shaped by national laws and policies is the case of political refugees, often in detention, awaiting the outcome of their applications for asylum (see also Chapter 41 by Nicholas Gill). Such individuals are often cast as 'illegal migrants', 'queue jumpers', or 'boat people', thus attesting to their deviant status, which in turn tends to rationalize the limits on their freedom and access to resources. As one sociologist notes: 'Human rights for non-citizens are far from popular.'[1]

Talk of human rights and claims that rights be recognized usually adopt legal language that appears dispassionate and above factional politics.[2] Who can disagree that human rights are a good thing? Human rights discourse often turns to law, and advocates demand the establishment of legal institutions—courts, tribunals, judicial personnel, legal representatives—for their enforcement at a supranational level, which in turn can bind the activities of particular nation states. Progressive social movements and activists often deploy human rights discourse to improve the plight of disenfranchised people and those suffering abuse and violence. Non-governmental organizations (NGOs) such as Amnesty International and Human Rights Watch draw attention to the activities and politics of organizations and governments that deny human rights or ignore atrocities being perpetuated. However, rights discourse is not the sole province of progressive social movements. Powerful actors such as international companies can adopt a framework of rights—for example, their rights to trade in particular markets or to access certain resources.

Thus claims for human rights can be invoked, or not, in a variety of circumstances and conditions. Like all law, global norms or international norms on human rights are general and abstract and require translation or transplantation into national or local laws and practices. To the extent that local experts, institutions, and legal cultures align with international laws regarding human rights, then it is reasonable to expect that human rights discourses and remedies will be available to citizens. This might mean that human rights claims must be framed in ways that resonate with the local community and its traditions, practices, and values.[3] Moreover, claims of human rights abuses can be successful in countries where there are strong economic ties with other nations that are responding to the claims.[4] The development of European human rights jurisprudence was facilitated by the early representation of the European Court of Human Rights (inaugurated in 1959) as legally conservative and no threat to national approaches to human rights law.[5]

At least four facets or manifestations of human rights discourses play out in everyday life:

---

[1] Kate Nash, 'Between Citizenship and Human Rights', *Sociology* 43, 6 (December 2009): 1080.

[2] Sharyn Roach Anleu, *Law and Social Change* (2nd edition, London: Sage, 2010).

[3] Sally Engle Merry, *Human Rights and Gender Violence: Translating International Law into Local Justice* (Chicago: University of Chicago Press, 2006).

[4] James C. Franklin, 'Shame on You: The Impact of Human Rights Criticism on Political Repression in Latin America', *International Studies Quarterly* 52, 1 (2008): 187–211.

[5] Mikael Rask Madsen, 'From Cold War Instrument to Supreme European Court: The European Court of Human Rights at the Crossroads of International and National Law and Politics', *Law & Social Inquiry* 32, 1 (March 2007): 137–59.

1

Claims of human rights violations are made by some nation states to condemn or control or influence other nation states and their domestic policies. A paradox for international law is the use of armed intervention (potentially violent, destructive, and causing loss of life and injury) in a state to prevent widespread atrocities and suffering. Human rights violations formed part of the justification on the part of some Western nations for the toppling of Saddam Hussein's regime in Iraq; it justified the US invasion of Mogadishu (capital of Somalia). Governments often tie aid to the establishment of particular politico-legal structures that are assumed to enhance democracy and political and civil rights. On the other side, injustices or harms closer to home or involving allies are often framed very differently. For example, it took a long time and a considerable amount of graphic evidence for claims that the occupying forces were engaged in violent, abusive acts against Iraqi prisoners which violated human integrity at the Abu Graib prison. The US government resolved these allegations by identifying the 'deviant' individuals who perpetrated such acts and closing the prison, rather than questioning the structural conditions and political context for such violations. The Australian government set up the Cole Inquiry following accusations that members of the government and public service had full knowledge of human rights abuses in Iraq but ignored them. For example, the government was accused of inaction in relation to the plight of David Hicks who was in detention in Guantanamo Bay from 2001 to 2007. He was released after pleading guilty to a charge of 'providing material support for terrorism'. However, it can be asked whether his plea was a free and voluntary acknowledgement of guilt or the means to achieve release from the military prison. Detention without trial has been the source of many claims of human rights abuses against governments, including the United States and the United Kingdom. Parallel claims have also been lodged against the Australian government's refugee and asylum-seeker policies which include mandatory detention, including of children, restricted access to the courts for judicial review of administrative decisions, and the establishment of offshore processing points.

2

In the current international political environment, human rights are often juxtaposed, usually less favourably, with concerns about national security and border protection. As part of the so-called war on terror, governments in the United States, the United Kingdom, Australia, and elsewhere have passed new legislation to combat terrorism, often with little public criticism or awareness. While many people might be aware of the introduction of anti-terror laws, it is likely that most people will know little or nothing about their rights under the new laws. Some of the provisions of these acts—mandatory detention, enhanced powers for police and other security forces, limits on freedom of association and expression, the outlawing of groups deemed to be engaged in terrorist activities, control orders, and reducing the scope of the court to hear some types of matters—can result in reduced political and civil rights for individuals and groups. Everyday discussion of these issues is usually embodied in the cases of particular individuals (for example, Jack Thomas, the first person convicted under Australia's new terrorism laws) or takes place in particular sites. Thomas's conviction was overturned on appeal as the court found that it was based on prosecution evidence obtained by improper inducement. Some questions about freedom of expression have arisen in discussions about the nature of limits of academic independence and the quest for knowledge and information and the place of institutions of higher education as locations of rebellious incitement. However, it seems that people respond to globalization by affirming their national and cultural identities, not by proclaiming global or cosmopolitan citizenship. Nowhere is this more patent than in the US anti-terrorism legislation passed one month after the 11 September 2001 attacks; this legislation is known by its acronym, USA PATRIOT (Uniting and Strengthening America by Providing Appropriate Tools Required to Intercept and Obstruct Terrorism) Act.

3

Human rights discourse is a strategy or claim often made by such NGOs as Amnesty International, Greenpeace, and Human Rights Watch. Such organizations have, among other things, pointed out some of the human rights implications of increasing economic deregulation and liberalization of trade policies via free trade agreements, for example, as leading to increased economic inequalities, especially among the poorest nations and among the poorest members of wealthier nations. Employees in Western nations have seen manufacturing and service jobs move offshore to countries such as India, China, and Fiji, where the hourly rate of pay is considerably lower, where child labour is used, and where working conditions are not subject to complex occupational health and safety regimes. Debates about human rights do not occur in an international environment where all participants are equal in economic and political power. For example, international banks are able to tie loans and repayments to social and political reforms, including human rights reforms and trade liberalization, in newly industrializing nations.

4

The occupation of a Mexican town in 1994 by impoverished peasants symbolizes the beginning of anti-globalization politics, in which human rights advocacy is a major strand. Other demonstrations against globalization and international corporations include protests against economic forums in major Western cities, including Seattle, Genoa, and Melbourne. Anti-globalization sentiment can have a number of effects at the level of everyday life. It can lead to consciousness raising among affluent, educated consumers in the West who pledge support for various NGOs or alter their daily practices, for example by switching to fair trade products or boycotting products from multinational corporations accused of unethical practices. On the other hand, bombardment by stories of despair and deprivation in faraway places can result in denial and indifference among publics, or at least a feeling of comparative well-being and complacency.

Conclusion

Human rights are typically cast as international and global issues. Their acknowledgement and remedy transcend the capacity of national governments, and rights should attach to individuals not as citizens of nation states but as humans. Human rights have become a general concept used to characterize a range of atrocities and deprivations in both contemporary and past societies. The move from abstract human rights to the practical recognition and enforcement of rights is highly complex and variable. The adoption of human rights discourse as a way of framing discrimination, inequality, loss of freedom, physical deprivation, and other harms will depend on local conditions, the activism of social movements, the available legal institutions, and political will.

Part VII
Classifications

46 Area-Based Classifications

Roger Burrows

The globalization of geodemographics—the technology of area-based classifications—provides an interesting case study of the recursive relationship that exists between the social sciences and the global machinations of capitalism. Geodemographic classifications, originally driven by the analytic concerns of urban sociology and the practicalities of urban policy, have transformed into:

> the basic fuel on which economic activity runs…Companies offering geodemographic profiling data are the 21st-century equivalents of the great energy companies of the 20th.[1]

The idea behind geodemographic classifications is a simple one. It is the notion that the physical spaces that people occupy say something profound about the sort of people that they are. It is a form of analysis premised upon the observation that 'people tend to live with others like themselves, sharing similar demographics, lifestyles and values'.[2] One of the major developers of geodemographic classification in the USA claims, for example, that their product is based upon 'the fundamental sociological truism that "birds of a feather flock together"…or that "you are where you live"'.[3] Empirically it is indeed the case that knowledge of where someone lives is a powerful predictor of all manner of consumption practices, values, tastes, preferences, and so on. Why should this be so?

There are many social scientific explanations for the socio-spatial zoning of populations, but one of the most recent displays a strong concordance with the views of 'commercial sociologists' working in the geodemographics industry. This is the idea that it is now 'place' and not 'class' that 'is determinant in the last instance'. Crudely, whereas occupation used to define social class, now it is residential location. We are thus witnessing nothing less than the

---

[1] Perri 6, 'The personal information economy: trends and prospects for consumers', in *The Glass Consumer: Life in a Surveillance Society*, ed. Susanne Lace (Bristol: Polity, 2005): 17.

[2] Michael J. Weiss, *The Clustered World: How We Live, What We Buy, and What it all Means About Who We Are* (Boston: Little, Brown, 2000): 305.

[3] Quoted in Jon Goss, 'Marketing the New Marketing: The Strategic Discourses of GIS', in *Ground Truth: The Social Implications of GIS*, ed. John Pickles (New York: Guilford, 1995): 134.

spatialization of class. The strongest codification of this position is in Savage et al., who conclude that:

One's residence is a crucial, possibly the crucial identifier of who you are...Rather than seeing wider social identities as arising out of the field of employment it would be more promising to examine their relationship to residential location.[4]

Why? Because:

people are comfortable when there is a correspondence between habitus and field...otherwise people feel ill at ease and seek to move—socially and spatially—so that their discomfort is relieved...mobility is driven as people, with their relatively fixed habitus, both move between fields...and move to places within fields where they feel more comfortable.[5]

In a sense, then, geodemographic classifications are codifications of complex spatial articulations of habitus—even though, until recently, geodemographers have been unaware of the work of Bourdieu.[6]

The first example of geodemographics is Charles Booth's *Descriptive Map of London Poverty.*[7] It is possible to trace a lineage from the work of Booth through to the myriad activities of the Chicago School of Sociology. The Chicago School instigated a research agenda that assumed that cities possessed a particular socio-spatial structure—an 'urban ecology'. This idea was given emblematic expression in one of the most famous diagrams in the social sciences—a combination of half-moon and dartboard depicting the five concentric urban zones of 1920s Chicago, representing the sorting of social and housing classes into distinct zones produced by 'ecological' determinants such as incomes, land values, race, class, and so on.

It was this Chicago School vision of urban ecology that, in the early 1970s, was combined with developments in multivariate statistical analysis that led to the creation of contemporary geodemographics. The person credited with this fusion is Jonathan Robbin, a faculty member of the Department of Sociology at New York University.[8] During the 1950s he contributed to the development of some of the first software for carrying out factor and cluster analysis. In the early 1960s he left the academy to become an entrepreneur by applying his analytic methods to a number of social and business problems.

---

[4] Mike Savage, Gaynor Bagnall, Brian Longhurst, *Globalization and Belonging* (London: Sage, 2005): 207.

[5] Ibid., 9.

[6] Richard Webber, 'The Metropolitan Habitus: Its manifestations, locations and consumption profiles', *Environment and Planning A* 38, 1 (2007): 182–207.

[7] Richard Harris, Peter Sleight, Richard Webber, *Geodemographics, GIS, and Neighbourhood Targeting* (Chichester: Wiley, 2005): 30–7.

[8] Weiss, *Clustered World*, 24.

Much of the background work to what was to become the first modern geodemographic system—PRIZM (Potential Rating Index for ZIP Markets)—was grounded not in the world of commerce but in urban policy. The US Department of Housing and Urban Development funded Robbin to develop a system for targeting housing grants to cities with a history of rioting, and out of this work grew PRIZM.[9]

At about the same time as Robbin was developing PRIZM in the USA, Richard Webber was developing a similar analytic technology in the UK. Webber, a social scientist, was working at the London Centre for Environmental Studies in the 1970s. Here he undertook work in Liverpool, the intention of which was to provide a better understanding of patterns of urban deprivation. This work led to the development of software specifically designed to identify clusters of neighbourhoods for which different types of policy interventions were appropriate.[10] Out of this grew the first modern UK-based geodemographic classification—Acorn (A Classification of Residential Neighbourhoods). Like Robbin in the USA, Webber left the domain of academia and urban policy to develop his system in more commercial directions.

As well as Acorn, Webber is also responsible for the development of Mosaic, now one of the most widely used geodemographic systems across the world. There are parallel Mosaic schemas for at least 25 different countries and there is a Mosaic global system that 'maps' each national Mosaic onto a common set of ten 'socio-spatial classes'. The Mosaic Global website claims that it is:

a consistent segmentation system that covers over 400 million of the world's households. Using local data from 25 countries ... [it] has identified ten types of residential neighbourhood that can be found in each of the countries, each with a distinctive set of values, motivations and consumer preferences. [It] is based on a simple proposition that the world's cities share common patterns of residential segregation ... In terms of their values and lifestyles, each type of neighbourhood displays strong similarities in whichever country it is found.

By way of illustration, Table 46.1 shows the schema as it pertains to Australia, New Zealand, and the UK.

Geodemographic classifications are then empirically driven area-based classifications based upon mutually exclusive and exhaustive categorizations of neighbourhoods that 'work' as variables in order to produce 'explanations' for subtle variations in consumption practices and 'lifestyles'. From an analytic point of view geodemographic classifications represent a radical collapsing of some common sociological variables onto small areas. The exact mixture of sociological 'elements' that become 'fused' together in each

---

[9] Ibid., 142.
[10] Richard Webber and John Craig, *A Socio-Economic Classification of Local Authorities in Great Britain* (London: HMSO, 1978).

Table 46.1 Mosaic global for Australia, New Zealand, and the UK; percentage of population in each country in each global mosaic type

Global mosaic	Australia	New Zealand	UK
A Sophisticated singles	10.4	7.7	6.6
B Bourgeois prosperity	22.4	6.1	21.6
C Career and family	3.5	11.3	9.7
D Comfortable retirement	2.0	3.3	3.5
E Routine service workers	3.8	3.5	11.4
F Hard-working blue collar	18.9	24.0	4.7
G Metropolitan strugglers	5.0	9.1	16.0
H Low-income elders	4.2	4.6	4.4
I Post-industrial survivors	16.8	16.5	16.8
J Rural inheritance	13.3	14.2	5.3

category is empirically determined by the statistical purchase each gives in explaining small-scale spatial variations in consumption patterns.

The specific algorithms used to create these classifications are largely proprietary, but most share a common methodological approach.[11] A large number of spatially referenced data items—about half from the Census and half from other (mostly commercial) sources—are subject to various forms of cluster analysis. This done, each category is given a 'label' that attempts to epitomize its dominant characteristics, accompanied by a narrative and visualizations that attempt to encapsulate the 'sort of place it is'.

This is then is not just a matter of the tools of the social sciences being put to work by the marketing industry. In an era of the 'automatic production of space',[12] the implications of the migration of area-based classifications into the digital assemblages generative of 'software sorted geographies'[13] needs attention. Are we already at a point where the characterizations of localities that geodemographics spawn have taken on a 'life of their own' over and above anything that might today pass for ground truth?[14] This author suspects so.[15]

---

[11] Harris et al., *Geodemographics, GIS, and Neighbourhood Targeting*, 147–83.

[12] Nigel Thrift and Shaun French, 'The Automatic Production of Space', *Transactions of the Institute of British Geographers* New Series 27, 3 (2002): 309–33.

[13] Stephen D. N. Graham, 'Software-sorted Geographies', *Progress in Human Geography* 29, 5 (October 2005): 562–80.

[14] John Pickles ed., *Ground Truth: The Social Implications of GIS* (New York: Guilford, 1995).

[15] Roger Burrows and Nick Ellison, 'Sorting Places Out? Towards a Social Politics of Neighbourhood Informatisation', *Information, Communication and Society* 7, 3 (2004): 321–36; Roger Burrows and Nicholas Gane, 'Geodemographics, Software and Class', *Sociology* 40, 5 (October 2006): 793–812.

47 First Names: Examples from Germany*

Jürgen Gerhards

Every newborn child receives a name. The combination of the newborn's first and last names serves as a marker of identity for both the child and for those with whom the child interacts. Names also label someone's social identity insofar as they indicate belonging to a certain group or society. If we meet a person named Doug, we can infer that he comes from an English-speaking country; and if we meet someone named Mohammed, we can expect him to come from an Islamic country. Traditionally, parents have marked their membership to their culture of origin by choosing names for their children from that culture.

David Held et al. define globalization as a 'process which embodies a transformation in the spatial organization of social relations and transactions'.[1] Following this definition we speak of a globalization process in naming when parents more often choose names from other regions of the world. Analysing the development of first names in Germany over the last century, this entry will illustrate what the globalization of names means, whether it has empirically taken place, and what the causes may be.

The pool of names that are traditionally used in Germany stems from German and Christian culture. At the beginning of the twentieth century, Ursula, Maria, Helga, and Sabine were among the top ten girls' names. Alfred, Hermann, Paul, and Wilhelm were among the leading boys' names. Names from other cultures were not used very often. How has the relationship between traditional German names and foreign names changed during the last century?

Figure 47.1 shows an increase in names with a non-Christian or non-German origin. Whereas in 1894 only 25 per cent of names came from foreign cultures, this number increased to 65 per cent by the end of the twentieth century. This increase in transcultural names began in the 1950s. This process was as marked in East Germany as it was in West Germany, even occurring at slightly

---

* In this article I rely heavily on a book in which I analysed the development of first names in Germany over the last hundred years: *The Name Game; Cultural Modernization and First Names* (New Brunswick: Transaction Publishers, 2005).
[1] David Held, Anthony McGrew, David Goldblatt, Jonathan Perraton, *Global Transformations: Politics, Economics and Culture* (Cambridge: Polity Press, 1999): 16.

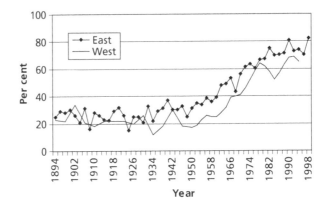

Figure 47.1 Globalization of first names in Germany (percentage of non-Christian and non-German names given to newborns by year)

higher levels.[2] Both East and West Germany witnessed a dramatic receptivity toward previously alien cultures.

The term 'foreign names' does not provide any information as to the specific cultural origin of the names parents choose for their children. After 1949 names such as Maurice, Marco, René, Natalie, Denise, Jennifer, Peggy, Sandy, Mike, Marvin, and Steve suddenly gained in popularity. A more in-depth analysis shows that the rise of foreign first names was mainly an increase in names from the Romance and Anglo-American cultural milieus; other foreign cultures were largely neglected.[3] In terms of first names, globalization is predominantly a process of occidentalization, similar to developments in art and science. Alain Quemin's study shows that beyond an increase in international exchanges, the art world still has a hegemonic centre consisting of a small number of Western countries, among which the USA and Germany are pre-eminent.[4] Jean Laponce illustrates that the number of articles in chemistry published in English was already high at the end of the 1970s; but the percentage of articles written in English still increased in the following years and sum up to 82.5 per cent in 1998.[5]

Interestingly, there was a Westernization of first names not only in West Germany but also in East Germany, where one might have expected a rise

[2] Germany was divided into the Federal Republic of Germany and the German Democratic Republic between 1949 and 1990.

[3] Gerhards, *Name Game.*

[4] Alain Quemin, 'Globalization and Mixing in the Visual Arts: An Empirical Survey of "High Culture" and Globalization', *International Sociology* 21, 4 (2006): 522–50.

[5] Jean Laponce, 'Babel and the Market: Geostrategy for Minority Languages', in *Languages in a Globalising World 2003*, ed. Jaques Maurais and Michael A. Morris (Cambridge: Cambridge University Press, 2003): 58–63.

of Slavic and Eastern European names as a result of its social affiliation to the Eastern bloc under Soviet domination. This affiliation, however, had no impact on first names. Names such as Ivan, Bronislaw, Wladimir, Nadia, and Tanja were not very widespread. East Germany as a whole remained Western-oriented and did not differ from West Germany in this respect. The publicly propagated solidarity with its socialist brethren in the Eastern bloc apparently did not impress the East German population, who took their cues from the West when naming their children.

How can we explain the globalization process of first names? From the parental perspective the choice of a first name is a decision process determined by three factors: (a) preference for certain cultures, (b) the known pool of possible names, and (c) the fit between traditional names and new names. The globalization of first names that took place after the Second World War was due to the interplay of changed parental preferences and a new name pool. The change in preferences as well as the change in opportunity structures was strongly influenced by societal change after the Second World War.

a) Children receive names their parents like. Hence, the choice of a name from a foreign culture expresses a certain preference for that culture in comparison to another culture. The increase of foreign names in Germany after the Second World War goes hand in hand with the decline of German names. The discrediting of nationalism that came with military defeat and the downfall of National Socialism in 1945 created an environment in which German names lost prestige. Both successor states abandoned the distinctive hallmarks of nationalism, and helped, in fact, to discredit it. This change of attitude toward the traditional German cultural heritage was reflected in first names, German ones losing in significance and suffering a radical curtailment. This created the possibility for a change in taste and a reorientation that focused on new kinds of names. These new names stemmed from Western societies and cultures with high prestige. Survey studies have shown that Americans and Western Europeans enjoyed the greatest prestige in Germany, while Eastern Europeans, Turks, Africans, and Asians are much less admired.[6] This seems to correspond to the trend in foreign names, as parents prefer those from Western cultures. This argument also explains why—somewhat surprisingly in view of the large number of Turks immigrating to Germany (Germany's largest group of immigrants)—Turkish names in West Germany have made no headway at all. There were nearly no Mehmets or Mohammeds among those names from other cultures that enjoyed a rise in popularity after 1949.

b) A parent must first be aware of a foreign name in order to choose it for their child. In this respect, the globalization of first names and other cultural

---

[6] Dieter Fuchs, Jürgen Gerhards, Edeltraud Roller, 'Wir und die Anderen. Ethnozentrismus in den zwölf Ländern der europäischen Gemeinschaft', *Kölner Zeitschrift für Soziologie und Sozialpsychologie* 45 (1993): 238–53.

symbols can be traced back to the expansion of mass media, primarily television and pop music recordings.[7] Starting in the 1950s, the proliferation of television, feature films, and recorded music permitted an exponential rise in access to the media world. The entertainment industry also proliferated globalization insofar as the percentage of English and Romance-language products increased sharply as compared to German-language ones. One can assume that foreign names were transported into the living rooms of German households in this way. John (e.g. Lennon), Steve (e.g. McQueen), Ernie (from Sesame Street), Jacqueline (e.g. Kennedy), and Kevin (from the film *Home Alone*) entered the German name repertoire. These names also originated from cultural milieus viewed as prestigious, likely heightening their appeal.

c) Not all names from foreign Western cultures made their way into the group of commonly used names. As Ulf Hannerz and others have shown, the acquisition of symbols and goods distributed worldwide is based on their respective cultural relevance.[8] If there is a local adaptation of globally distributed goods and symbols, the resultant interaction leads to 'creolization'. The success of certain names from foreign cultures is due to the interplay between the parents' cultural dispositions and the respective exogenous offerings.[9] Successful foreign names introduced into Germany have to enjoy a certain phonetic similarity to German names. For example, the German name Markus was already among the top ten names in 1970 and remained there until 1976. In 1974 Marc entered the top ten, as did Marco two years later, where both names remained for an extended period. In 1992 the French name Marcel broke into the top ten. Marc, Marco, and Marcel are 'mutations' of the German name Markus. A similar process took place with the German Andreas entering the top ten and then the French André following in its wake. Successful foreign names are those that have phonetic commonalities with the ones currently fashionable. Out of the entire pool of foreign names available to German parents, only a small portion ever entered the top ten.

Although our data refer to the developments of names in Germany only, the explanatory model may hold true for the analysis of globalization processes in other countries as well: a precondition for the globalization of names is that parents must become familiar with names from other cultures. Mass media and the worldwide circulation of popular culture bring new names—mostly from Western culture—to parents' attention. Parents only choose one of these newly introduced names, however, when the name comes from a highly appreciated culture. Finally, out of the pool of new names, parents are most likely to choose those names that are similar to ones they are already familiar with.

---

[7] Scott Lash and Celia Lury, *Global Culture Industries: The Mediation of Things* (Cambridge: Polity Press, 2007).

[8] Ulf Hannerz, *Cultural Complexity. Studies in the Social Organization of Meaning* (New York: Columbia University Press, 2003).

[9] Stanley Lieberson, *A Matter of Taste; How Names, Fashions, and Culture Change* (New Haven: Yale University Press, 2000).

48 One of My Top Ten Days

Lucy Kimbell

I wake up in my (*Wallpaper* magazine top ten) hotel and look out the window. It's a stunning view, so I take a photo and realize it's similar to one I noticed on the (Dopplr traveller recommendations top ten) website. I decide to upload it quickly to my blog, where I'm doing a reportage of my trip visiting the emerging design capitals of the world, but there seems to be some problem linking my (*Wired* magazine top ten latest gadgets) phone and the (top ten by market capitalization) mobile network connection. So I go straight down for breakfast. On the way my phone vibrates and it's my friend Dan who has just flown in for the exhibition opening that we are both attending tonight. He suggests breakfast at a café a friend of his recommended, who is originally from this city but is now in a (top ten by billings *Business Week*) consultancy, which involves travelling a lot, and, according to Dan, makes an effort to share his local knowledge with his friends via Facebook. I check where the café is on the map on my phone and as I set off, I notice a couple of other venues that have popped up, prompted by the (*Global Foody* magazine top ten) recommendation engine I signed up to.

After breakfast I decide to buy a packet of coffee. As we wait while it's ground and bagged, we check out some of the other beans available in the café's monthly (top five staff picks) menu, which come from several different countries, some ethically sourced and some organic, according to the logos, but you never know. I tweet the producer's name quickly to see if my Twitter followers know the beans. Then it's time to head to the museum for the invitation-only private view before the official reception later this evening. This is a new design museum, which has been endowed by a (*Forbes* magazine top ten) philanthropist and a few other (*Corporate Social Responsibility* journal's top ten) corporate sponsors. The design world does not yet have a critical mass of museums, fairs, festivals, or private galleries, so I am not sure if today's event will attract the right people. But here we are.

While Dan catches up with a (top ten by mentions in *Monocle* magazine) gallerist, I wander round the show on my own. I know much of the work, mostly iconic pieces by well-known (Phaidon's top ten bestselling) contemporary designers but there are also a couple of more idiosyncratic works by names I'm not familiar with. My phone is again having problems connecting to the network, so I have to rely on the press pack the museum prepared, which cites a journalist who writes for a (top ten by international sales) newspaper, a (top ten Amazon non-fiction bestseller) historian, and a management scholar from a (*Financial Times* MBA rankings top 20) business school. Including the last is unusual. The design world tends to keep itself at one remove from scholarship that de-emphasizes the particular qualities of artefacts, which is what designers are celebrated for attending to. At least that's what I think and probably so do my (top ten by numbers of followers, connections, and friends on Twitter, LinkedIn, and Facebook) colleagues and peers. But I learn from reading further in the press pack that a strand of innovation management does pay attention to objects and so, presumably, this academic is from that world.

The museum has a small bookshop where I spend time looking at the predictable collection of glossy (top ten by advertising revenue) magazines, mixed with a few hand-printed fanzines which have more of an anti-aesthetic and are not even in English. Definitely need some of them. One of the books is about the museum itself. As I flick through it I decide the architecture is impressive, giving plenty of space to the objects on display but conveying a sense of unspectacular modernity which fits well with the rest of the (top ten by awards and commissions) architect's oeuvre. I already have a couple of other books about this architecture practice, so decide not to get this one. Or not here, anyway. Maybe when it pops up on Amazon.

Once Dan is free we look round the exhibition together, this time trying out the new interpretation system the museum has installed, a co-development with the local (national top ten by research income) university and a (top ten by global revenues) IT company. The assistant gives us each a handset with an earpiece through which we can listen to a commentary in three languages and also leave our own comments which will later be uploaded to the website, presumably checked for obscenities and defamation. I see one of the curators watching us as we get a bit frustrated with the handsets. We go and talk to her to find out why they set it up in this way. This turns into a longer conversation about curating strategies and designing interpretation systems based on ideas of co-production with users rather than telling them how to experience the show. They have also copied the lo-tech feedback system used at a (global top ten by visitor numbers) museum in London for its annual art prize exhibition. This invites visitors to make handwritten notes on small cards that are put up on a huge wall, providing a range of responses to the artwork. Although the show we are viewing is not yet open to the public, quite a few of the cards have already been filled in and put on the wall, presumably by the staff to get things going. Dan playfully fills in one of the cards, writing on it the name of a designer who is not even in the show and adding five stars and a web address for his online auction house. Lunch is laid on in the museum's restaurant, which is surprisingly good, lots of locally sourced ingredients and a small deli where you can buy produce, with its own bags which I see quite of few of the visitors and those of us with the press pack are carrying around.

After lunch I pop out to have a look around the city, which I have never visited before. There's a museum I have always wanted to see with a particularly good (BBC History website top ten) Roman mosaic that I remember my stepfather mentioning from a trip here when he was a student. The museum is currently showing an exhibition of (Wikipedia top ten historically significant) scientific inventions, although as I scan the images on the hoarding outside I have to question how they picked that curator. I decide not to go in after all. Instead I wander in the direction of the old city that, according to my pre-trip research, mixes high-end international fashion boutiques with independent, local retailers. Piped all around this area is whatever the current (top ten iTunes chart) hit is, some awful grime that does not sit well with my desire to be a *flâneuse*. I drown it out by listening to my smartphone, so the choice of music is driven by recommendations on Spotify, not a local facilities manager. As I walk around I note the considerable amount of building work taking place, evidence of the city's emerging role as a (top ten foreign direct investment) holiday destination following the (regional top ten by passenger numbers) airport extension a couple of years ago.

Then it's time for the official opening of the exhibition. There are speeches by the mayor, the benefactor, the museum director, and some rent-a-celebrity who apparently likes culture. I'm sure I saw him a week ago on someone else's arm at an art biennale. I keep looking around to see how many of the designers whose work is shown in the exhibition are here. I do not recognize anyone so am not sure if the funds ran dry or whether they just decided not to come. Maybe I'm missing something somewhere else. A couple of other people here today have been tweeting. I wait to see if any of them have got anything to say about the show.

With some other people I slip off for a quiet dinner. We pick a restaurant that one of them went to the previous night, although I can't find out anything about it when I look it up. I share my observations from my walk around the city and am interested to hear my companions' views. Considering I woke up quite ignorant about what this city had to offer, I am delighted with my discoveries. I decide not to post anything on my blog, to keep this city unknown a little bit longer.

49 Barcodes and RFIDs

Rob Kitchin and Martin Dodge

Introduction

One of the key phenomena of the globalization of commerce has been the internationalization of goods and brands. A set of diverse practices and processes, including the transformation of transport infrastructure and logistics and the virtualization of money, have enabled both producers (e.g. goods manufacturers) and sellers (e.g. wholesalers, supermarkets) to massively extend supply chains, to globally expand their markets, and to increase their turnover and profits. A key technology in improving the efficiency and productivity of logistical organization and operation has been the development of sophisticated identification systems that overcome the anonymity of manufactured products by assigning unique numerical identifiers—'digital thumbprints'—to material products. These identification systems allow products to be effectively and unambiguously processed, shipped, and traced through complex logistical networks, to monitor sales, aid account management, refine supply chains, and inform marketing strategies. Conceptually they have two distinct components, first an agreed allocation of unique identification code numbers and, second, an agreed medium to physically store the code. The most obvious manifestation of this technology for product identification and tracking is the parallel black-and-white printed stripes of barcodes.

Barcodes

Barcodes, visible on nearly all retail products, are the physical manifestation of a UPC (universal product code)—a code that uniquely identifies a product regardless of location or language. The original UPC concept can be traced back to the 1940s but gained widespread acceptance and usage in the 1970s with the development of a UPC standard by a group of US retailers and food manufacturers, based on a design by IBM.[1] This standard consisted of two

---

[1] Stephen A. Brown, ed., *Revolution at the Checkout Counter: The Explosion of the Bar Code* (Cambridge, MA: Harvard University Press, 1997); David Savir and George G. Laurer, 'The

distinct components: the 13-digit-code numbering system and the particular barcode design. The resultant barcode system was first used on 26 June 1974 in a supermarket in Troy, Ohio to scan a pack of chewing gum.[2] Instead of manually keying in the price of the product being sold, the barcode could be scanned by a laser, automatically looking up both the product type and the price in a stock database. Working in parallel with the replacement of manual tills by computerized point-of-sale technologies, barcodes quickly became an ubiquitous part of any packaging, and a vital part of logistical organization and marketing know-how, so much so that by April 1976, some 75 per cent of goods in US supermarkets had a UPC barcode.[3] In short, barcodes linked material objects to their virtual representation, making them machine readable, and thus facilitated computational efficiency to be bought to bear on production, distribution, and sale. Hosoya and Schaefer thus describe them as the 'bit structures' that organize and synchronize flows, acting as 'the mechanism by which the virtual establishes its logic in the real'.[4] Today barcodes also appear on nearly all manufactured goods, letters, and parcels, and an increasing number of documents. Many large organizations and industrial sectors have developed their own particular form of barcode and protocols for allocating numbers and tracking products.[5]

Importantly, the barcode system provides a single identification code number, with all other details concerning the object (e.g. product type, date of manufacture, price) being held in an information system. Further, each UPC barcode is unique to a single product class, not to each item being produced and sold. As such, a product barcode lacks granularity—that is, discrimination at the item level. For example, every bottle of a particular brand and type of shampoo has the same barcode. Each bottle cannot be uniquely identified. A second major weakness with barcodes is that the product needs to be handled to facilitate line-of-sight scanning. As a consequence, barcodes are being replaced by new smart labels and tags that have finer granularity and can be read remotely and en mass by radio signals.

Characteristics of and Decodability of the Universal Product Code', *IBM Systems Journal* 14, 1 (1975): 16–35.

[2] Alan Q. Morton, 'Packaging History: The Emergence of the Uniform Product Code (UPC) in the United States, 1970–75', *History and Technology* 11, 1 (1994): 101–11.

[3] J. T. Dunlop and J. W. Rivkin, 'Introduction', in *Revolution at the Checkout Counter: The Explosion of the Bar Code*, ed. Stephen Brown (Cambridge, MA: Harvard University Press, 1997): 1–38.

[4] Hiromi Hosoya and Markus Schaefer, 'Bit Structures', in *Harvard Design School Guide to Shopping*, ed. Chuihua Judy Chung and Sze Tsung Leong (Köln: Taschen, 2001): 157.

[5] Martin Dodge and Rob Kitchin, 'Codes of Life: Identification Codes and the Machine-Readable World', *Environment and Planning D: Society and Space* 23, 6 (2005): 851–81.

Radio Frequency Identification (RFID) Tags

RFID tags represent and communicate product information quite differently from barcodes. RFID tags have been developed to provide a means to 'identify any object anywhere automatically'. Each tag consists of a small chip composed of a simple digital circuit into which is embedded a unique identification code with attendant information, and an antenna that broadcasts the information and can be queried via radio signal at a distance by a reader without handling. RFID systems greatly increase the granularity of product identification to enable individual object recognition.

The first commercial RFIDs were developed in the 1970s and entered the mainstream in the 1980s with respect to farm-animal tagging and transportation transponders. They are still most widely used in vehicle dashboard tags for automatic toll payment (the main system in the USA is known as E-ZPass) and in livestock to facilitate ' "farm-to-fork" traceability'.[6] Their main application, though, is likely to be in retail and logistics where their increased granularity is seen as a major advance in inventory management (for example, improving just-in-time logistics and facilitating 'smart shelving' that is aware of its own stock levels), in combating shoplifting and staff pilfering, and in enhancing customer profiling.[7] Other forecasted uses include household appliances interacting with RFIDs so that microwave ovens automatically check the best cooking settings for ready meals, washing machines choose the most appropriate cycle for clothing, and medicine cabinets are able to identify out-of-date or recalled pharmaceuticals. There could also be potential for tracking goods at the end of the life cycle, alerting waste companies to items containing toxic substances, for example. In turn, the many potential, sophisticated uses of RFIDs raise many concerns relating to consumer privacy and individual confidentiality that are beyond the scope of this short chapter.[8]

In the 1990s a number of RFID standards were developed. The leading standard RFID data standard is Electronic Product Code (EPC), developed by the Auto-ID Center, an industry-sponsored R&D lab at MIT, and now being commercially implemented by EPCglobal Inc. (<http://www.epcglobalinc.org/>; a joint venture of the Uniform Code Council and EAN International, the main players in UPC barcode management). The definition of the EPC standard defines a number range large enough to uniquely identify every object on the planet. RFID tags and their EPCs will be part of a global information network

---

[6] Wired News, 'Mad Cow Spurs Livestock Tracking', Wired News, 31 December 2003, <http://www.wired.com/news/medtech/0,1286,61770,00.html>.

[7] Glover T. Ferguson, 'Have Your Objects Call My Objects', *Harvard Business Review* 80, 6 (June 2002): 138–43.

[8] See Katherine Albrecht and Liz McIntyre, *Spychips: How Major Corporations and Government Plan to Track Your Every Move with RFID* (Nashville: Nelson Current, 2005).

providing the means to automatically 'look up' details on any tagged object from any location. Borrowing the domain name schema used on the Internet, the EPC network will use a distributed Object Naming Service (ONS) to link each EPC number to an appropriate naming authority database. Importantly, the querying of the ONS by RFID-tagged products as they move through supply chains will automatically create a richly detailed audit trail, including geographic location. The result will be a much greater degree of routine 'machine-to-machine'-generated knowledge on the positioning of many millions of physical objects through time and space. In other words, RFIDs will lead to the creation of what Bleecker terms 'blogjects'—'objects that blog'; that is, objects that can interact across distributed networks and which record their histories with respect to other blogjects and databases and thus are searchable and trackable.[9] Over the next few years, it is likely that RFIDs will replace/supplement barcodes on retail packaging and be embedded in all manner of manufactured goods to facilitate asset management, as well as automating access through keyless entry and smoothing the payment process through contactless cards.

Conclusion

Barcodes and RFIDs are everyday and seemingly banal technologies. And yet, by enabling a transfer from manual coding to a standardized, universal identification, and from manual, anonymous data entry to laser scanning and radio identification, over the past 30 years they have had a profound effect upon how production, logistics, and retail are organized and function. As part of larger technical systems, barcodes and RFIDs have reshaped modes of production and the processes of capital accumulation at a variety of scales. As such, their influence on the global processes and everyday practices of logistics and retail should not be underestimated.

---

[9] J. Bleecker, 'A Manifesto for Networked Objects—Cohabiting with Pigeons, Arphids and Aibos in the Internet of Things', <http://research.techkwondo.com/files/WhyThingsMatter.pdf>.

50 ISO 9000
Wendy Larner

The impetus for international standardization is usually attributed to the need to better align defence industries during the Second World War, and indeed the first technical committee was established to write guidelines for screw threads. As the International Organization for Standardization (ISO) itself explains, it is standardization of screw threads that keeps chairs, children's bicycles, and aircraft together, and solves the maintenance and repair problems that were once a major headache. In 1947 the ISO was formally established as *the* global international standardizing body, following the merger of the International Federation of the National Standardizing Associations (established in New York in 1926, and administered from Switzerland) and the United Nations Standards Coordinating Committee (established in 1944, and administered from London), in order to address these concerns in the post-war engineering and manufacturing sector.[1]

Today the ISO is a Geneva-based worldwide federation, made up of 158 country-specific accreditation bodies, which oversees the development and dissemination of ISO standards. In January 2009 there were 18,500 standards, and this number continues to grow steadily. ISO standards establish internationally recognized measurements and processes for a wide range of taken-for-granted aspects of everyday life such as the qwerty keyboard, ISBN (International Standards Book Numbering), and foot sizes. Moreover, efforts to standardize now extend well beyond the characteristics of physical products such as computers, books, and shoes into fields such as environmental management, food safety, and corporate social responsibility. Recent developments include ISO 26000 that aspires to become the overarching standard for 'social responsibility', and ISO 31000 that aims to develop standardization in the field of 'risk management'.

ISO 9000 is perhaps the best known of the ISO standards developed to date. The ISO 9000 process involves the use of standardized management tools that provide a methodology for documenting, adapting, and improving organizational processes. The first set of ISO 9000 standards, 9000–9004, was published in 1987, and was subsequently revised and updated in 1994 and 2000 (see Figure 50.1). To gain ISO 9000 accreditation, the organization prepares written documentation of its processes, including a quality policy statement, and

---

[1] 'The Founding of the ISO', International Organization for Standardization, <http://www.iso.org/iso/founding.pdf>.

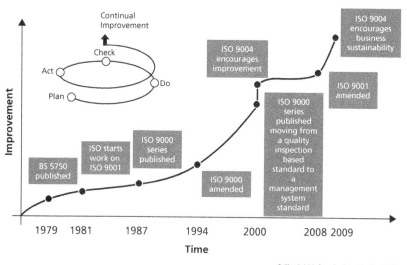

Figure title: **Evolution of ISO 9000 series**

© The British Standards Institution 2010

Figure 50.1 The evolution of the ISO 9000 series

Source: Permission to reproduce extracts from BSI publications is granted by BSI. No other use of this material is permitted. British Standards can be obtained in PDF or hard-copy formats from the BSI online shop: <http://www.bsigroup.com/Shop> or by contacting BSI Customer Services for hard copies only: Tel: +44 (0)20 8996 9001, email: cservices@bsigroup.com.

details of the purpose, scope, content, and procedure for each activity it under-takes. The aim of preparing the documentation is to ensure that consistent processes are being applied throughout the organization. This documentation is then internally and externally audited by an accredited third-party registrar. If no major problems are identified, an ISO 9000 certificate is issued, usually for three years, which the organization can use in promotions and publica-tions. It is explicitly recognized that the ISO 9000 process does not determine what organizations should actually do, nor does it guarantee the quality of end products and services. Rather than providing a ready-made set of procedures, the intention is that each organization has space to design its own processes. Moreover, because the ISO 9000 certificate is awarded for only three years, the management system ensures that organizations are constantly engaged in efforts to improve the quality of their processes.

While adoption of the ISO 9000 process is voluntary rather than mandatory, since the establishment of the series over one million certificates have been issued to organizations in 170 countries.[2] Initially ISO 9000 certification was

[2] 'The ISO Survey–2009', International Organization for Standardization, <http://www.iso.org/iso/survey2009.pdf>.

sought by engineering and manufacturing industries, especially those aiming to export into international markets. It was a way for externally oriented firms to signal their commitment to effective management systems and quality assurance. Today there remains a strong connection between globalizing economic ambitions and ISO certification, with China, Italy, and Japan currently the top three countries for numbers of ISO 9000 certificates awarded annually. However, ISO 9000 processes have also extended well beyond their origins in engineering and manufacturing into the service sector, including not only the private-sector providers of health and education but also government departments, state agencies, and a wide range of publicly funded organizations such as schools (New Zealand), police departments (United States), and indeed even professional soccer teams (Mexico).

Despite its apparent popularity and growing ubiquity, the ISO 9000 process is not without its critics. Most immediately, gaining accreditation can be extremely costly, with one study dating from the late 1990s showing that the cost of certification could range from US$50,000 to several million dollars. Relatedly, implementing ISO 9000 processes is time consuming and requires extensive administration. There is also considerable debate over its alleged benefits, with even the ISO itself admitting that there is limited evidence to show that the ISO 9000 process boosts quality.[3] Indeed, there is an oft-repeated adage—attributed variously to an anonymous manager, Motorola's quality manager, and the CEO of Microsoft—that a manufacturer of concrete life jackets could be ISO 9000 registered as long as there were systems in place to assure these were well made. These criticisms suggest that the astronomical rise of the ISO 9000 process needs to be explained in terms other than the immediate benefits to the organizations involved. It is here that various links can be made with broader discussions of economic globalization.

First, the phenomenal rise of ISO processes can be seen as a consequence of the increased importance of multinational corporations in the global economy and the consolidation of global supply chains. Empirical studies show that multinationals prefer ISO 9000-certified providers when they source products and services from offshore as this provides them with a degree of certainty about the nature of the organization involved. As one journalist observes, 'if you don't go through the processes you can't work for the big guys'.[4] In this context, ISO 9000 not only provides multinationals with a promise of quality in relatively unknown settings, it also facilitates coordination amongst geographically distant firms, a challenge that is seen as critical to the success of globalizing production networks. Seen in this context, ISO 9000 is a key aspect

---

[3] S. Clifford, 'So Many Standards to Follow, So Little Payoff', Inc., <http://www.inc.com/magazine/20050501/management.html>.

[4] Ibid.

of the process through which global economic integration is occurring. It is a way for geographically remote organizations both to recognize each other and to imagine themselves in the shared economic space of a global supply chain. The stakes in such ventures are high, as is underlined by the well-known cases of Betamax versus VHS formats in VCRs, and the ongoing debates over standards in operating systems in personal computers.

Second, the ISO 9000 process exemplifies the rise of the non-governmental and private-sector actors whose activities are understood by many to be displacing nation-state authority. Discussions of global governance, emerging predominantly out of political science, highlight the rise of what is called 'private authority'. Seen in this context, the ISO 9000 process can also be seen as part of a broader shift in governance away from legally binding rules and regulations towards 'softer' forms of governance such as standardization and harmonization. In this context it is important to note that the ISO process is voluntary; that neither the ISO process itself nor third-party certification is formally required but organizations opt for it because of the external perceptions it generates and the opportunities that subsequently ensue. As more countries and organizations opt to join these processes, so too there is a degree of 'regulatory convergence' around these new governmental forms. The ISO process, for example, is now being used in efforts to settle WTO trade disputes.

Third, the ISO 9000 process illustrates the rise of what political scientist Peter Haas calls 'new epistemic communities'.[5] Discussions of global policy transfer, knowledge, and training emphasize how management techniques such as ISO 9000 travel in both embodied and codified forms. In this context it is important to recognize that ISO 9000 processes are not overseen by governments; rather, in the member countries, accredited third-party registrars can include organizations as diverse as laboratories, private testing organizations, firms that were early adoptors of ISO, industry trade groups, and major accounting firms. Moreover, as ISO 9000 has become more visible, so too independent 'quality consultants' have begun to proliferate, particularly as the ability to modify ISO standards to local circumstances has been recognized in the new ISO initiatives for social responsibility and risk management mentioned above. These new economic intermediaries offer both products and services to organizations wanting to put ISO quality management processes in place. The globally networked industry of certification and consultants that has emerged around ISO standards makes manifest new forms of expertise that also help constitute globalizing processes.

Finally, ISO 9000 processes reconstitute the organizations and individuals subjected to them by making manifest specific understandings of economic and social life. Seen in this context, ISO 9000 is an exemplar of the diverse

[5] Peter Haas, 'Epistemic Communities and International Policy Coordination', *International Organisation* 46, 1 (1992): 1–35.

range of calculative practices, including audit, benchmarking, and standards, through which the activities of organizations and individuals are now being governed. It makes manifest the new emphasis on constant learning, organizational improvement, and futurity understood to be characteristic of 'advanced liberalism' more generally. It also encourages entrepreneurial, empowered, organizational actors to adopt a systems view in which connections are made between otherwise discrete activities. Seen in this light, ISO 9000 processes, and indeed the broader ambitions of the ISO for standardization of economic, environment, and social life, are not simply trivial aspects of globalization. Rather, these mundane practices are a key aspect of the ways in which organizational subjects are being reconstituted, and are reconstituting themselves, as part of a globalizing world.

51 Number

Helen Verran

At 2 pm on the first Sunday of every month, Waterwatch Victoria volunteers gather to test the water quality of Merri Creek on the upstream side of St George's Road Bridge in Melbourne's inner-city suburb of North Fitzroy.[1] Their 'kit', donated by a sponsoring water company, has various-sized tubes and bottles, some empty, a few already equipped with reagents, conductivity and pH probes, plastic spoons and bowls, ice cube trays, and plastic syringes. Usually by 3.30 pm a nice set of numbers has been assembled. The quality of the creek's water emerges as a complicated arithmetical composite of aggregated numbers generated in chemical and physical tests set alongside another complicated arithmetic composite representing aquatic life and derived from estimates of numbers and types of 'bugs' counted in a sample of sludge. Later in the week these numbers are added to the Waterwatch Victoria database by the group's coordinator.

Begun in 1993, Waterwatch is an environmental NGO providing services mainly under contract to governments. It now has many thousands of Australians regularly attending their streams with bottles, thermometers, and pH meters, peering at tiny creatures they have scooped up with a net, trying to identify what they are and count their numbers. In part Waterwatch aims to sensitize citizens to the failing health of Australia's rivers. But more substantively and certainly of significance to the people who do the measuring, the numbers that Waterwatch volunteers produce 'fill-in spatial and temporal monitoring gaps', contributing to Australia's ongoing environmental audit. In Victoria there are a mere 270 official water-monitoring sites; in contrast Waterwatch Victoria collects data from 1,454 places.

Animated by the slogan 'You can't sustain what you haven't measured', the enthusiasm that pervades Waterwatch evidences Australians' enthusiasm for ecological sustainability. What is much less evident is the way these numbers so enthusiastically generated by volunteers with the best of intentions towards Australia's nature are contributing to constituting water as commodity-expanding possibilities for 'doing business with nature'.

To the chagrin of Waterwatch Victoria's thousands of volunteers who go out of their way to wade about in streams and lakes and understand their labour

[1] Acknowledgement: I am grateful to Christian Clark who in his undergraduate honours project research was alert to the puzzle of the separation between the Waterwatchers' community water data and official water data.

as generating important information, the numbers they generate in attesting water quality are not be added to the official register of water quality in Victoria: the Victorian Water Resources Data Warehouse. That website contains only 'official data' gathered by personnel employed and supervised by state instrumentalities and water companies. Why the cordon sanitaire? Surely two websites, separate institutions and databases, are counter-productive in a project assembling information on the state of the environment?

Unlike the 'official data', the confidence limits of the 'community data' are not specifiable. While it has a network of coordinators providing training in water quality and biological monitoring, the measuring activities of Waterwatch's various volunteer groups are still murky. The provenance of numbers arising in their unreliably disciplined gestures with hands and eyes, probes and tubes, buckets and nets, words spoken and figures recorded, cannot be guaranteed by the institutional location nor by attested skill levels of the number generators. These people who in their spare time muck about in gumboots and waders in dams and billabongs, creeks and rivers do not verifiably possess at least the Level III Community Environment Certificate. The numbers they record may cohere well enough to give an alarming general picture of the state of Australia's waters, but their consistency is not quantifiable.

Nevertheless, the expressed hope is that when the level of discipline embedded in the hands and eyes of Waterwatch volunteers can itself be reliably witnessed and quantified, the data sets will be consolidated. If and when this does happen, a peephole which allows us to see some inner workings of globalizing capitalism will close up. What does this (perhaps) soon-to-be-closed peephole allow us to see? Among other things it reveals the wonder of cadastral number. The mismatch between the provenances of 'community water data' and 'official water data' enables us to see that cadastral numbering projects such as the Victorian Water Resources Data Warehouse hold two distinct moments of numbering in tension. The moments articulate distinct ends. Cadastral number embeds two separate and distinct purposes while appearing merely as means to assembling information.

The Victorian Water Resources Data Warehouse has to be particular about confidence limits. It must manage risks and provide only data of quantifiable provenance, for much is at stake—the emerging Australian water market. Per capita, for each Australian, the amount of water extracted from the environment and held in storage far exceeds that for citizens of other nations. Australia has in the past invested vast sums, and in today's world this past obsession with storing water is evident as infrastructure, which translates water's use value into exchange value. Extracted and stored water is a potential commodity. Extracted, stored, and recorded water is capable of realization as a commodity. Through its trade, capital gains can be realized.

The Victorian Water Resources Data Warehouse invisibly manages dual and mutually interfering moments: on the one hand exhaustively registering

Victoria's water resources, and on the other contributing to expanding the markets that exploit those resources. To appreciate the complexity and flex-ibility embedded in the sets of numbers that populate the Victorian Water Resources Data Warehouse databases we need to remember that numbers' remarkable capacities lie in their being the relation unity/plurality, a relation that might be expressed as the relation between one and many, or alternatively as the relation between a whole and its parts.

The numbers that constitute the Victorian Water Resources Data Warehouse are about knowing the state of Australia's nature. This purpose depends on numbers being the relation of one to many: single instances of defined meas-urement are cumulated. Simultaneously the numbers that constitute the Victorian Water Resources Data Warehouse make a whole—a marketplace for Australia's emergent water trade. This whole, articulable water resources, has many parts: surface water, groundwater, return water, and increasingly reuse water, and each of these parts has manifold sub-parts. These parts and sub-parts are not given, but are continually proliferating as new configurations are ingeniously designed, while other configurations wither or are killed off. The whole, the Australian water market, is necessarily vague and emergent.

Considering the contrast in more detail, the numbers representing water for the purpose of exhaustive environmental audit work the relation one–many. As part of a precise, specifying, and definitive process the Victorian Water Resources Data Warehouse contributes to a register of quantity and quality of located water in all Australia's catchments. Ones—specified units of flowing or stored water, with specified space–time coordinates and specified physical, chemical, and biological properties are collected together as a many. They add up to a general picture of the states and places of Australia's waters. In some ways a fantasy of exhaustive cumulation, the purpose of the audit project is nevertheless identified as a common good endeavour: developing better rep-resentations of the evidently deteriorating state of the waters that are crucial in sustaining Australia's nature.

Yet sets of consistent 'official' numbers stored in the likes of the Victorian Water Resources Data Warehouse, soon (perhaps) to be supplemented by the vast stores of numbers that Waterwatchers produce, also serve quite different ends. A fantasy of quite a different type is sustained by the existence of these numbers: the vague, emergent, and unspecifiable notion of ' 'the Australian water market'. Here the sets of numbers are no longer a representation but are now constitutive of the entity itself. The wholeness of the Australian water market emerges as its continually reinvented parts, commodities, are conjured into existence by various ingenious means of bundling, tracking, partitioning, and so on. These parts of the whole are literally made feasible by the cumu-lated numbers. Surface water, groundwater, return water, and reuse water are phenomena generated in disciplined interrogation of knowable water in place. Each of these parts of the water market has its sub-parts, each made separable as a product, a commodity, by the social, literary, and material technologies through which it is borne. Ingenious tinkering—separating water entitlements from land rights, rebundling water as low-, medium-, and high-security licences, inventing tamper-proof flow meters, is continually coming up with new sorts of parts in the vague emergent whole of Australia's water market; new water products designed for new markets. Here the waters and the numbers are one and the same. The work, the human labour that separates and connects them becomes invisible, or it would if only the confidence limits of the 'community water data' were specifiable.

Recognizing the origins of numbers' capacities to carry human endeavours is important, for the ease with which they enable one project to become quite another is uncanny. Where does this ease of shape-shifting come from? Numbers, coming to life originally as rule-bound sequences of words, are radically incomplete. In use they are both agile, a property deriving from the rule-boundness, and needy, this latter mode bequeathed by their origins in the patterns of events, not in the events themselves. In this combination of needy agility is found numbers' unnerving capacity to continually evert themselves, flipping imperceptibly from their one–many manifestation to their whole–part form of being. A one, invoked as a defined unit, can be collected together with many other similar units. This plurality can with an almost imperceptible alteration in the criterion of completion invoke a whole. The cumulated defined units of water in many linked locations can with a self-evidently useful alteration in the defining criterion become 'regulated water'. The usefulness of the slide obscures the flip from cumulus to whole, and more significantly the change in numbers' role from representation to constitution. The elision accomplished, however, parts can be evoked utilizing differential completing criteria: 'dam-water bodies' evoked in one criterion can be the subject of trade with landholders; 'regulated river flows' evoked through another criterion can be subject to trade as environmental flows, and 'weir pools' through yet another criterion might allow trade in high-security water licences.

If not for the glitch that the numbers so earnestly recorded by Waterwatch volunteers do not have specifiable confidence limits because of the unreliability of the volunteers' gestures with hands and eyes, tubes and meters, words and figures which generate those numbers, the elision of a many—numerous observations/measurements—to a whole, Australia's tradable water resources, would be less visible. The conflation of a project whose explicit purpose is to better picture for the public good the deteriorating state of the waters that make up Australia's rivers and creeks, and swamps and lakes, with a project whose stated purpose is to trade those waters and enable a few to reap private capital gain from that trade, would be more seamless. The numbers in Australia's water resources data warehouses are not innocent means.

INDEX